Integrated Children's Centres

Designed to be a one-stop-shop to meet the needs of local communities, children's centres represent a revolutionary shift in the way children's services are delivered to families. *Integrated Children's Centres* looks at the way in which children's centre development has built upon the research and experiences of initiatives such as the HeadStart programme in America and the Sure Start programme. Exploring the component elements of truly integrative services and the key players in ensuring positive outcomes: families, the local authority, PCT, private and voluntary sectors, and faith groups, this book covers:

- the challenges faced by children's centres
- how to tackle social issues through the medium of children's centres
- achieving effective multi-agency working and true collaboration
- the essentials of leading and managing children's centres
- the benefits of early intervention
- how to effectively deliver health care, education and children's services.

Providing a wealth of case studies, this highly topical book will be of interest to nursery and children's centre managers and early years practitioners enrolled on the NPQICL or EYPS programmes, as well as students working towards a degree in Early Childhood Studies or MA in Early Years.

Carole Beaty is a currently setting up a children's centre in West Sussex. She was previously Programme Manager at the Littlehampton Children's Centre and a tutor on the NPQICL programme run by the National College of School Leadership. She has also lectured in Early Years at the University of Chichester.

Integrated Children's Centres

Overcoming barriers to truly integrated services

Carole Beaty

Routledge
Taylor & Francis Group

LONDON AND NEW YORK

This first edition published 2011
by Routledge
2 Park Square, Milton Park, Abingdon, Oxon OX14 4RN

Simultaneously published in the USA and Canada
by Routledge
270 Madison Avenue, New York, NY 10016

Routledge is an imprint of the Taylor & Francis Group, an informa business

Typeset in Bembo and Frutiger by
Book Now Ltd, London
Printed and bound in Great Britain by
CPI Antony Rowe, Chippenham, Wiltshire

British Library Cataloguing in Publication Data
A catalogue record for this book is available from the British Library

Library of Congress Cataloging-in-Publication Data
Beaty, Carol.
Integrated children's centres: overcoming barriers to truly integrated services/by
Carol Beaty.— 1st ed.
    p. cm.
1. Children—Services for. 2. Children with social disabilities—Education.
3. Children with social disabilities—Services for. 4. Community and school.
I. Title.
HV713.B4 2011
362.71—dc22   2010003399

ISBN13: 978–0–415–47914–1 (hbk)
ISBN13: 978–0–415–47915–8 (pbk)
ISBN13: 978–0–203–84702–2 (ebk)

To all the children, families and staff who make the wonderful alchemy of children's centres possible; most particularly to past and present members of Littlehampton Children's Centre

Contents

Contents

Contributors

Carole Beaty has been in the field of Early Years education and care for 35 years. She started her teaching career in Peckham South, London. She was Deputy Head of a rural primary school before moving into higher education, first at King Alfred's College Winchester and later at University College Chichester. At Chichester she was part of a multi-disciplinary team that wrote and set up a Childhood Studies degree programme that started in 1999 and was Programme Manager of this degree until 2003. She moved to Littlehampton Children's Centre in 2004, first as a teacher in the centre and later as acting Programme Manager and worked on the NPQICL (National Professional Qualification in Integrated Centre Leadership) programme teaching, mentoring and assessing across the South East. Carole worked as a freelance consultant in Higher Education. She is currently setting up a Phase Three children's centre in West Sussex.

Christine Blanshard taught in schools in South Yorkshire before moving to West Sussex to teach in both key stages within a village school. In 1995, as a Senior Lecturer in Early Years at the University College of Chichester, she became involved in writing, establishing and teaching on Early Years foundation, undergraduate and postgraduate degree levels. She later became the education lead at a Sure Start children's centre in Littlehampton, West Sussex, working closely with different agencies and local families. Further work as an Early Years Advisory Teacher for both West Sussex and Hampshire Education authorities and more recently as a freelance trainer, have reinforced her belief that to truly provide the very best start for a child's route to learning we have to have a deep understanding of early attachment, child development, and the significance of the adult role in nurturing, developing and caring for a child's individual needs and self-worth.

Sim Dendy is part of the leadership team of New Community, a network of churches and projects based in Southampton, UK. Sim has a passion to see the Church take its place within the community and has developed a number of successful community action projects in partnership with the Church and statutory bodies in the areas of health, education and social care. He also leads one of the congregations based at Central Hall, which is a thriving family-focused community. He serves as a trustee of Links International developing Micro Enterprise and Primary Healthcare in 55 countries overseas.

Antonia Hopkins has worked as a social worker, a State-registered nurse and a part-time lecturer in health studies courses. She was formerly vice chair of the Professional Executive Committee and Board nurse for the Adur Arun and Worthing Primary Care Trust and project and more recently led a health team at a local Sure Start programme in Littlehampton, West Sussex where she fully immersed herself and her team in integrated working. Antonia is currently the Public Health Nurse/Programme Manager for Children and Young People's services.

Steven Popper originated the first University of Chichester Early Years teacher education route in 1997, and has led it successfully ever since. He has a long previous background as a teacher, mainly in nursery and reception classes, and before that worked in several social services nurseries.

Jeannette Sax, after having three children and enjoying helping in schools, completed her PGCE in primary teaching at Chichester University via the articled teachers route and then taught in reception and nursery classes for seven years. After this she trained in personal and professional development and worked with teachers and sixth-form students to make good life choices. She was then asked to set up and manage a Neighbourhood Nursery Initiative daycare facility run by the voluntary sector for 60 children alongside the Sure Start local programme at a Phase One children's centre in West Sussex. She was one of the first in the country to gain Early Years Professional Status and now mentors other students. Whilst there she also completed her NPQICL and has recently moved on to manage two Phase Two children's centres in Worthing, West Sussex.

Preface

Integrated children's centres: myth or reality?

Recent years have seen a sea-change in the way that services for Early Years children have been conceptualised, organised and assessed. All professionals and services working for young children now share a common set of five 'outcomes' originating from the 'Every Child Matters' agenda (2003 onwards). All local authorities now employ one central Director of Children's Services to lead and oversee the entire range of provision for children in their area. The new statutory 'Early Years Foundation Stage' (EYFS) applies from birth until children start Year One at school, and all professionals working with children have to work within its parameters. Better integration of all local authority departments, personnel and services has been promoted by professionals and researchers from virtually every perspective, whether to do with smoothing transition between settings for children, assessing and respecting children's achievements properly, improving the quality of Early Years training and provision or avoiding the sad pitfalls that some child protection services have, unfortunately, fallen into.

The most obvious and explicit manifestation of this national concern with better integration has been the astonishing growth of children's centres. These would seem to represent integration of Early Years services and professionals in a most explicit manner, and, one would hope, stand as shining examples of how the quality of young children's lives can be enhanced through the existence of personnel with different training, different expertise and different professional responsibilities all pulling together in one smooth, co-ordinated (and properly budgeted) manner for the common good.

But are they? Rarely in life are things that simple. If children's centres are successful in running as well-integrated units, then they and their staff will have had to work at it. Communication between staff with different professional backgrounds and levels of training will have had to be clear and well-organised. Shared expectations of high quality will have had to be developed in a way that gives all staff a sense of ownership over them. The leadership of these children's centres will have had to be careful not to appear to favour or value any one profession over another. The practical organisation of the different services available to children and their families will have had to be efficient, well-co-ordinated and sensible. None of this is easy.

There are other issues too. How do children's centres avoid enhancing the possible attachment and behavioural problems identified by some research (such as that carried out by Biddulph 2006, and UNICEF 2008)? Will the statutory nature of the new EYFS mean that all services for Early Years children improve in quality through having such a common framework, or will the bureaucratic demands of demonstrating compliance with the EYFS get in the way of actually working with children? Can any Director of Children's Services who has, for example, a background in either education or social services, really understand the other major strand and make sound judgements about it?

This book, therefore, does not seek to suggest that everything in the garden is lovely; rather, it seeks to explore some of the nitty-gritty issues that might affect the effectiveness of integrated children's centres. The authors of the following chapters are wedded to the principle of better integration, but all recognise the difficulties that can arise in practice, and explore these in search of ways to overcome such difficulties.

Early Years practitioners, leaders and students at all levels should, therefore, find this book immensely informative and helpful towards enhancing their own understanding of integrated work in children's centres and developing their personal practice as a result. It is on such improved practice that the future success of integrated children's centres rests.

Steven Popper
Advanced Study of Early Years Co-ordinator,
University of Chichester

References

Biddulph, S. (2006) *Raising Babies*. London: Harper Thorson.
UNICEF (2008) *Report Card 8: The Childcare Transition*, December, p. 15. Available at www. childwellbeing.org.uk

Introduction

Carole Beaty

Having worked in two Sure Start children's centre and visited many others, it is always such a privilege to walk in the door. It may be in a church hall, in a mobile unit, or in a brand-new purpose-built building. The effective centre will be full of activity, and for the uninitiated it will come as a tremendous surprise, for there will be a sign directing parents and visitors to: 'Baby Massage' with the community nursery nurse; 'Story Telling' with the librarian; 'Baby Clinic' with the midwife; a 'Childminders' Drop-In'; a 'Play and Stay'; a 'Pre-Natal Exercise Class'. There will also be a chance to meet with a representative from Jobcentre Plus to discuss training options, and to see a tutor from adult education. There will be children playing, and parents and practitioners chatting over a coffee, coming together to make a difference. And of course much, much more. There will be a rich mix of services and opportunities, with people working together to make a things happen in each community for every child – a 'one-stop shop' for children and families.

> Sure Start is the jewel in the crown of Labour's social policy, the missing link in the welfare state's promise of cradle-to-grave assistance. Rolling out in every neighbourhood, starting in the most deprived, new children's centres are becoming a hub for local communities, a meeting place for young families, where young lives may be turned around before it's too late. Here, ideally, are sited all the services a family might need, from midwives to training programmes helping mothers find jobs, from speech therapy for small children to debt advice, from tai chi classes and parenting support to childcare, cafés, chatting and fun.
>
> (Toynbee and Walker 2008:133)

We still live in a divided society. While some throw up their hands in horror at communities that appear to have split off from the mainstream, some appear to willingly accept the status quo and a feeling of inertia often seems to pervade political intent. When the Labour government came to power in 1997, it was with the mandate of ending child poverty by 2012. In September 2008 Gordon Brown committed one billion pounds to the fight to end childhood poverty.

With the promise of one billion pounds there is a clear determination to invest in the lives of the 3.8 million children who are being held by issues of poverty in the United Kingdom. The UNICEF report on child well-being (2007) provides a measurement of child well-being in six dimensions: health and safety, material well-being, education, peer and family relationships, behaviours and risks, and young people's own subjective sense of their own well-being. This report provides a valuable picture of children's lives. What this study found was that Northern European countries came out most favourably, with child well-being seen at its highest in Finland, Sweden, Denmark and the Netherlands. The United Kingdom is in the bottom third of those countries studied for five out of the six areas studied. It is in the areas of relative poverty and deprivation, quality of children's relationships with both peers and parents, health and safety, behaviour and risk-taking, and in subjective well-being that this country scores less well. However, significant improvements in child well-being in rich societies are likely to depend much more on the reduction in equality rather than on expenditure alone. What this study suggests is that it is a complex mixture of interwoven factors that leads to a better sense of well-being for children. What it rightly emphasises is that what is needed is a multi-dimensional approach to improve our overall understanding and the effectiveness of both policy and practice in supporting the well-being of all of our children (UNICEF 2007:39).

The Labour government, when it came to power introduced a raft of initiatives apparently to address issues of social exclusion, and what they started with were reforms that would affect every young child, responding to research both in the United States and in Europe that money spent on excellent Early Years provision and preventative services would pay significant dividends in the future. They started to introduce measures that would enhance the life chances of each and every child. The original intention of the Sure Start programme was to provide autonomy to local communities and to present services that were relevant and accessible to families. The whole ethos of the original Sure Start local programmes was based upon community development lines, the notion that local people, most specifically parents should own their programme and should bring to each and every Sure Start a sense of the local community and its particular needs. This was a revolutionary vision that sought to move away from the monoliths of central and local government and its often hidebound and bureaucratic services, and instead place children and families at the heart of service design and delivery. Rather than families being done-to by well-intentioned professionals, parents should help to create the services and the opportunities that they needed, and these would be delivered in a more informal and user-friendly manner. Services were to become more individualised centred upon what was needed rather than what was on offer.

Post Laming (2003) and the Children Act 2004, there was a requirement to co-operate for all services working with and for children. The government was, it seemed, putting into practice what all members of the Early Years lobby had been saying and campaigning for, for generations: a comprehensive, fully funded, integrated Early Years policy that took into account the holistic nature of children's development and placed the child firmly within the context of family and of community. What is self-evident from research and what this book will seek to explore is that the quality of Early Years education and care both in the home and in excellent childcare settings and within the community can make an enormous difference to enhancing life chances for young children into adulthood. Children and ultimately families are the building blocks of our community and of our economic, social and cultural success. We ignore children's rights and needs and individuality at our peril. The whole area of Early Years practice, in health, education, the voluntary sector and social care is changing, and what educationalists and philosophers spoke of so eloquently two hundred years ago is now verified by modern scientific research. The development of neuroscientific study on the impact of early life experience on the developmental architecture of the brain echoes powerfully the work of Rousseau (1712–1778) who famously advocated young children learning through the power of the emotions and from their senses. Today we have more concrete proof that those experiences of early childhood are hardwired into our brain and will make a difference to how we react and how we respond as our lives unfold. That notion of the way in which the brain is responsive to early experiences must now be central to policy design.

> The infant brain starts to form connections at a very rapid rate during this time [*the first year of life*]. In fact, 90 percent of the growth of the human brain occurs in the first five years of life. Over these crucial years, millions

of brain connections are being formed, unformed, and then re-formed, directly due to your child's life experiences and in particular his emotional experiences with you.

Around age seven, this massive sculpting activity is slowed down. This is because more and more brain cells are being myelinated (myelin is a whitish material made up of protein and fats that surrounds the brain cells in sheaths like a form of insulation). This enables better communication between brain cells. It also strengthens brain pathways, fixing them in place.

(Sunderland 2006:21)

This book seeks to explore the development of the Sure Start/children's centre initiative and its possible impact upon the way in which services are designed and delivered for young children and how the move towards the more generalised children's centre rollout has impacted upon the original sense of autonomy and child-centred philosophy.

Integration of services is the ideal that is explored in this book. It is achievable if families, communities, local authorities, health services and voluntary services accept the challenge. In Sure Start children's centres we have the opportunity to fully embrace the integrated practice agenda. The voices in this book come from different backgrounds with different training and experience to record their ideas and their passion for making a difference in every community. Parents and families present their own ideas and their experiences of working within this framework. We need to learn every day from what works for them, what is truly making our communities stronger, more resourceful and more self-sustaining. Children's centres are so different across the country because they are part of the local structure and respond to the unique set of circumstances and needs of their area. Yet they must all be the same in the commitment from all who work in partnership to the central vision to create a community in which each and every child can realise their potential.

We have a tremendous opportunity here to make a difference to all families. The time is right to embrace it now.

References

Laming, H. (2003) *The Victoria Climbié Inquiry*. London: House of Commons Health Committee.

Sunderland, M. (2006) *What Every Parent Needs to Know*. London: Dorling Kindersley.

Toynbee, P. and Walker, D. (2008) *Unjust Rewards*. London: Granta.

UNICEF (2007) *Child Poverty in Perspective: An Overview of Child Well-being in Rich Countries*. Florence: UNICEF Innocenti Research Centre.

Further reading

Camgoz, S. (2008) 'UNICEF UK welcomes government commitment to tackle child poverty', UNICEF, online.

Glass, N. (2005) 'Surely some mistake', *Guardian*, 5 January.

Websites

UNICEF:
www.unicef.org.uk/press/news

CHAPTER 1

Why integrated children's centres?

Carole Beaty

What is a children's centre?

If you talk to people about hospitals, nurseries and schools, and about health centres and dental practices they know what you mean, but if you talk about a children's centre they will often look at you blankly and ask you what you mean. Children's centres are a key arm of the Labour government's drive to abolish child poverty and to ensure that every child has the very best opportunity to fulfil their potential in all areas of their life in every community. They build upon the successful work of the Sure Start programmes that were introduced in 1999; they are diverse and individual programmes that lie at the heart of the 'Every Child Matters: Change for Children' programme. They are a central mechanism for providing services that meet families' needs. It was estimated that by 2010 there would be 3,500 children's centres, one in every community (DfES 2006:6). The idea is for children's centres to bring services for young children, usually under five, but in some areas this has extended to nineteen, together under one umbrella. So a centre is a hub of health, social care, voluntary sector activities, employment and training opportunities. This may be in one building, but more likely it will be spread across a community. Most importantly the children's centres will be there to offer advice and support, and information. There are many different models of children's centres and this can cause some confusion. Some children's centres are located in substantial purpose-built buildings, with training rooms, nursery and crèche facilities, possibly a community café, and much more. Others may have a couple of rooms in the local school or library, and will offer services out and about in the local area. In some areas children's centres have combined with social services family centres. At the heart of all centres is the idea of providing early support for families and their children in an integrated and co-ordinated manner. They provide universal to targeted services to serve the whole community.

Children's centres: the vision

Children's centres play a key role in improving outcomes for all children in all areas; most particularly they have a central role in addressing issues of inequality between the most and the least advantaged children in our country (DfES 2006:6) and now a universal service for all. Children's centres should provide accessible services that are led by parent and family need and are offered in such a way that parents feel fully involved. For example, parents in a local area might identify a need for a group that supports families with children who are fostered or adopted; it would be the children's centre that could make this happen, ensuring that the way that it was organised enabled parents to be part of the process and fully contribute their own ideas, experience and feelings. Parents with children with additional needs might wish to have multi-professional assessment and planning meetings more locally rather than having to travel to their nearest hospital or child development centre.

Integration is fundamental to the children's centre vision – the idea that the child lies at the heart of services, and that health, education, social care, training, employment and the voluntary sector work together in clear partnership to ensure that every child has the possibility of realising their potential. This just seems to be common sense that saves money and makes services user-friendly and cohesive. So at a children's centre, a family might come to a drop-in post-natal group, and at the same time find out about activities in the summer holidays for the older children in the family talk to an adviser about possible training opportunities for the adult members of the family. More specific targeted services can be planned around the needs of children through partnership working using the CAF (Common Assessment Framework) or through regular children's centre practitioner meetings when partners build strong, informed professional alliances. Children's centres also provide intervention and support in those vital early years of life, when it can make such a difference: providing help, for example, to a mother who feels isolated within the local community, with obtaining childcare, getting support with housing, and considering her own training needs. Just providing a place for the family to meet up for a drink and a chat can be such a positive start.

Most importantly children's centres are aspirational for families, children and communities and for changing professional practice.

Making children's centres statutory?

Children's centres have already made an enormous difference to how services are provided and to the work of practitioners; however, there is clearly a need to embed this practice into professional and public consciousness and to ensure the future of children's centres. To this end the Apprenticeship, Skills and Learning Act gained Royal assent on 12 November 2009. This Act gives children's centres statutory status, and a duty to Ofsted to inspect all centres (DCSF website).

Section 191 of the bill defines children's centres as:

A place, or group of places –

a   Which is managed by or on behalf of, or under arrangements made with, an English local authority, with a view to securing that early childhood services in their area are made available in an integrated manner,

b   Through which each of the early childhood services is made available, and

c   At which activities for young children are provided, whether by way of early years provision or otherwise.

(DCSF website, accessed July 2009)

It is interesting to note that this bill emphasises that the role of children's centres is to directly provide activities for children, as there had been a fear that with the widening remit of the children's centre and the move to local authority control that centres might just become places where you pick up information and are signposted. Under this bill, centres must be a hub of activity and of provision for children and families. However, a significant challenge in making children's centres statutory is to come up with some form of recipe for centres, a standardisation without losing their unique sense of individuality. A challenge indeed, but one well worth embracing if it means that children's centres will become part of the infrastructure of every community, providing support and care for every child in every family.

This is an exciting bill and one which sees children's centres firmly on the map in terms of service provision and part of the furniture for community-led practice.

Why do we need children's centres?

So we have nurseries and schools, child development centres, hospitals and health centres, why do we need children's centres?

We live in a unequal society and one in which we see the impact of poor health, educational opportunity and the lack of community cohesion leading in some parts of our society to a sense of disaffection and hopelessness. Social isolation for many in all communities, rich and poor, is a real issue in some of our communities, both for the elderly and the young; this can and does have enormous implications for individuals' mental health. Poor housing and lack of adequate, safe and challenging spaces for children to play and young people to meet has a real impact upon health and upon social well-being. Social class and where we live makes a real difference to how we live our lives and to the possible realisation of our own personal potential. Social policy, the way in which governments spend our money and the say that we have in this choice daily creates the context for each and every life. The good health, in every sense of that word, of our communities, makes a difference to all of us and is our collective responsibility. Sadly children's centres do not hold the key to all the challenges of our communities, but they have the ingredients to make a substantial change.

What we know is that the social, geographical, educational and emotional conditions in which individuals live make a difference to their life expectancy, to their attainment and their sense of well-being and to their aspiration. It is not just about money spent on health and education, but about looking at issues as a whole. The foundations of life are laid down in the womb and in the very early stages of life. Those first few years are crucial for the child's later health and well-being. In July 2009 we saw the impact that inadequate housing has on sections of our population when a tower block, Lakanal House, in Camberwell in South East London caught fire and caused the death of six people, including children. A tower block with one central stairway is an unsuitable place to house young families, which must be, you would think, self-evident. If we are to address issues of children's life chances and of each of them realising their potential then our commitment must be multi-dimensional in nature and must look at all aspects of children's lives. Increasing expenditure is one thing, but resources must be deployed effectively and involve those who are in receipt of them. We need to anticipate need and be skilful and imaginative in the deployment of resources.

> Good health involves reducing levels of educational failure, reducing insecurity and unemployment and improving housing standards. Societies that enable all citizens to play a useful role in the social, economic and cultural life of their society will be healthier than those where people face insecurity, exclusion and deprivation.
>
> (Wilkinson and Marmot 2003:11)

The reasons for poor health, poor educational attainment and social exclusion are myriad and complex, and are interconnected; what is clear is that all these evils blight lives as they blight communities. Children's centres are certainly not the cure-all in the government's armoury of social policy, but they certainly have a great deal to offer. We just need the courage and tenacity for radical changes to practice and to keep our collective heads for the long haul.

Children's centres need to be unique to their local community and respond to local need, but all should exemplify excellent practice in providing accessible, multi-agency services. They need to be welcoming and dynamic, places you want to go to.

Sure Start children's centres are vital, exciting places where children under five years old and sometimes young people up to the age of nineteen, and their families, can receive seamless integrated services and information, and where they can access help from multi-disciplinary teams of professionals. Children's centres should be a 'one-stop shop' for families. Wherever they are they need to be a central part of the community, building upon existing services. They need to house proactive, friendly staff with a good understanding of community-based practice and of the local community and its needs.

If we are to address issues of social exclusion and poverty, and poor educational attainment, then we need to be aware of why these evils persist in our society; just spending more money is a start but it is not enough. We all need to be aware of the context in which children grow and learn and those elements that impact upon their life chances, like housing, opportunities to play in appropriate spaces, family employment, diet, exercise, aspiration, and so on.

A theoretical context

In considering the development of integrated children's centres it is important not just to respond to government edicts, but also to firmly root complex development within an understanding of appropriate theory and an appreciation of societal indicators that drive this initiative. For those working within this exciting development they need to be aware of the philosophical and developmental theory that forms the starting point for practice.

Sociocultural theory

Sociocultural theory provides a thoughtful model for grounding discussion on children's-centre development. The Russian psychologist Lev Vygotsky (1896-1934) has strongly influenced the whole field of education, most particularly the area of Early Years practice. According to Vygotosky, social interaction, in particular co-operative dialogues between children and more knowledgeable members of society, are necessary for children to acquire the ways of thinking and behaving that make up a community's culture (Berk 2002). Vygotsky believed that the child's developing sense of their own identity and initiation into their social and cultural world was supported by parents and adults. Children's developing brain architecture is enabled by the experiences presented to them; language, communication and play are part of the framework that structures that development.

> The child brings with them to any early years setting a range of behaviours and a cultural identity that they have learnt from home, family and from community. This identity is wrapped up in that community evolution. A children's centre can support this aspect of the child's identity by drawing upon the wide range of professionals who have a sound knowledge of their local community.
>
> (Beaty, in Knowles 2006:34)

Ecological systems theory

The American psychologist Urie Bronfenbrenner (1995) put forward the idea of ecological theory when describing influences upon the developing child. It is one that is of particular value when conceptualising the foundations on which the children's centre development rests. He described this theory using a series of concentric circles, each illustrating a field of influence that shapes the child's experience of the world and impact on their developing brain and on their personality (Figure 1.1). It is also interesting to see that the child will influence in their turn the contexts in which they grow and learn.

Berk (2002) in referring to this theory said:

> It offers the most differentiated and complete account of contextual influences on children's development. *Ecological Systems Theory* views the child developing within a complex system of relationships affected by multiple levels of surrounding environment. Since the child's heredity joins with environmental forces to mould development, Bronfenbrenner (1998) recently characterized his perspective as a *bioecological model.*
>
> (Berk 2002:27)

The microsystem

The innermost circle of influence is the microsystem, which is the closet to the child in everyday life. This level will consist of parents and siblings, maybe grandparents as well. These close relationships will be fundamental to the growing child. The quality of warmth in these relationships will have a lasting impact upon the child's developing potential and their ability to capitalise on later life chances. Patterns of interaction are forged in this crucial circle of influence.

Bronfenbrenner reminded us that to consider child development in this way we must see the way in which children grow and learn as bidirectional. That is, the adult's behaviour will affect the child as they grow, and at the same time the child's behaviour will elicit adult responses.

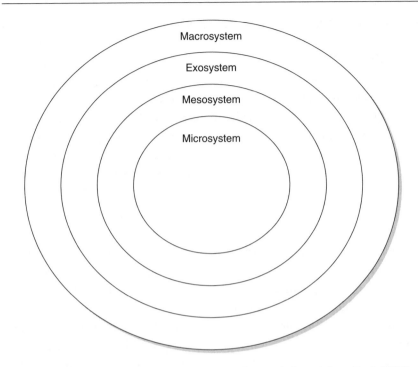

Figure 1.1 Bronfenbrenner's ecological systems theory (adapted from Berk 2002)

The mesosystem

The second level in Bronfenbrenner's theory is the mesosystem. Within this circle we see the wider context of care and support offered to the child, so within this circle we might see the local playgroup or nursery, a childminder or a member of the family who regularly cares for the child. Here reciprocal relationships are central to the developing child. So communication both ways is vital in building upon home experiences and ideas and experiences taken back from the care setting can be reinforced and consolidated at home. Where care settings and childminders have effective systems of communication and excellent relationships, they are more likely to foster the child's development.

The exosystem

The next level, the exosystem, is the wider social context in which the family operates; it does not necessarily contain children, but can affect the child's growth and learning. So this level would contain parents' employment status and workplace, and health and welfare services. Whether or not either or both parents are in employment will affect the growing child; the level of flexibility offered to parents in enabling effective child-rearing practices will have considerable implications for both child and adult well-being. Parents' sense of themselves and their self-esteem will radically affect the child–adult relationship and will provide models of living that will help to create the child's developing sense of identity; this can form either a positive or negative effect. This level will also contain more informal contact for the family; friends and extended family will form an important part of the family's wider network of support. Research shows us the negative impact of the break-down of these forms of support possibly leading to social isolation, which could have a profound effect upon the family and society as a whole.

The macrosystem

Bronfenbrenner refers to the outer level of the circles as the macrosystem. This consists of the values, the culture ideology and the way in which childhood is conceptualised by a society. This element of the circle of influence will influence both policy and practice in the way education, health care and social care is offered. For example, the way in which responsibility is apportioned in a society, the way that policy is designed and the underlying value systems on which that policy is constructed will impact upon each child and ultimately affect their life chances. There is an old African proverb: 'It takes a whole village to raise a child'.

The amount of GDP that each government allocates to fund Early Years services is an indication of how much is understood about the crucial nature of early development. The media will also fall within this circle. The impact of advertising upon young children is well known, targeting families to buy inappropriate unhealthy food is often implicated in rising levels of obesity and the increase in type-two diabetes. Where many Scandinavian countries restrict advertising to children under the age of twelve, there are limited restrictions currently in practice in this country.

The ecological model provides us with a very valuable framework in which to consider the efficacy of integrated working. It urges us to bear in mind not just the child but also the different contexts that revolve around that child, constantly impacting upon their development. So the parents' self-esteem, relationships, employment and contact with educational, health and social caring services will temper the child's growing identity and whether or not they might be able to benefit from opportunities as they present themselves (Beaty, in Knowles 2006:37).

When considering the design and delivery of services through children's centres it is essential to bear in mind the ecological model of child development and create services that are innovative and client friendly and provide genuine support for families. Services and activities need to respond to that interrelationship between those circles of influence, and build effective partnership working. Every day in every children's centre across the country we are seeing the relevance of those circles of influence upon the life of a child and their relevance to their life chances. Each practitioner needs to be aware of the unique way in which each context might affect the growing child.

Early experiences/attachments

The first five years of life are a time of rapid growth and of learning, a time in which the child takes enormous steps in finding out about the world and establishing patterns of learning. Ignatius of Loyola (1491-1558), founder of the Jesuits, recognised the importance of the early years when he said 'Give me a child until he is seven and I will give you the man'.

In the mid twentieth century, John Bowlby's work on the developing infant gave groundbreaking insights into the growing life of the brain and personality and the way in which a baby is responding to those early experiences of relationships.

More recently, neuroscientific research has recognised the importance of early experiences in shaping the brain and enabling brain plasticity and allowing response to life chances. The washing of the brain with emotion is seen as fundamental in creating the individuals we become. To see the scan of a child's brain that has experienced domestic violence or trauma in some form, is to see the physical evidence of the effect of emotion on the brain, and the atrophy this can cause.

Children who are subject to poor early experiences are generally less able to take hold of the opportunities that nursery and school can offer. Social skills may well be impaired and cognitive function damaged. From the 1950s John Bowlby demonstrated the importance of early attuned attachments in supporting healthy growth and psychological adjustment. Most particularly he emphasised the importance of a responsive, reciprocal, loving relationship from the prime care-givers. Current family life can be disparate in nature, fractional and at times dysfunctional. Parents may live a long distance from family and support. The media provides quick fixes on parenting, often portraying a very behaviourist, simplistic approach, that rarely reflects the responsibility and complexity of effective parenting. Families need local support with childcare and sometimes support with parenting.

Integrated children's centres have the opportunity to provide excellent informal support to parents and families, with access to health, education and social care professionals, as well as to good quality peer support. Support can be offered to enrich early attachment, and that 'dance' between caregiver and child that is so fundamental to healthy bonding. We have the opportunity to strengthen communities by strengthening the building blocks of our society – human relationships. Early intervention can be light-touch and must always be client centred as it offers services in an open, non-judgemental fashion.

Central to children's progress in school is their ability to communicate effectively. Appropriate language development is critical as they settle into school, make relationships and begin to make sense of this new environment. Good communication skills are also important for early literacy development and to help children access the curriculum. Poor language skills can be attributed to a wide range of causes, but one area that is of central significance to integrated children's centres is post-natal depression, which affects one in ten mothers, and research suggests that the mother–child dynamic can be adversely affected by it. Early diagnosis and support is critical in cases of post-natal depression if the functioning of the infant is not to be adversely affected. A multi-professional team has the capacity to diagnose and provide sensitive, low-level intervention. For example, infant massage may provide a vital tool for re-establishing the parent–child dynamic, promoting early attachment. Peer support may enable new mothers to explore their feelings in a safe and empathetic context, with people who have experienced those feelings themselves. If we are to lose that 'long-tail of underachievement' we must work with parents and communities to provide the very best foundation for learning and ensure entitlement for every child.

Integrating services

The move towards effective integration of services for children and families was given momentum by Lord Laming's enquiry into the tragic death of Victoria Climbié. The subsequent Children Act 2004 provided the framework for radically altering the way in which children's services are offered to families. Most particularly the 'Every Child Matters' agenda enables an understanding of the holistic nature of children's development and the need for cohesive, complementary services that put the child at the centre.

Victoria's story is a particularly horrific example of child abuse and the failure of the agencies involved in her care to help her. However for all the cases brought to the attention of the nation through media coverage there are many cases where children are not being properly protected and looked after, cases that need to be addressed. ECM recognises that all those who work with children in whatever capacity, have a duty, now enshrined in law, to be responsible for the overall welfare of those children and young people with whom they work. Through the ECM policy all agencies that work with children and young people will be brought together as Children's Services to work in a cross-agency, multi-disciplinary way to ensure that children are healthy, safe, achieving at school and making a positive contribution to the community and achieving economic well-being.

(Knowles 2006:13)

In 2008, Lord Laming expressed his frustration at the lack of progress in creating truly integrated services. However, the exhortation to provide integrated services for children and families seems at times to entirely underestimate the complexity of the task, and the need to dismantle years of hierarchical, demarcated practice. If integration is to be effective at all then we all need to address the following:

- working towards a common set of agreed values and working practices across professions;
- training in all professions working with children and families on the contribution of different services and the building blocks of integrated services, how it might happen on the ground;
- regular in-service training for all agencies working with children and families on integrated work;
- transparent integrated work at senior management level in local authorities and primary care trusts, pooled management and finances;
- work on what is meant by effective communication across all agencies;
- information-sharing protocols across different agencies, with a clear understanding of what constitutes effective practice;
- clear community and parental involvement in the design, delivery and evaluation of services;
- clear organisation of family-based services to enable partnership working
- successive governments committed to integrated working;
- streamlining of information technology systems and paperwork;
- parity of pay and working conditions across agencies;
- clear protocols for supervision across different agencies;

- clear understanding of safeguarding children practice across all agencies with a clear understanding of roles and responsibilities;
- children's centres to become a statutory part of the infrastructure of children's services.

The Children's Plan

In December 2007 the government launched the Children's Plan, basing their ideas on a comprehensive set of research that establishes how children might be best supported to make the best possible use of their potential. The Children's Plan established the following set of objectives:

- At age five, 90% of children will be developing well across all areas of the early years foundation stages
- At the age of 11, 95% of all children will have reached expected levels of literacy and numeracy
- At the age of 19, 90% of pupils will have achieved the equivalent of five good GCSEs
- At the age of 19, the majority of children will be ready for higher education with at least 6 out of 10 pupils achieving the equivalent of "A" levels
- Child poverty will be halved by 2010 and eradicated by 2020
- There will be clear improvements in child health, with the proportion of overweight children reduced to 2000 levels
- The number of first time offenders will be reduced so that by 2020 the number receiving a conviction, reprimand or final waning for an offence has fallen by a quarter.

(Children's Plan, DCSF 2007:20)

A key principle of the Children's Plan is that intervening early should be the objective for schools and other agencies to support children. However, rhetoric is one thing, but it is the people on the ground who need to make that happen. It is only by working closely with parents and communities that we can come close to making this a reality. The revised version of the Children and Young People's Plan (CYPP) (DCSF 2009) recognises the importance of consultation, and requires that local authorities draw up their own plan to meet the needs of their individual communities, ensuring full involvement of all stakeholders, working together in partnership.

A central aim of the CYPP is to demonstrate how local services will help to reduce inequality between children. There is no fixed blueprint stipulating how local priorities will be met. All CYPPs should provide evidence for the following:

- secure the well-being and health of children and young people;
- safeguard the young and vulnerable;
- close the gap in educational achievement for disadvantaged children;
- ensure that young people are participating and achieving their potential to 18 and beyond;
- keep children and young people on the path to success; and
- deliver system-wide reform to the way services for children and young people work together.

(DCSF 2009:23)

The whole notion of Sure Start children's centres is a highly complex, challenging yet rewarding idea that already has made an enormous difference to the way in which services are delivered to communities. The challenge is to embed good practice into every children's centre across the country. With the promise of a children's centre in every community, our purpose now is to make each centre count in maximising the potential of each and every child. This book draws upon a wide range of different experiences and different perspectives in considering how those elements work together. It is the bringing together of those highly diverse elements, in excellent partnership, that is the key to successful practice. This is never easy and as the work with families is relational so is effective inter-agency communication.

References

Berk, L.A.E. (2002) *Infants and Children* (4th edition). Boston: Allyn & Bacon.
Bronfenbrenner, U. (1995) 'The bioecological model from a life course perspective: reflections of a participant observer', in Moon, P., Elder, G.H. and Luscher, K. (eds) *Examining Lives in Context*, Washington, DC: American Psychology Association, pp. 599–618.
DCSF (2007) *Children's Plan*.
DCSF (2009) *Children and Young People's Plan Guidance 2009*.
DfES (2006) *Sure Start Children's Centres: Practice Guidance*.
Knowles, G. (Ed.) (2006) *Supporting Inclusive Practice*. London: Routledge.
Wilkinson, R. and Marmot, M. (Eds) (2003) *The Social Determinants of Health: the Solid Facts*. World Health Organisation.

Further reading

Murry, L. and Cooper, P.J. (Eds) (1997) *Postpartum Depression and Child Development*. New York: Guildford Press.
Sunderland, M. (2006) *What Every Parent Needs to Know*. London: Dorling Kindersley.
Whalley, M. (2007) *Leadership in Integrated Centres and Services for Children and Families: A Community Development Approach Engaging in the Struggle*. Corby: Pen Green Research.

Websites

Every Child Matters:
www.everychildmatters.gov.uk/planningandcommissioning/cypp

CHAPTER 2

The background

Creating a fairer society?

Carole Beaty

This chapter considers the national context for the development of the Sure Start programme and discusses some of the initiatives that lay behind its inception and development. It also reviews some of the barriers to effective working, as well as those elements of policy and practice that can make a difference in helping this dream to become a reality.

Definitions of poverty and social exclusion

When considering the development of the Sure Start programme and its evolution into the children's centre initiative it is essential to consider the underlying drivers that gave rise to such a groundbreaking movement in Early Years policy and practice. It is also important to see how such a philosophy of child-centred practice and community empowerment is living up to those original aspirations.

Any community large or small must be judged, held to account for the way in which it treats its most vulnerable members. Poverty in children is just one such indicator of our sense of ourselves as a civilised nation. Yet poverty amongst young children still remains a significant barrier to achievement and development to many in our society.

In March 1999, Tony Blair the then Labour Prime Minister made a promise to eradicate child poverty by 2020. 'Our historic aim will be for ours to be the first generation to end child poverty forever, and it will take a generation. It is a twenty-year mission, but I believe it can be done' (Tony Blair, 18 March 1999).

What do we mean by poverty?

Poverty, like success, happiness and sadness, is hard to define; maybe it is something that we recognise when we see it. It is certainly an element of our communities that we still seem to live with and almost to accept. When that great social reformer and exposure of social injustice Charles Dickens described Oliver Twist, we recognised the symptoms of poverty:

> I wish some well-fed philosopher, whose blood is ice, whose heart is iron, could have seen have seen Oliver Twist clutching at the dainty viands the dog had neglected. I wish he could have witnessed the horrible avidity with which Oliver tore the bits asunder with all the ferocity of famine.
>
> (*Oliver Twist*, Dickens, 1838)

We see a scene of abject and terrible poverty; however, while such sights would be less familiar in twenty-first-century Britain, maybe what Dickens would recognise today is an insidious form of poverty that disempowers the individual and allows certain sections of our community to experience barriers to their own sense of personal fulfilment and agency in their own lives. Poverty still stalks the streets of our country and is every bit as dangerous and disempowering to the whole of society. It lies at the heart of many social evils that contaminate our communities and give rise to feelings of insecurity and hopelessness; it can also provoke feelings of dissatisfaction. While the intentions to nail child poverty are eloquent and passionate, the rhetoric often lacks the detail that might just make the difference that might really enable us to be the generation that eradicates child poverty. The policies that seek to address issues of child poverty and of social exclusion sometimes seem to be short on the courage to grasp the whole complex nettle.

How do we define poverty at the beginning of the twenty-first century? The Child Poverty Action Group uses the following criteria as measures of poverty:

1 Children experiencing relative low income. Defined as children in households with 'needs-adjusted' incomes below the poverty line (60 per cent of the current national median income).

2 Children experiencing material deprivation and relative low income combined. Defined as children in households with needs-adjusted incomes below 70 per cent of the national median and who are experiencing material deprivation.

3 Children experiencing absolute low income. Defined as children in households with needs-adjusted incomes below 60 per cent of the 1998/99 national median income.

(Child Poverty Action Group 2008:5)

What Dickens might recognise in our current society is the attitude that somehow the poor bring the misfortune upon themselves and that a bit of initiative, a bit of resourcefulness, would end their problems. Maybe this way of thinking was reinforced in a Thatcherite Britain in which Norman Tebbitt (the then Under Secretary in the Ministry of Trade) made his famous remark about the unemployed: 'I grew up in the 1930's with an unemployed father. He didn't riot. He got on his bike and looked for work'.

Today with the current government committed to eradicating child poverty, employment often seems to lie at the heart of their strategy. We know that the cycle of poverty and social exclusion is cyclical and that it is sometimes seen to be passed down from generation to generation. However, this government, as many others, can see employment as a cure-all, and miss the complex reasons that entrench poverty and minimise life chances, and the specific reasons that employment may prove impossible or very difficult for some. Highly diverse and sensitive issues often lie at the heart of poor communities: the lack of employment; single-parent households, where childcare is often not affordable or does not fit around working arrangements; poor transport, most particularly in rural areas; the inaccessible nature of some forms of benefit; the stigmatization of some portions of the population; complex policies that often contradict each other, most specifically those that relate to asylum seekers. Sure Start children's centres are central to the government's policy to end child poverty and to provide a possibility of prevention rather than cure, but we have a long way to go if we are to achieve that much vaunted aim of eradicating child poverty by 2020.

What needs to happen to end child poverty?

- Truly joined-up services from the top to the person working on the bottom rung of the ladder;
- adequate housing that meets the needs of individual family;
- housing that considers the very specific needs of families with children with additional needs;
- excellent health care, with good health visiting in all areas;
- adequate maternity and paternity leave that enable parents to be with their infant children in the crucial moments of their life;
- adequately resourced childcare/education that is free at the point of use. staff that are well trained to degree level and paid accordingly;
- a clear professional structure for childcare/education staff so that it is seen as a valued and valuable profession;

- education that enables children of the less well-off to access all areas of learning, so that they feel part of the school and can fully benefit from everything that is on offer;

- flexible working/training that fits around the individual;

- a benefit system that is understandable and accessible;

- adequate child-friendly outside spaces to be enjoyed by both adults and children;

- communities who have a real say about the development of their own area;

- children's centres that are a statutory part of the children's services;

- a more truly equal society; this means addressing both ends of the spectrum.

The development of the Sure Start programme: a new dawn

The creation of Sure Start offered a wonderful opportunity to parents, practitioners and members of the community to learn from each other in an exchange of ideas creating imaginative and dynamic ways of meeting the needs of a local community. It was an irreplaceable time that I fear will never come again for those of us who had the opportunity to experience it. It was a time to get off our metaphorical 'high horse' whether we were a parent, teacher, social worker, member of the voluntary sector, health visitor, community nursery nurse, or midwife. We could ask those difficult questions, be in a position of not knowing, of not being the expert, without feeling vulnerable. It was a melting pot of creation in supporting children. However, this sense of integration and mutual exchange did not materialise from nothing; it arose from a government, and practitioners determined to give every child the best possible start in life. At last those of us working in Early Years saw what we and those who came before us had been saying for generations: if a society invests in young children and in the well-being of families we are investing in the long-term prosperity of our whole society. We are helping to create the seedbed of a more confident, happy, valued society.

The Sure Start programme is the cornerstone of the government's push to address issues of poverty and social exclusion to build upon that long-held understanding that it is by working effectively in the Early Years that we lay secure foundations for the future. Sure Start drew upon the work of the Head Start programme in the United States for some of its inspiration; we explore these links further in Chapter 3.

The vision for Sure Start and its birth

The Labour government came to power in 1997 with a mandate to improve standards of education, indeed their mantra was: 'Education, Education, Education'. A supporting plank of their policies aimed at raising standards in education was to concentrate on practice in the Early Years, to create a more equal start for very young children. Noted educationalists such as Rudolph Steiner and Maria Montessori, to name but two, had seen the power and the possibility of working more effectively with children in a dynamic and imaginative manner to provide excellence in these vital early years. Early Years policy and practice, often conceptualised as the Cinderella of the education arena, was at last being recognised for its possibilities.

When the Labour party came to power the provision for young children was fragmented and disjointed with little sense of cohesion across different areas. A review of services at this time found that (Glass 1999):

- Children living in poverty had a greater chance of performing poorly in school, getting a criminal record, and becoming teenage parents.
- These children were more likely to be unemployed as adults.
- Services for young children are highly variable and haphazard.

In 1997, Sure Start developed as a result of the discussions of the United Kingdom's Government Comprehensive Spending Review (CSR), a group that was tasked with looking at public spending in the light of government priorities. Norman Glass stated:

> One of the first duties of the Ministerial Steering Group, on which all major departments with an interest were represented, was to agree terms of reference for the review. These were:

> To look at the polices and resources devoted to children aged seven and under, in order to secure effectiveness in providing preventative action and the necessary support to ensure the development of their full potential throughout their adult lives

> To consider whether the multiple causes of social exclusion affecting young children could be more effectively tackled at the family and community level, using a more integrated approach to service provision to take account of policy developments and initiatives being taken forward in other fora.

> (Glass 1999:2)

This multi-professional review recognised the growing problem of social disadvantage in many areas of society; they saw that provision for the pre-school child was often patchy and unco-ordinated. Some inner-city areas had excellent provision while other areas lagged woefully behind.

There was a growing sense that it was not just throwing money at Early Years provision that would make a difference, there also needed to be a new way of working in this area, a challenge to existing practice. The Sure Start movement required professionals and parents, families and community members to think and act in entirely new ways, to be experimental and radical in the way in which we might view our work. The scheme demanded 'empowerment' of those people who had often had the least say in their own and their children's destinies. It asked practitioners in all fields, health, education, social care and the voluntary sector to consider that they may not always have the answers. It asked everyone to challenge certainties and this made working in Sure Start unsettling and radical. What was called for was a more cohesive joined-up approach to service design and delivery, at all levels of different organisations. This move towards increased integration of service design and delivery was not always welcomed, nor was the full involvement of service users.

Sure Start local programmes (SSLPs) were locally defined, but every Sure Start had to contribute to the following objectives (Eisenstaedt 2000):

- to improve children's health;
- to improve children's ability to learn;
- to improve children's social and emotional development;
- to strengthen families and communities.

To meet these goals SSLPs had to provide a key set of services, known as the Core Offer:

> Sure Start Children's Centres in the most disadvantaged areas will offer the following services:
>
> - Good quality early learning combined with full day care provision for children (minimum ten hours a day, five days a week, 48 weeks a year)
> - Good quality teacher input to lead the development of learning within the centre
> - Child and family health services, including antenatal services
> - Parental outreach
> - A base for a childminder network

- Support for children and parents with special needs
- Effective links with Jobcentre Plus to support parents and carers who wish to consider training or employment.

In more advantaged areas, although LAs will have flexibility in which services they provide to meet local need, all Sure Start Children's Centres will have to provide a minimum range of services including:

- Appropriate support and outreach services to parents and carers, and children who have been identified as in need of them
- Information and advice to parents and carers on a range of subjects, including local childcare, looking after babies and young children, Local Early Years provision (childcare and early learning) education services for 3- and 4-year-olds
- Support for childminders
- Drop-in sessions and other activities for children and carers at the centre
- Links to Jobcentre Plus services

(Every Child Matters homepage, accessed 19/7/2009)

This notion of 'cultural change' lay at the heart of the Sure Start programme and was emphasised in future policies; however, whether it really took root and was accepted was another matter. Often initiatives that had been hailed as groundbreaking saw a quick return to orthodoxy and to the status quo.

Where many countries in Europe had already invested substantially in Early Years services, with significant outcomes, the United Kingdom still saw the whole area of child development as the province of the family. Now the Cabinet approved a £200-million-per-year expenditure on an upgrade of services for young children and their families. This money was part of the DfEE budget, but was to be ring-fenced so that it could only be spent on Sure Start. Thus began a new era in the development of Early Years practice, a time that saw agencies at last communicating more clearly with each other and building upon research-based practice. Glass emphasised this idea of integrated policy in ensuring better outcomes for all children:

> Sure Start local programmes represented a new way of doing things, both in the development of the policy and in its delivery. It is an attempt to put into practice 'joined-up thinking', but it is also an outstanding example of evidence-based policy and open consultative government. At a policy level it represents a commitment to investing in our children for a

long-term future and a commitment to the belief that statutory and voluntary agencies working together with a common goal can achieve more than the sum of the individual parts.

(Glass 1999:5)

In January 1999, sixty trailblazers were launched by David Blunkett and Tessa Jowell, programmes that were concentrated in areas of identified disadvantage. These new programmes were to be guided and managed by local partnerships. Representatives from different agencies from health, education, social services, and from the private and voluntary sector, would work together across a neighbourhood to support the interests and children under five and their families. Neighbourhoods were to be small, maybe just a mile or two in radius, so that services were as accessible as possible for the local community.

The whole Sure Start programme emphasised from the start the notion of consultation and full community involvement. The vision was that by asking families what they wanted, expensive mistakes would be avoided. However, consultation and agreement is a laudable aim and sounds wonderful in theory, but it is complex to achieve successfully. Many fun-days and family outings, picnics and parties were organised to facilitate the gathering of information and ideas and often to recruit parents to the partnership board. It seems that at times this very complexity was misunderstood by policy-makers, and interpreting that rhetoric into a reality took a lot longer than was initially anticipated.

Selection process

Areas were selected to develop Sure Start local programmes according to level of deprivation within their areas, but decisions about catchment areas were decided locally. Catchment areas cover wards in the 20 per cent of the most deprived wards (as measured by the ODPM (Office of the Deputy Prime Minister) Index of Multiple Deprivation).

The building blocks of the Sure Start programmes were:

- health, education, social care and the voluntary sector working in an integrated way to improve the life chances of children and their families;
- senior managers in all sectors working in a multi-agency, multi-professional manner;
- frontline staff who can stay with ambiguity and change;
- easily accessible services, offered in a user friendly manner;

- services that are community/parent led and professionally facilitated;
- health, education, social care and the voluntary sector viewing the child as a whole person within the context of family and community;
- building upon existing services on the ground that already offer good practice rather than starting from scratch;
- supporting the development of children's early learning and attachment, through play-based experiences;
- being innovative in practice and having the freedom and resources to try out new ideas to reach aspects of the community;
- building upon evidence-based practice;
- being ambitious about supporting community regeneration;
- holding on to a child-centred approach to policy and to practice.

The barriers to effective working in Sure Start programmes

New ways of working can often throw up issues that need to be addressed as programmes develop and show that the success of true partnership working is dependent on everyone having a will to tackle potential threats to long-term success:

- inertia in statutory services that saw new ways of working as a threat;
- hierarchal nature of statutory services who found learning from service users unfamiliar and threatening;
- professional boundaries sometimes become more entrenched at the start of the programme;
- hard-to-reach groups and services remain hard to reach;
- poor or non-existent communication, most particularly communication overly dependent upon electronic means of communication, rather than using real-time communication;
- a top-down model, with scant integration of ideas at the top.

After Gordon Brown's comprehensive spending review in 2002 the Sure Start Unit merged with the Early Years and Childcare Unit to create a new cross-departmental programme. Baroness Ashton led this unit as Minister of Sure Start, Early Years and Childcare. This merger then brought together Sure Start and the government strategy for childcare, which was published in 2004 and gave a commitment that by 2010 there would be a Sure Start children's centre in each community, serving the needs of young children and families. Providing universal services in partnership with other agencies and targeted intervention and support as necessary.

The Laming Report and increasing emphasis on joined-up working

The tragic case of Victoria Climbié in 2000 emphasised again the need for a greater sense of co-operation and communication between agencies in supporting issues of child protection. Victoria was one of a long line of children who experienced abuse at the hands of those family members charged with her care. Victoria, who had come from Sierra Leone to England in the care of her great aunt, was the subject of repeated and horrific abuse. When Lord Laming produced his report in 2003, he said he wanted to emphasise most particularly the failure of agencies to work co-operatively to ensure an understanding of children's well-being.

During the winter of 1999/2000 Victoria spent her last days in circumstances of the most desperate abuse and neglect.

> When Victoria was admitted to the North Middlesex Hospital on the evening of the 24th February 2000, she was desperately ill. She was bruised, deformed and malnourished. Her temperature was so low it could not be recorded on the hospital's standard thermometer. Dr. Lesley Alsford, the consultant responsible for Victoria's care on that occasion, said 'I had never seen a case like it before. It is the worst case of child abuse and neglect that I have ever seen'.
>
> (Laming 2003:1)

Victoria tragically died on 25 February 2000, after being transferred to the paediatric unit of St. Mary's Hospital, Paddington, in a valiant attempt to save her life.

What Lord Laming wanted to bring to the public's attention was the need for every individual, whatever their professional position, to take hold of issues of child protection and of the general well-being of children, emphasising yet again that it is each and every one of us that can and must make a difference. The report makes desperate, but salutary reading for all those working with and for young children. What Laming emphasised was that it is too easy to vilify those front-line staff who have failed to make that connection, failed to file a report or follow-up adequately on a referral; however, it is the failure of the whole institution or collective that must be addressed, along with the accountability of senior managers, in ensuring that everyone has a clear sense of their responsibility and an understanding of lines of accountability.

> It is not the handful of hapless, if sometimes inexperienced staff, that I direct most criticism for the events leading up to Victoria's death. While the standard of work done by those with direct contact with her was generally of poor quality, the greatest failure rests with the managers and senior managers of the authorities whose task it was to ensure that services for children, like Victoria were properly financed, staffed, and able to deliver good quality support for children and families. It is significant that while a number of junior staff in Haringey Social Services were suspended and faced disciplinary action after Victoria's death, some of the most senior officers were being appointed to other, presumably better paid, jobs. This is not an example of managerial accountability that impresses me much.
>
> (Laming 2003:1.23)

Laming's criticism of the local authority department's inability to work together led him to recommend the setting up of directorates of social services in each local authority. There was an increased understanding that it was not just the specialised services working to promote the safety of children that must be on their guard for possible problems, but that all professionals working with children must be appropriately trained and empowered to take responsibility: 'The term "safeguarding" replaced "child protection" to emphasise the message that it is the responsibility of all professionals working with children to promote their health and development' Anning and Ball (2008:6).

The report called for better lines of communication and comprehensive systems of information sharing, and Laming's final recommendation was for a universal database. He also recommended that when children's services were inspected, government inspectors should focus both on the quality of children's services provided and essentially the 'effectiveness of inter-agency arrangements for services to children and parents' (Laming 2003:para. 17:97).

Laming saw good practice in integrated, multi-professional work as fundamental to the well-being and safety of children. Centrally, Laming called upon the government to set up a central database that would facilitate effective communication between professional agencies.

The main points of Laming's 2003 report were:

- The creation of a children's and families board chaired by a senior government minister to coordinate policies and initiatives that have a bearing on the wellbeing of children and families

- A national agency for children and families, led by a children's commissioner, should be established to ensure local services meet national standards for child protection and implement reforms
- Committees for children and families should be established by councils, with members drawn from social services, education, housing, the NHS and the police
- New local management boards – chaired by council chief executives with members from the police, health, social services, education, housing and the probation service-should be set up. The boards should appoint a local director of children and family services to monitor effective interagency working on child welfare and protection.
- The creation of a national children's database that keeps a record of every contact a child has with a member of staff from the police, health and local authorities.

(Batty 2003:1)

The Laming Report set out the blueprint for a fundamental change in practice for services for young children and gave a new and urgent impetus for action. Has this really happened?

Following the tragic death of 'Baby P. (Peter)', Lord Laming was asked to review safeguarding children's services. Again his report flagged-up issues to do with leadership, recruitment, training, learning from experience, partnership working and the availability of resources. He felt that there were improvements and that committed front-line staff were daily making an enormous difference to the safety of children. However, he urged national and local government to grasp the responsibility of implementation more firmly. He asked that the leaders of local services 'accept their responsibility to translate policy, legislation and guidance into day to day practice on the frontline of every service' (Laming 2009, in Pugh 2009:5).

Every Child Matters (Green Paper 2003)

The appalling death of Victoria Climbié was not a tragically isolated case, but one of several that we have witnessed over the years; however, it stands out both for its horrific nature and for initiating the range of changes that Laming identified in his 2003 report.

In January 2003 the then Secretary of State for Health, Alan Milburn, made a statement to the House of Commons in response to the Laming Report; he emphasised the need for all services at all levels to facilitate real change in respect of creating a more cohesive approach to children's services, and to ensure that as a society we look at prevention rather than cure:

The safety of children is a priority for the government. The most effective safety net is prevention. We want to stop children falling into a spiral of ill-health, anti-social behaviour or social exclusion, as well as prevent the worse forms of ill-treatment and abuse. We are looking at how we can create a system where children are provided with the most effective preventative services we can develop. Local Preventative Strategies are being put in place by local authorities across England this year, which will draw together all agencies working with children to provide appropriate services.

The Green Paper 'Every Child Matters' was published in 2003; this document sought to strengthen protection for children and to create a more cohesive service for children. However, it went beyond this in helping to maximise life chances for every child. There were four main areas for action:

- supporting parents and carers;
- early intervention and effective protection;
- accountability and integration;
- workforce reform.

Early intervention was seen as pivotal to the Every Child Matters agenda to ensure that families and communities were provided with services that met their needs and that families were fully involved in the design of those services. To further ensure the best interests of children it was anticipated that working with young children and supporting their progress and development would become an increasingly attractive and high-status career. This workforce would become increasingly flexible in meeting the needs of young children and it was expected that there would be a common training framework that would facilitate more effective joint working.

The Children Act 2004 provided the legislative framework for establishing the recommendations laid out in 'Every Child Matters'. This signalled the most fundamental change in how children's services were perceived and delivered. Central to this was the principle of integrated practice at every level of service design and delivery. The key outcomes are for every child, whatever their circumstances and background, to:

- be healthy;
- stay safe;
- enjoy and achieve;

- make a positive contribution;
- achieve economic well-being.

What Laming had done was to indicate that tinkering with aspects of services was not sufficient; what was required was a fundamental sea-change in how we see childhood services and how we value and respect the vulnerability of individual children. What was needed was parents with a greater sense of their own agency, children who were genuinely listened to, and service providers at all levels who know the score, know what is going on in their local communities and are empowered to help create the climate in which children reach out to achieve their potential. This does not happen overnight and needs robust frameworks to help facilitate such a change. Central to Laming's message was that better communication and true integration was essential.

The National Service Framework for Health

The promotion of children's health was seen as a key element of the Children Act 2004 and central to the Every Child Matters agenda. If professionals working with children were to respond fully to the recommendations laid out by Laming then the holistic understanding of children's needs was essential. In the past, children's health was visualised as an addendum to adult health and not given validity in its own right. 'The National Service Framework for Health' would require that practice changed and that health professionals saw the unique needs of children, and that children were viewed holistically, with appropriate engagement between health, education and social care. Again the message is clear from this document that services must be centred around the needs of the child, not around the needs of the providers. It also requires that health services for children and for pregnant mothers be seen as far as possible as community based resources with accessible patient led provision. Clearly, Sure Start children's centres are vital to the design and delivery of community-based practice:

> The vision of the national service framework is huge and implies considerable cultural change in the NHS and beyond. The aim is child and family centred services, designed and delivered around their needs rather than those of the organisation. The NHS must grasp this opportunity. The national service framework is government policy, strengthened by concurrent reports, and signals a higher priority for children and maternity services

across all areas of government. If the services and all clinicians working with women and children do not respond, children will be the losers.

(Lachman and Vickers 2004:693–4)

What is fundamental to this document is that it promotes children's health and proactive early support in enhancing the positive life chances of the child within the wider context of family and of community.

The Key Standards for the National Service Framework for Children, Young People and Maternity Services

Promoting Health and Well-being. Identifying Needs and Intervening Early

The health and well-being of all children and young people is promoted and delivered through a co-ordinated programme of action, including prevention and early intervention wherever possible, to ensure long-term gain led by the NHS in partnership with local authorities.

Supporting Parents

Parents or carers are enabled to receive the information, services and support which will help them to care for their children and equip them with the skills they need to ensure that their children have optimum life chances and are healthy and safe.

Child, Young People and Family Centred Services

Children and young people and families receive high quality services and support which are co-ordinated around their individual and family needs to take account of their views.

Growing Up into Adulthood

All young people have access to age-appropriate services which are responsive to their specific needs as they grow into adulthood.

Safeguarding and Promoting the Welfare of Children and Young People

All agencies work to prevent children suffering harm and to promote their welfare, provide them with the services they require to address their identified needs and safeguard children who are likely to be harmed.

Children and Young People Who Are Ill

All children and young people who are ill, or thought to be ill, or injured will have timely access to appropriate advice and to effective services which address their health, social, educational and emotional needs throughout the period of their illness.

Children and Young People in Hospital

> Children and young people receive high quality, evidence-based hospital care, developed through clinical governance and delivered in appropriate settings.

Disabled Children and Young People and Those with Complex Health Needs

> Children and young people who are disabled or who have complex health needs receive co-ordinated, high quality child and family-centred services which are based on assessed needs, which promote social inclusion and, where possible, which enable them and their families to live ordinary lives.

The Mental and Psychological Well-being of Children and Young People

> All children and young people, from birth to their eighteenth birthday, who have mental health problems and disorders have access have access to timely, integrated, high quality multidisciplinary mental health services to ensure effective assessment, treatment and support, for them and their families.

Medicines for Children and Families

> Children, young people, their parents or carers, and health care professionals in all settings make decisions about medicines based on sound information about risk and benefit. They have access to safe and effective medicines that are prescribed on the basis of the best available evidence.

Maternity Services

> Women have easy access to supportive, high quality maternity services, designed around their individual needs and those of their babies.

> (Ibid.)

If the recommendations set out in the National Service Framework for Health are to work successfully then all those involved in policy making and in delivering services need to work together in a cohesive and comprehensive manner. The further roll-out of children's centres provides an ideal opportunity to ensure that this might happen. In his report on safeguarding in children's services Laming emphasises the role of health professionals in working with families. Most particularly, health visitors are uniquely placed in their relationship of trust with young families, and are central in supporting effective practice.

Children's Trusts

Fundamental to the change in children's services was the establishment of Children's Trusts. The idea for these trusts was to bring together all services supporting children and families; they are local-area partnership arrangements for co-ordinating key agencies in line with the Children Act 2004, 'duty to co-operate'. The essential features of the Children's Trusts were:

- A child-centred, outcome led vision;
- Integrated front-line delivery: organised around the child, young person or family rather than professional boundaries or existing agencies – for example, multi-agency teams, co-located staff in extended schools or children's centres, joint training, and arrangements for identifying a lead professional wherever a child is known to more than one targeted or specialist agency and a co-ordinated response is required;
- Integrated processes: effective joint working sustained by a shared language and shared processes. These include a Common Assessment Framework, effective information sharing agreements;
- Integrated strategy (joint planning and commissioning): joint assessment of local needs; the identification of all available resources; integrated planning to prioritise action and a move towards preventative services; and joint commissioning of services from a range of providers, supported appropriately by shared resources and pooled budgets. Voluntary and community organisations, and other providers, should be able to contribute to planning and commissioning of services on an equal footing with other partners;
- Interagency governance: whilst each partner is responsible for the exercise of its own functions, robust arrangements for inter-agency co-operation are needed to set the framework of accountability for improving and delivering effective services.

(DfES 2005:7)

Who are the partners?

A key flaw in the Victoria Climbié case as indentified in the Laming Report was the failure of different agencies to work together to assess the needs of a child and to respond appropriately. Anyone who works in this area or has experience of accessing services will be only too aware of the complexity of agency protocol and of the wide range of agencies who might be involved with one child. The Children's Trust seeks to identify these agencies and facilitate more confident and robust communication and joint working.

The 'relevant partners' must co-operate with the local authority in making arrangements to improve children's wellbeing. This duty requires them to work together with the local authority at every level in making the arrangements. The relevant partners are as follows:

- The district council in two tier authorities. Services provided by the district council which impact upon children's well-being include housing, leisure and recreation
- The police authority
- A local probation board
- The Youth Offending Team (YOT)
- A Strategic Health Authority (SHA) and Primary Care Trust (PCT)
- Agencies providing services under section 114 of the Learning and Skills Act 2000, i.e. the local Connexions Partnership
- The Learning and Skills Council for England.

(DfES 2005:6)

To facilitate good integrated practice between agencies the Children Act provided the local authority and the partner agencies with the power to establish pooled funding for the purpose of co-operative arrangements.

Bronfenbrenner identified the wide range of contexts that affect children's life chances in his model of ecological systems (see Chapter 1). He looked at the way in which family, friends, childcare, street, and parent's employment all impact day-to-day on a child's feelings about themselves and the world around them. If children's services are to make a true difference they need to address the wider context in which children grow and develop. So further agencies that might be involved with the Children's Trusts might include:

- Children and young people themselves;
- Voluntary and community sector agencies;
- Agencies with responsibility for delivering other front-line statutory services to children young people and their families, e.g. not for profit and private sector bodies, colleges, work-based learning providers of health services (including NHS Trusts and General Practitioners, Jobcentre Plus and, where appropriate the immigration service;
- Childcare, culture sport and play organisations;
- Families, carers and communities. The Act also specifically requires authorities to 'have regard to' the importance of parents and other persons caring for children when making arrangements under section 10 of the Act (The Guidance on the duty to cooperate).

(DfES 2005:10)

However, although the Act made mention of the involvement of schools as essential in promoting children's life chances within the framework of integrated practice, their involvement has been at times patchy and has at times appeared to lack commitment.

Are Children's Trusts making a difference?

The Department for Education and Skills and the Department of Health commissioned the University of East Anglia in association with the National Children's Bureau to carry out a national evaluation of Children's Trust pathfinders. This showed that Children's Trusts have:

- Acted as a catalyst for more integrated approaches to the diagnosis of provision of services for children;
- Drawn together a variety of statutory and local services with the aim of enabling them to make a difference to the well-being of children and young people;
- Begun to develop expertise in joint-commissioning of services across traditional organisational boundaries;
- Sometimes found it difficult to engage partners in key sectors, notably where there were funding difficulties or complex accountability frameworks;
- Enabled joined-up approaches to workforce development and training;
- Facilitated the development of new types of professionals who are able to work across long-standing organisational and professional boundaries;
- Reported early indications of local positive outcomes for children and young people.

(Husbands 2007:1)

The Common Assessment Framework (CAF)

If we are to promote the well-being of children and young people and if those people who work directly with children are to communicate and co-operate effectively then they need robust systems of multi-agency assessments to identify children's specific needs and to work together to provide appropriate and targeted services. The CAF is a key element for delivering front-line services that are focused around the needs of the child, not around the perceived needs of the service provider. The CAF should be about ensuring earlier intervention to support the needs of families it needs to be a proactive rather than reactive service.

One of the main purposes of 'Every Child Matters' was to 'mainstream preventative approaches' (DfES 2003:1.18). 'As part of this initiative, the common assessment framework is intended to shift thresholds downwards and change the focus of dealing with the consequences of difficulties in children's lives to preventing things going wrong in the first place' (Brandon *et al.* 2006).

Everyone who works with children and young people should have received appropriate training in the use of the CAF and in the key role of the lead professional in supporting truly integrated assessments and remediation. The Common Assessment will help:

- the early identification of specific additional needs of children and young people;
- the fully co-ordinated designation of services around the needs of the child;
- to avoid the duplication of services;
- eliminate the need for children and families to re-tell their story to a wide range of different agencies.

Common Assessments are a tool for identifying children with 'additional needs' before they escalate into more serious and damaging problems. 'Additional needs' are defined as those which need specific, targeted support within universal settings.

This might include situations where there were issues with:

- Disruptive anti-social behaviour
- Involvement in or risk of offending
- Overt parental conflict or lack of parental support/boundaries
- Poor attendance or exclusion from school/disengagement from education, training
- Bullying
- Special educational needs
- Disability
- Employment post-16
- Poor nutrition and ill-health
- Substance misuse
- Anxiety or depression

- Housing
- Pregnancy or parenthood

Common Assessment will not be appropriate for the majority of children as they will make satisfactory progress with the support of universal services. Nor will it be appropriate in situations where an immediate statutory or specialist assessment is the most appropriate way to determine the support required.

(Northamptonshire County Council website, accessed 19/10/2008)

When completing a CAF, practitioners will be required to review the following three domains:

1 how well a child is developing, including in their health and progress in learning;
2 how well parents or carers are able to support their child's development and respond appropriately to any needs;
3 the impact of wider family and environmental elements on the child's development and on the capacity of their parents and carers.

The CAF provides a challenging way of working for all practitioners working with families, most particularly because it requires all those professionals to subscribe to a common vision of practice that is child-centred and child-led. It also requires practitioners in all areas of practice to view the child in a holistic manner, seeing all of their needs and their progress in a global manner. The health worker needs to be aware of the child's attitude to life in school or nursery; the teacher needs to know about the child's attitude to friends and family. The child-minder needs to be aware of the impact of a mother's post-natal depression on a child's emerging language. For some people this is part and parcel of their work, part of their training; for others this type of assessment is new. It requires dedicated staff working in each sector of practice; it requires excellent initial and ongoing training and appropriate supervision. It also requires that managers in all sectors of practice understand what is going on in front-line practice and support key workers appropriately, in highly sensitive, often emotive practice. Most importantly, it requires that society as a whole recognises the excellent work that professionals working with children and families undertake and that these staff are seen for what they do and valued appropriately.

The lead professional

The lead professional plays a central role in the way in which the CAF is co-ordinated amongst different agencies and with the child and their family. They are also crucial in helping to draw up a plan across different professional boundaries that will support the child's specific needs and monitor progress. This person might work in education, health, social services or the voluntary sector; they might, for example, be the child's health visitor or their teacher. The important thing is that they are known to the family and trusted by them; they will help the child and family to navigate through the process of assessment and of service provision. They need to be a single point of contact for the family and for the agencies working with the child. At times this may seem to be additional work for that professional acting as lead professional, as some professionals working in the front line with children are likely to be called upon to take on considerable responsibilities for lead professional work. However, the idea is to streamline work with children and to make assessment and remediation a process that is fully addressed by all agencies.

How is the CAF working?

The University of East Anglia was asked to conduct an independent evaluation of the twelve English areas chosen by the DfES to the CAF and the use of the lead professional ahead of the national roll-out in April 2006. Its main research question was 'What helps or hinders practitioners in implementing the Common Assessment Framework (CAF) and lead professional (LP) working?'

The study sought to identify holistic ways of addressing the needs of children. What this piece of research found was that largely the new initiative had been well received across the twelve areas and that practitioners had already seen quite significant benefits for children and families. Practitioners welcomed the co-ordinated way of working and the move towards a more holistic way of addressing the needs of children.

> There was considerable enthusiasm at both grass roots and management level for CAF and LP work in the areas studied and a widespread willingness to make these processes work. Over half of the practitioners and managers interviewed felt that even in this early stage, CAF and LP work was promoting better multi-agency working, helping agencies to come together much faster and enabling more rigorous follow-through in

delivering services. Practitioners were already identifying some positive impact on the lives of children, young people and their families and three quarters spoken to thought the work would lead to better outcomes for children.

(Brandon *et al.* 2006:6)

In this study of recommendations for the national roll-out of the CAF the authors identified a common theme which was the need for a true will to see child-centred practice as fundamental across all of service design and delivery. They emphasised that the important thing was the will to put children at the very heart of service planning and delivery right from the top of government thinking down to the front line along the continuum from early support to child protection risks (Brandon *et al.* 2006).

The Children's Plan 2007

The Children's Plan was launched with a great fanfare as part of the government's strategy to reduce poverty and tackle the causes of social exclusion. When launching the Children's Plan, Ed Balls (Minister for Education) said that he wanted to 'make England the best place in the world for children to grow up.' The Children's Plan sought to acknowledge that children have lives outside school, and that as Bronfenbrenner showed in his ecological model of human development all those contexts in which the child lives will contribute to their sense of well-being and to their capacity to achieve their potential. It recognised that children live within communities and are both affected by them and contribute to them. The Children's Plan brings together a range of already established initiatives, including the whole Sure Start children's centre philosophy of early intervention and community-based practice.

This is a ten-year strategy that sets out a series of ambitions for all areas of children's lives (DCSF 2008a):

- At age 5, 90 per cent of children will have reached expected levels in language and literacy.

- At age 11, 95 per cent of children will have reached expected levels of literacy.

- At age 19, 90 per cent of young people will have achieved the equivalent of five good GCSEs.

The Children's Plan draws upon a wide range of research upon which to base their policy. Early Years research findings emphasise the role of the foundations of learning in creating the 'seedbed' for learning so vital in creating the best opportunities for every child. Most specifically these findings show that children from challenging backgrounds in terms of early life experiences are less likely to be able to be able to make the best use of statutory education. Central to the role of Children's Plan are children's centres in supporting young children and their families. The notion of early support and proactive rather than reactive services form the central vision of this document.

The Children's Plan one year on

In 2009 the government published a review of achievements so far in relation to the Children's Plan objectives and refocused its efforts. It published its priorities for 2009 to help children and families get the support that they need. These were to:

- enshrine in law our commitment to eradicate child poverty by 2020, and publish a 'route map' to achieving it;
- extend our offer of a free childcare place to more 2-year-olds, making sure more children benefit from early learning;
- work with schools to help more parents get involved in their children's learning, for example by ensuring that all new teachers are trained to work with parents;
- introduce new ways to support parents at times when their relationships come under strain, and give more support to children when family relationships break down, and
- publish for the first time, guidelines on young people's alcohol consumption, helping parents to help their children make sensible decisions about the amount they drink.

(DCSF 2008c:7)

The Foundation Stage Curriculum

There has been much rhetoric around 'excellent' Early Years practice; a great deal has been said about the importance of providing free childcare and education so that parents can have greater flexibility around their own working arrangements. The challenge, however, in the whole Early Years debate is not just about provision, but about the quality of that provision; this is a term that is often used in the rush to increase access. However, real 'quality' in childcare and education comes at a price and requires well-trained, highly motivated and well-rewarded staff who have a profound knowledge of child development and can provide consistent care for all children. The REPEY (Researching Effective Pedagogy in the Early Years) study looked at different childcare settings to try to identify the building blocks that support excellent experiences for young children, and promote learning:

> We found that qualified staff in the most effective settings provide children with more academic activities (especially literacy and mathematics) and they encourage children to engage in activities with higher cognitive challenge. While we found that the most highly qualified staff also provided the most direct teaching, we found that they were most effective in their interactions with the children, using the most sustained thinking interactions. Further we found that less qualified staff are significantly better pedagogues when they are supervised by qualified teachers.
>
> (Siraj-Blatchford *et al.* 2003:12)

The whole development of good Early Years practice was founded upon a belief that children should have the very best start in life if they are to make the best possible use of their individual potential. The introduction of the Foundation Stage Curriculum was in many ways a controversial move, giving rise to concerns that too much formality would be introduced to children too early and that the freedom of childhood would in some ways be compromised. However, what the new guidelines have provided is a sense of entitlement for children wherever they are cared for, in a maintained nursery, a private nursery or with a childminder.

The revised version of the Early Years Foundation Stage (EYFS) Statutory Framework and Practice Guidance was published in May 2008. It brings together the Curriculum Guidance for the Foundation Stage (2000), Birth to Three Matters (2002) and the National Standards for Less than 8 Daycare and Childminding (2003). This document would seek to build a coherent flexible approach to care and learning. All providers are required to use the EYFS to ensure that whatever settings parents choose, they can be confident that their child will receive experiences that supports their development and learning (DCSF 2008b).

It is expected that all Early Years' providers and schools in Ofsted registered settings will provide a learning framework in line with the EYFS. That is, for all children in such settings from birth to the end of the academic year in which a child has their fifth birthday.

The EYFS vision needs to guide the work of all practitioners, and is grouped into four distinct but complementary themes (DCSF 2008b):

- a unique child;
- positive relationships;
- enabling environments;
- learning and development.

These themes seek to provide a philosophical base upon which to plan and organise comprehensive learning experiences that recognise the unique nature of each child's learning.

The six areas of learning

The Foundation Stage Curriculum is organised around six areas, with the early learning goals detailing the knowledge, skills and understanding which young children should have acquired by the end of the academic year in which they reach the age of five (DCSF 2008b):

- personal, social and emotional development;
- communication, language and literacy;
- problem solving, reasoning and numeracy;
- knowledge and understanding of the world;
- physical development;
- creative development.

The development of children's centres

By 2003 there was a growing recognition that Sure Start local programmes were making a difference to local communities, and that innovative practice was helping to create more sustainable communities. Evidence from the NESS (National Evaluation of Sure Start), although patchy at first, was beginning to show an impact upon children's lives. While the original intent was to set up Sure Start local programmes in areas of specific deprivation, starting in 1999 with the trailblazer programmes, in 2003 the government decided to move towards a national programme of Sure Start children's centres offering universal mainstream services for children who are under five and their families. This roll-out of a more universal service represented a long-term commitment to 'joined-up' thinking and to an understanding that it is only by all areas of professional endeavour putting the child and family at the centre of our thinking that we can create appropriate, accessible services.

However, not everyone was enthusiastic about the expansion of the Sure Start programme to a more universal service offered through children's centres. Some saw it as a dilution of intent and a compromise that might well lose the essential vision of community and parental involvement that was the backbone of Sure Start.

Norman Glass in his article in *The Guardian* in 2005 spoke of the 'abolition' of Sure Start and some of those essential principles that provide its future and its potential for community ownership:

> What I have learnt from visits to successful Early Years programmes and local communities was that it is necessary, in the case of Early Years at any rate, to involve local people fully in the development and management of the programme if it is to take root and not simply be seen as another quick fix by middle-class social engineers. 'What works' is important but 'how it works', at least in this policy area, is equally, if not more, important.
>
> (Glass 2005:3)

The roll-out of children's centres has seen a move to local authority control and the lack of ring-fencing on funding, this may be challenging for the future of children's centres. It is also the case that the government is not good at promoting the excellent work that children's centres achieve in their local community. We all, including the government and local authorities, need to be better at promoting the work of the children's centre. We need to be shouting it from the roof-tops, because we need everyone to know about it, everyone to be supporting this innovative exciting work that really can make a difference to every child and to every community. We must not allow this great piece of work to get lost to get sidelined under a plethora of rhetoric.

Will children's centres become statutory?

As discussed in Chapter 1, there is a move to make children's centres statutory.

The NESS 2008

The National Evaluation of Sure Start has provided some valuable insights into the way in which this approach is supporting children and families. Key findings for this study are:

Comparison between children and families living in SSLP areas and those in similar areas not having a SSLP revealed the following benefits associated with living in a SSLP area.

- Parents of three-year old children showed less negative parenting while providing their children with a better home learning environment.

- Three-year old children in SSLP areas had better social development with higher levels of positive social behaviour and independence/ self-regulation than children in similar areas not having a SSLP.

- The SSLP effects for positive social behaviour appeared to be a consequence of the SSLP benefits upon parenting (i.e., SSLP>Parenting> Child).

- Three-year-old children in SSLP areas had higher immunisation rates and fewer accidental injuries than children in similar areas not having a SSLP: (it is possible that instead of reflecting positive effects of SSLPs these health-related benefits could have been a result of differences in when measurement was taken of children living in SSLP areas and those living elsewhere).

- Families living in SSLP areas used more child and family-related services than those living elsewhere.

- The effects associated with SSLPs appeared to apply to all of the population, rather than suggesting positive and negative effects for different subgroups as detected in the earlier (2005) report.

- The more consistent benefits associated with SSLPs in the current study compared with the earlier study may well reflect the greater exposure of children and families to better organised and more effective services, as SSLPs have matured over time (though it remains possible that differences in research design across the two studies could also be responsible).

(Anning *et al.* 2008)

While the impact of the Sure Start approach remains positive, but tentative at national level, there are beginning to be encouraging signs that this approach really is making a difference. By June 2008 2,907 children's centres had been established offering services to over 2.2 million young children and their families. By 2010, the number of children's centres increased to 3,500 with the aim that every family will have access to high-quality integrated services in their immediate community. While there has been widespread recognition of the need for community-based services for children, the general roll-out of children's centres has caused concern in some areas. Most particularly the concern has related to the possible watering down of the original philosophy of Sure Start, and its specific emphasis on parent-led services and a move towards a more target-driven, centralised ethos that might compromise the vision of keeping the child at the heart of the process. The fact that children's centres have now come under the central control of local authorities has led to some concern that the innovative, creative nature of the Sure Start programmes might be lost to a more service-driven model that might sidestep the needs of the child and family and re-create existing services along defined sector tramlines. The need to keep early intervention at the heart of the process needs to be paramount and the sensitivity and training of all staff working is this area will continue to be a priority. Essentially it is keeping the child at the heart of thinking, planning and delivery.

What are the key messages from all these initiatives?

- Always build on what is already there in the community, rather than constantly reinventing the wheel. Give initiatives the chance to grow and flourish.

- All services must work together at every level to create dynamic responsive services.

- Parents and families need to be involved in all aspects of service design and delivery right from the start.

- Services, where possible need to be co-located and community based to enable them to be accessible to families.

- Services need to look at the needs of the child, not the needs of the service when designing opportunities for families.

- Services must be offered in a holistic manner taking into account the whole experience of the child and the context in which they grow and learn.

- It is important to offer universal services with practitioners who are aware of the continuum of need.

- Early intervention is essential in addressing issues of social exclusion; practitioners from all areas of practice need to be skilled in working with individual families and children and sensitive to their concerns.

- An over-dependence on electronic ways of communication can stifle the spontaneity of the in-the-moment communication which is the very stuff of relational-based joined-up working.

- Strongly hierarchical ways of working can get in the way of effective communication and good practice. It is important to challenge hierarchical practice which can impede the development of integrated working.

- The temptation for 'empire building' must be constantly challenged, it just gets in the way.

- 'It takes a whole village to raise a child' is relevant today. We are all responsible. A strong community-based approach is essential if all these new initiatives are to make a real difference to children's life chances.

References

Anning, A. and Ball, M. (2008) *Improving Services for Young Children*. London: Sage.

Anning, A., Hall, D., and Meluish, E. (2008) *The Impact of Sure Start Local Programmes on Three Year Olds and Their Families*. National Evaluation of Sure Start (NESS) Institute for the Study of Children, Families and Social Issues, Birbeck University of London. HMSO.

Batty, D. (2003) 'Main points of the Laming Report', *Society Guardian*.

Brandon, M., Howe, A., Daglev, V., Salter, C., Warren, C. and Black, J. (2006) *Evaluating the Common Assessment Framework and Lead Professional Guidance and Implementation in 2005–6*. Norwich: DfES/UEA.

Child Poverty Action Group (2008) *Child Poverty: the Stats Analysis of the Latest Poverty Statistics*. London: CPAG.

DCSF (2008a) *Every Child Matters – Change for Children*.

DCSF (2008b) *Early Years Foundation Stage (EYFS) Statutory Framework and Practice Guidance*.

DCSF (2008c) *The Children's Plan: One Year On*.

DfES (2003) *Every Child Matters*.

DfES (2005) Children's Trusts: Statutory Guidance on Inter-agency Cooperation to Improve *Well-being of Children, Young People and Their Families*.

Dickens, C. (1838) *Oliver Twist*. Harmondsworth: Penguin Classics.

Eisenstadt, N. (2000) 'Sure Start: research into practice: practice into research', *Public Money and Management*, Vol. 20, No. 4, pp. 6–8.

Glass, N. (1999) 'Origins of the Sure Start Local Programme', *Children and Society*, Vol. 13, No. 4, pp. 257–264.

Glass, N. (2005) 'Surely some mistake', *Guardian*, 5 January.

Husbands, C. (2007) *Children's Trust Pathfinders: Innovative Partnerships for Improving the Well-being of Children and Young People. Findings from the National Evaluation of Children's Trust Pathfinders*. Norwich: UEA.

Lachman, P. and Vickers, D. (2004) 'The national service framework for children', *British Medical Journal*, Vol. 329, pp. 693-694.

Laming, H. (2003) *The Victoria Climbié Inquiry*. London: House of Commons Health Committee.

Pugh, J. (2009) 'The protection of children in England: a progress report. Lord Laming's findings and the government's response'. DCSF (Power Point presentation).

Siraj-Blatchford, I., Sylva, K., Muttock, S., Gilden, R. and Bell, D. (2003) *Researching Effective Pedagogy in the Early Years (REPEY)*. London: Institute of Education.

Further reading

DCSF (2008) *The Sure Start Journey – A Summary of Evidence*.

Department of Health (2004) *Executive Summary, National Service Framework for Children, Young People and Maternity Services*. HMSO.

Laming, H. (2008) 'Child protection plans failing', *File on Four*, BBC News.

Preston, G. (2005) *At Greatest Risk*. London: Child Poverty Action Group.

Websites

Every Child Matters:
http://everychildmatters.gov.uk/deliveringservices/contactpoint/about/

Northamptonshire County Council:
www.northamptonshire.gov.uk/child/CAF/whatis-cafhtm

CHAPTER 3

Lessons from abroad

Carole Beaty and Christine Blanshard

Maybe it is our island mentality that makes us an eclectic nation generally eager to learn from other countries and other cultures. The Sure Start programme drew upon the work of Head Start and the Nurse-Family Partnership for its inspiration. Both projects are significant in that they demonstrate the importance of support early in children's lives, most particularly where children are born into challenging circumstances.

Perhaps the most important way in which we can prepare a pre-school child for later schooling is to give them the opportunity to be the age they are and enjoy the freedom and creativity that early childhood can offer. The way in which any society views childhood and enables children to grow and flourish in their early years is indeed the mark of the efficacy of that society. This chapter looks at the different Early Years practices and initiatives in other countries and how these have and might in the future influence the development of integrated children's centres.

When we consider the development of sound Early Years practice, we can learn a great deal from considering the work of other nations and the way in which they offer care and education to young children. A great deal has been said about the work of Loris Malagussi and the Reggio Emilia approach in northern Italy, and of the Scandinavian approach to a play-based way of working that places the child very firmly at the centre of practice. The Sure Start vision drew on the work of the Head Start programme when creating its overall philosophy and design. Sure Start originally aimed to meet the needs of children living in areas of deprivation and to create opportunities not just for the child, but the whole family and by doing so help to lift children out of poverty and give each and every child the very best possible life chances. The whole philosophy of the original Sure Start programme was one of early intervention and support, and of a community-based approach to nurturing the whole family. The possibilities of learning from other ways of working are infinite and exciting in this essential aspect of practice for young children. However, it is always important to remember that it is not possible to entirely transplant a way of working with children from one culture to another.

Head Start

Head Start was part of US President Lyndon Johnson's War on Poverty and was incorporated within the Economic Opportunity Act of 1964. Part of the development of this programme was attributed to Robert Kennedy, who provided the impetus for such initiatives in his desire to address juvenile behaviour, and to create pre-school opportunities that might create a lasting impact upon young people and their families. Head Start was originally launched as a summer programme in 1965, by the Office of Economic Opportunity. In 1995 the Early Head Start programme was formed, reflecting the growing understanding that it is the very first years of life that are crucial in establishing positive patterns of behaviour and in ensuring children's sense of well-being.

The Head Start mission statement states that its overall aims are to address issues of poverty and of social exclusion: 'Head Start is a national program that promotes school readiness by enhancing the social and cognitive development of children through the provision of educational, health, nutritional, social and other services to enrolled children and families' (US Department of Health and Human Services website, accessed 1/8/2009).

What did the Head Start programme provide?

Head Start is essentially a child-focused programme that provides a comprehensive set of services designed at breaking the cycle of deprivation. Head Start was part of the US programme to address issues of poverty and social exclusion and key to this particular way of working was the basic notion that if a child is not in a position, because of reasons of health, poverty or lack of self-esteem, to learn, then education programmes will be worthless for that child. So as with Sure Start programmes there is a fundamental recognition that to tackle social exclusion we must see the child as a whole within the context of family and of community. Services include pre-school education to agreed national standards. Health services include screening programmes, health checks and dental checks. The social services aspect of the programme includes family advocates to work with parents, parenting support groups and training.

Head Start programmes

Head Start originally began with children from low-income families, from three- to five-year-olds, offering a wide range of services across different agencies. It sought to positively influence children's development through the following programmes:

- *Early Head Start:* this built upon the work of the Head Start programme which increasingly recognised the significance of early life experiences in shaping the architecture of the brain.
- *American Indian and Alaskan Native Program Branch:* provides health care and education services to Alaskan and American Indian children.
- *Migrant and Seasonal Program Branch:* provides services to children of migrant and seasonal farm workers.

Early Head Start

The Early Head Start (EHS) programme built upon the work of the initial Head Start in that it is a two-generational programme which is designed to provide effective child and family services to low-income parents. EHS began in 1995 with 68 programmes and has now developed into 708 community-based programmes serving 61,500 children. It is a federally funded, community-based programme that serves low-income families with young children and pregnant women.

Its aim is to:

- Promote healthy prenatal outcomes for pregnant women
- Enhance the development of very young children
- Promote healthy family functioning

(US Department of Health and Human
Services website, accessed 1/8/2009)

The EHS programmes are designed to facilitate positive outcomes in four specific domains:

1 Children's development (including resilience, social competence, health, cognitive and language development)
2 Family development (including family functioning, family health, parenting, parental involvement and economic self-sufficiency)
3 Staff development (including relationships with children and parents)

4   Community development
(Mathematica Policy Research Inc. Overview of the Early Head
Start Research and Evaluation Project, accessed 1/8/2009)

As with the Head Start programme, EHS offers families a full programme of
both centre-based and community-based services or sometimes a combination of both. The EHS programme is based around a specific vision of child-
centred, early intervention. Most specifically the principles for EHS are:

- *An emphasis on high-quality* – which recognises the crucial nature of
  early support and its potential for making a difference in the Early Years
  and later stages of life
- *Prevention and promotion activities* – promotes healthy development and
  recognises atypical development as early as possible
- *Positive relationships and continuity* – having a full understanding of the
  importance of early attachment on healthy development. Helping to
  support early relationships
- *Parent involvement* – Ensuring that parents are as fully involved as possible in the design and delivery of services and in governance
- *Inclusion* – creating strategies that respect the unique development of
  each child, ensuring the inclusion of children with disabilities
- *Cultural competence* – this principle acknowledges the essential role that
  culture plays in a child's development. The programs also recognise that
  we all bring with us both families and staff a set of cultural values which
  will impact upon our approaches to child development. Programs work
  within the home languages of all families who are receiving services
- *Comprehensiveness, flexibility and responsiveness* – enabling services to be
  responsive to the changing needs of families
- *Transition planning* – respecting the needs of families as they move across
  programs as their needs change
- *Collaboration* – is central to all the work of the Early Head Start program, strong partnerships enabling comprehensive services for children
  and families
  (Early Head Start National Resource Center 2009:1)

The absolutely critical aspect of the EHS programme is its ability to
respond in a sensitive and appropriate manner to the needs of the child and
their family. A key element of this programme is a comprehensive assessment to clearly establish the needs of the family within the context of their
community. As the child grows and develops so their needs change, so this
assessment is ongoing to map the family's need of services.

The programme includes:

- *Center-based services* – providing enrichment experiences and care in an early education and care environment. EHS staff would also visit families in their homes
- *Home-based services* – this takes EHS staff into family's homes to facilitate child-development and to nurture that essential parent-child bond. Twice a month families would have the opportunity to come together for discussion, maybe a social group and for specific areas of learning
- *Combination services* – this provides a combination of both the above services
- *Family Child Care services* – this provides both care and education to children in a family-like setting

(Early Head Start National Resource Center 2009:2)

Research into Head Start programmes

Research into the effects of Head Start has been mixed, but those studies assessing the long-term benefits have largely been positive, and have demonstrated that where the intervention has been of high quality it has made a difference to children's life chances. Not all studies into the impact of Head Start are positive, however, in their results, and some research has identified a phenomenon known as 'Head Start fade' which sees children who benefited from the programme in the early stages of life begin to fall behind their peers as they progress through school.

However, research shows that:

- Poverty costs society money and early intervention can save money on rates of delinquency, crime and training in later life.
- There is a link between pre-school programmes and reduced youth violence and crime.
- Early intervention raises the performance of children from deprived backgrounds, particularly in the area of developing early communication and literacy, and supports later academic achievement.

Benefits of Early Head Start

The Early Head Start Research and Evaluation Project (2006) involved 3,001 families and children across 17 sites. Half were receiving services from the Early Head Start programme, while the others were not in receipt of the programme, although they may have been receiving other services. The affects on parenting style and on cognitive and language development of these programmes both centre-based and home-based was significant. The study also demonstrated that the programmes that combined centre-based and home-based services had the most significant impact upon children's overall development. Significantly, this study also found that programmes who recruit families during pregnancy or in the very early stages of a child's life have the 'greatest chance to effect change'.

It was most particularly the wide range of services, and these services responsiveness to individual needs that most significantly supported later development and was more likely to affect school readiness:

> The broad impacts on child development, combined with changes in parents' support for language and literacy (such as daily reading and enhanced literacy environments) provides a foundation that subsequent programs can build on to continue the Early Head Start gains.
>
> (Administration for Children and Families website 2006:4)

High/Scope

Head Start programmes are often linked with the High/Scope way of working in Early Years settings and they can be seen as mutually complementary in providing a firm base for later development and a platform for communicating with families. High/Scope is based upon a developmentally appropriate curriculum and on a set of principles and practices which encourage children's independence and growing sense of autonomy and sense of personal agency. High/Scope practices are fundamental to good Early Years work:

- the environment, room arrangements;
- daily routines;
- child–adult and child–child interactions;
- a developmentally appropriate curriculum.

Many Early Years practitioners and parents will be familiar with this approach which provides a framework for children to become increasingly independent. It enables children to plan ahead, using the 'plan, do, review' pattern. This enables young children to begin to take charge of their own choices; with adult support this cycle provides an opportunity for children to reflect upon their own work and that of their colleagues. The High/Scope approach is often used within Head Start centres. Supporting the central importance of very young children becoming increasingly responsible for their own learning, within the supportive framework of adult involvement. The consistent pattern of the day provides a predictable sequence of events within which young children can begin to set their own goals within the play environment. A day in a High/Scope nursery would follow a clear pattern:

- meeting the families and children upon arrival;
- planning time usually carried out in small groups;
- work/play time;
- clean-up time;
- recall time;
- large-group time;
- outside time;
- leaving;
- staff planning.

A most important element of the High/Scope way of working is the nature of the relationships fostered by the adults with the children and the way in which the adults support the creation of positive and productive ongoing relationships between children. Early Years practitioners seek to facilitate relationships of mutual respect and interest so that children feel listened to and empowered.

The High/Scope curriculum

The High/Scope curriculum is based upon a young child's natural learning styles and is appropriate to their holistic development. It is founded upon a play-based experiential approach which puts the child at the centre of the learning experience and encourages them to take charge of their own challenges.

It is based on key learning experiences and offers children the foundation of knowledge, skills and ideas that they will build on throughout their lives. These key experiences involve:

- Using language
- Representing experiences and ideas
- Developing logical reasoning involving classification, seriation and number concept
- Understanding time and space.

(High/Scope UK website 2007)

A High/Scope setting

Working within a High/Scope setting is an exciting and stimulating experience for both adults and children. The learning environment is set up in such a way that children feel able to make their own choices about whom they will play with, how they will play, and what materials they will use. When they have planned and completed their activity, they will know where they can return the materials and most important how to tidy up. Children in a High/Scope setting will both plan and review their activities, fostering a sense of anticipation and of reflection.

Research on the High/Scope approach

What has emerged from the study of the High/Scope approach are the incredible long-term benefits of encouraging children from a very early age to take charge of their own challenges, and to develop a sense of personal initiative. Thirty years of research study into this approach have shown how this way of working with pre-school children can produce quite dramatic outcomes for children and as a result for society as a whole.

Most specifically the findings from a range of research studies found that children who had experienced this approach went on to have an:

- Increased social responsibility
- Increased chance of higher income status
- Improved educational performance
- Increased commitment to relationships

(Early Years, Learning and Teaching Scotland
website, accessed August 2009)

Portage

Portage originated in a town called Portage in Wisconsin, USA, in the 1970s and is a telling example of working in an integrated manner in Early Years practice.

It was introduced into the United Kingdom in 1976. It offers a way of working with children with additional needs and their parents to support a child-centred approach to enhancing personal potential. Central to this method of working is the idea of putting the parents or carers at the very centre of the process. A Portage worker will use a developmental framework to assess a young child's 'can dos' to observe where they are at this moment in time, to consider their particular learning styles, and then to develop a set of goals with the parent, and help to achieve a continuum of small steps leading to that identified goal.

A Portage approach would involve:

- using play and fun as a central way of learning;
- developing a 'can-do' approach to the facilitation of new confidence and skills;
- working in partnership with parents/carers and other professionals to support the developing needs of the child;
- using a 'small steps' approach to reaching an identified goal;
- a commitment to ensuring full inclusion for the child.

Portage home visitors work within the home setting with parents to provide an empowering framework of play opportunities for the child within the context of the family.

Portage home visitors work alongside parents to offer them help and ideas in order to:

- make learning fun for all the family
- encourage a child's interests
- address problem situations.

(National Portage Association website, accessed August 2009)

The very significant aspect of a Portage approach when considering it in relation to a children's centre model is the way in which it provides such a valuable model of integrated practice, a range of professionals working towards a common goal and providing a shared experience to move development forward. Portage also puts the parent and the child at the very centre of the process, enabling both to have their say and have the opportunity to talk about their needs and aspirations. They are the people who know what the child needs, what their aspirations are. They see their development day to day and can gauge achievement.

The Nurse–Family Partnership

Making a difference for young mothers and their children is key to the children's centre agenda. In the Nurse–Family Partnership, which originated in Elmira, New York, we find a way of intervening early in a possible cycle of impoverishment that might limit children's later life experiences. The Nurse–Family Partnership was originally established as a research demonstration project by David Olds and his colleagues in 1977; subsequently this increased to serve between 9,000 and 10,000 families in twenty-three different states. The Nurse-Family Partnership is operated out of the National Center for Children, Families and Communities at the University of Colorado. The USA does not currently have a universal system of health visitors who work with pregnant and new mothers; however, it is interesting to see that this intense and personal involvement of a nurse with a vulnerable family can make a considerable difference to the life chances of both mother and child. Helping to build that bond between mother and child and to provide consistent ongoing support that may have been absent from some at-risk family groups can make a considerable difference to each parent's aspirations and then to a child's life chances.

> David Olds conducted the Nurse–Family Partnership Project in 1977 in Elmira, New York. Four hundred women, most of whom were young, unmarried, lower-income and pregnant for the first time, participated in the study. The participants of this study were put into different groups: a treatment group of mothers who received an average of 9 nurse home visits during pregnancy and 23 home visits from the child's birth until the child's second birthday, and a control group of mothers who did not receive visits. During the visits, the nurse discussed 1. Health-related behaviours during pregnancy and the Early Years of the child's life; 2. The care parents provide to their children; and 3. Personal life course development for mothers (family planning, educational achievement, and work force participation).
>
> (Eckenrode 2008:1)

Nurses visiting families have three fundamental goals:

1 The nurses would help the women to improve their health outcomes during pregnancy by looking with them at their health behaviours, considering their diet and exercise and supporting them in reducing the use of cigarettes, alcohol, and illegal drugs. They would also identify possible obstetric problems in the early stages. The nurse would always

work in close partnership with other professionals to support both mother and baby.

2   The nurses would help the parents to improve their babies' health outcomes by helping them to provide responsible and thoughtful care of their child.

3   The nurses would support the parents in developing a vision for their own future, helping them to plan ahead in the process of becoming economically self-sufficient.

(www.nursefamilypartnership.org)

Research findings

The nature of this programme of early support and intervention, most specifically the nurturing aspect of the work proved to have positive long-term benefits both for the families involved and for society as a whole.

After 15 years, Eckenrode and Olds (Eckenrode 2008) investigated the long-term benefits of this intervention, both to families involved and to society as a whole. Eckenrode showed that the effects of the nurse home-visiting programme included a reduction of the following:

* the number of reports of child abuse and neglect;
* subsequent pregnancies and births;
* use of welfare;
* behaviour problems caused by drug and alcohol abuse;
* criminal behaviour.

Most importantly in this and subsequent studies was that the ongoing support of a consistent person in the families lives would indicate the reduction of child-maltreatment and subsequent anti-social behaviour amongst children and young people born into the at-risk groups.

This programme has significant implications for the way in which health visitors, community-nursery nurses and midwives are deployed within an integrated children's centre. In the United Kingdom the project is called the Family–Nurse Partnership and is already demonstrating enormous potential in terms of helping health professionals intervene and support families at significant risk. Health professionals have unique knowledge about families and in most circumstances have the quality of relationship to really make a difference at the time that counts really early in the child's life. This is a very exciting project.

Reggio Emilia

Reggio Emilia is a large town in the Emilia Romagna area of northern Italy. It is famous for its cheeses and ham. It is an area that was devastated by the war, but has subsequently become prosperous. What it has become famous for is its innovative Early Years provision that has now influenced practice all over the world. The end of the Second World War saw the population diminished and there arose within them a conviction that the future must be shaped by the nature and quality of education, most specifically those precious early years. They saw the shaping of Early Years provision as a political act, one of defiance and of resting control from the church and from Mussolini's government which had largely dominated education. They wanted to move towards a way of working in which children and families were listened to and in which children, even young children were empowered to have their own minds and their own thinking, and most important to express this in many different ways, through the 'hundred languages of children'.

It was the educator and psychologist, Loris Malaguzzi (1920-1994) who founded the 'Reggio Emila approach'. He spoke of the catalyst of war as an impetus for change:

> War, in its tragic absurdity, is the kind of experience that pushes a person toward the job of educating, as a way to start anew and live and work for the future. This desire strikes a person, as the war finally ends and the symbols of life reappear with violence equal to that of the time of destruction.
>
> (Malaguzzi 1993)

> So the local people of this area used what resources were available to create environments for young children. Malaguzzi considered that the education of young children to be a public task for the community at large; parents, citizens and politicians.
>
> (Oberhuemer and Ulich 1997:134)

The Reggio Emilia approach to early education shows a commitment to facilitating an environment that will enable the child to construct their own learning and enhance each child's abilities to think constructively and independently. The idea is to help the child to construct their own meaning through 'The Hundred Languages of children', that is, through the different modes of expression: drama, puppetry, sculpture, painting, drawing, etc.

The whole Reggio vision of the child as a competent, empowered learner, has led to the development of a curriculum which is strongly child directed. 'The curriculum has purposive progression but not scope and sequence' (Brainy–Child.Com 17/5/2009:1).

Central principles of the Reggio Emilia approach

The role of the teacher

- The teacher is seen as a researcher, alongside the child. So together they explore the world, resources and ideas and become 'co-constructers' of meaning. The teacher is not so much there to instruct, but rather to act as guide and model and to be a co-worker.

- The teacher needs to be a skilled observer and a skilled listener in their pursuit of finding the child's starting points, their interests and their skills.

- Working with Howard Gardner's idea of 'multiple intelligences', this approach calls for the 'integration of the graphic arts as tools for cognitive, linguistic, and social development' (Brainy–Child.Com 17/5/2009:2).

- The teacher needs to be committed to ongoing reflection on the impact of their teaching on learning.

The environment

The environment is seen in the Reggio approach as 'the third teacher' and a very significant means of stimulating learning and development. It needs to be aesthetically attractive and fully reflect the children's interests and enthusiasm. Areas are separated to support aspects of children's work, for example into art spaces, dramatic areas, etc. Architects and town planners are seen as essential in helping to create beautiful and workable spaces that are truly child-centred. Angela Nurse describes a visit to Reggio in 1999 saying:

> I was impressed firstly by the beauty and quality of the environment each of the nurseries provides for its children. Each is unique and an integral part of its own community, whether purpose-built or adapted from an existing building. Architects meet with the community, parents, children and staff to decide on each design. Buildings utilise existing features well. Tiled floors, wooden staircases and balustrades are retained, for example, and the community's cultural priorities are reflected in the organisation of every nursery, with the kitchen and dining rooms at the heart of each. Most importantly there is an understanding of the needs of children of this age and what they like to do.
>
> (Nurse 2003:1)

The children's space needs to enable the child to express themselves, and they need skilful adults to work with them.

The centrality of creativity

Creativity is a central theme of the Reggio approach. In their nurseries everyone is a creative being, seen as having great potential. They focus not so much on the product, but on the process and what that process can tell the teacher or parent about the child's developing intellect.

> Creativity becomes more visible when adults try to be more attentive to the cognitive processes of children than the results they achieve in various fields of doing and understanding.
>
> (Malaguzzi 1993:77)

However, although the focus may be on the process, the work which the children produce is truly astonishing, for its imagination and for the skill with which it is composed. This may owe a great deal to the richness of experiences to which the children are exposed, working through specific projects, where children are expected to experience the world in a very sensual way before they seek to encode their thoughts, feelings and experiences. Children are also given high-quality materials, as well as using everyday materials to create. Within each setting there is an artist in residence, an *alterista*, who supports the children's emerging skills, as well as supporting and observing the cognitive aspect of their learning.

Projects as a way of capturing children's learning

The curriculum within a Reggio Emilia setting is characterised by an understanding of the way in which children learn. So building upon children's real-life problem-solving skills their desire for exploration and play becomes a key part of the work in nurseries. Adults will often work with small groups of children on topics while the rest of the group are engaged on self-selected activities. Topics might arise from the adult's observations of children play, from a particular social concern that has arisen in the local community.

> Projects form the basis of the programmes in the preschools. The children are very much at the centre of this, selecting topics that have caught their imagination, with the final decision taken after group discussion. No subjects are taboo. Children have chosen to investigate birth, angels, lions and

the rain in the city. Problem-solving is central to developing children's thoughts; teachers prompt but do not give answers.

(Nurse 2003:2)

The curriculum develops from children's interests and concerns and thus they have a momentum of their own and work is by its very nature differentiated to meet the learning needs of the children within a setting, including those with additional needs. Crucial to the Reggio approach to the curriculum is a balance between child-initiated and teacher-directed work. Through problem-solving work, children are encouraged to depict their findings through different languages and different media, what the Reggio Emilia approach calls the 'hundred languages of children'. In the Reggio approach to learning and development, children's learning styles and their engagement with the world are celebrated and cherished.

> Within the Reggio Emilia schools there are no planned goals or standards indicating what is to be learned as 'these would push our schools towards teaching without learning' (Malaguzzi, in Edwards *et al.*, 1993). The children are encouraged, in collaboration with teachers and one another, to construct their own personalities and to determine the course of their own investigations and learning.
>
> (Directorate for Education, OECD 2004:13)

The hundred languages of children

Within the Reggio Emilia pedagogy it is the primary role of the teacher to be guided by the child as they begin to construct their meaning, and to listen to the child as they move through their learning. Children are given time and opportunity to select and to develop different modes of expression. Settings employ trained *alteristas* to work both with the adults and the children within a setting and help children to sustain their interest in a particular topic.

Children are helped to be competent users of many skills with clay, brushwork, puppetry, woodwork, drama, etc., enabling them to use both their imagination and their experiences to interpret the world.

With an absence of a curriculum document to follow, as with the EYFS (Early Years Foundation Stage, DCSF 2008) which clearly sets out a more prescribed route for the learner, teachers are trusted to work within a commonly shared set of principles that reflect a clear philosophy based on a constructivist way in which children grow and learn. Pertinent to the success of this philosophy are the bonds which are established between the teacher, family and child within the school environment. Parents and families play a large part in the running of each nursery and often come in and eat with the children at lunch time.

The people who work within Reggio Emilia settings would be the first to acknowledge that they owe a great deal to other traditions such as the High/Scope model in the USA and the nursery tradition within the United Kingdom (Nurse 2003). It is also important to remember that Reggio Emilia is firmly rooted within the background and culture of northern Italy; however, there is a great deal that we can learn from this challenging and inspiring way of working.

Sweden

The Swedish approach to the care and education of the pre-school child provides a great deal of inspiration for all those working with the young child. Like the Reggio Emilia approach, Sweden bases its way of working on the entitlement both of the child and of the family to high-quality experiences, based on the learning needs of the child. A fundamental principle behind the Swedish conceptualisation of Early Years practice is that their view that care and education are linked and are mutually complementary. Most significantly, access to early childcare and education is viewed as the child's right.

In 1966, the government established committees to review the overall content and working practices in pre-school classes for six-year-olds. People who work both in daycare and in the pre-school are expected to have similar training.

The curriculum

An important aspect of the Swedish system is its commitment to both decentralisation and to deregulation. Decisions about learning are meant to be taken at municipal level, at the

> level of pre-school centres, and in classrooms, by children and their teachers. The curriculum is based on a division of responsibility where the state determines the overall goals and guidelines for the pre-school and where the municipalities-and staff working in the centres-take responsibility for implementation.
>
> (OECD 2004:21)

It appears that Sweden's attitude to pre-school education is incredibly relaxed, with play being the central vehicle to children's learning. There is very little structured learning; it is very child-centred and each child is enabled to develop in their own way and at their own pace. However, there is recognition in Sweden that the pre-school years are central to children's later success and therefore there is good investment in this period of a child's life. Sweden spends three times the amount on their Early Years provision than we do in the United Kingdom. So the ratio of staff to children is much higher than is generally seen in the United Kingdom. Staff have the opportunity to work alongside individual children, and really enable them to flower. While there is little formal teaching, the whole pre-school is seen as a strong base for later more formalised learning.

> Most Swedish children who leave school at the age of six are not able to read or write. Yet within three years of starting formal school at the age of seven these children lead the literacy levels in Europe.
>
> (Teacher's TV 2006)

The child in Swedish pre-schools is seen as a whole being with all their different dimensions catered for within the environment. The health and well-being of the child is paramount to delivering an exciting, healthy and challenging learning experience. Meal times are social experiences which emphasise healthy food and interactions across the age groups. Children are expected to take responsibility for preparing and serving food (Figure 3.1), and are encouraged to pay attention to the needs of others. The nature of the environment both inside and outside is paramount to the underlying principles of the Early Years curriculum. The inside environment is often set up as a homely space in which children can feel safe and reassured. There are plenty of opportunities for children to explore the world around them and to engage in play experiences. The outside space is central to developing children's individual personalities, and helping them to take charge of their own challenges. The weather is no bar to taking the children outside, they just put on extra clothes, where they can truly engage in learning through all of their senses. The role of the teacher is of facilitator and support. There is not the emphasis on observing every minute detail or upon a specific adult-led agenda; rather it is on attuning to each child, to their interests and to their developing skills. The unique aspect of each child is celebrated in a Swedish pre-school, rather than trying to shoe-horn them into a defined curriculum, the adults follow them, and pedagogical practice is designed around them.

Figure 3.1 Developing early learning through a creative curriculum based upon everyday experiences

Goals of the Swedish curriculum

The Swedish curriculum defines five groups of goals which each centre should aim to achieve:

1 Norms and values
2 Development and learning
3 Influence of the child
4 Pre-school and home
5 Co-operation between the pre-school class, the school and the leisure time centre.

(OECD 2004:22)

Central to this curriculum is the idea that to develop an effective pedagogy within pre-school we must pay attention to the underlying value system within which we place the learning and from which other aspects of learning grow and develop.

An important task of the pre-school is to establish and help children acquire the values on which our society is based. The inviolability of human life, individual freedom and integrity, the equal value of all people, equality between the genders as well as solidarity with the weak and vulnerable are all values that the school shall actively promote in its work with children.

(Swedish Ministry of Education and Science 1998a,

in OECD 2004:23)

The Swedish pre-school is characterised by an environment in which the development of care, nurturing and learning are paramount to their pedagogical approach, therefore learning is about growing up with a strong sense of personal identity, self-respect and respect for others. Collaboration and shared experiences with both adults and with other children are seen as crucial to the developing child.

Key messages: what can we learn from these different approaches?

There is always a consideration that we need to bear in mind when we look at any practice in different countries and in different cultures that we cannot transport an entire way of working into our existing practice. We must also bear in mind the British habit of deprecating what we have and wanting to throw the baby out with the bath water, rather than celebrating what we have in Early Years practice and building upon it rather than tearing it down. But the review of other countries does shed light on very important issues which we need to bear in mind as we continue to develop more children's centres across the country.

- Investing in Early Years practice, creating excellent spaces for young children with practitioners who are trained to degree level and who have a good understanding of the developmental needs of young children is paramount. What all of these different countries showed us is that while we are investing more in Early Years we are still not seeing it as a sufficiently urgent priority. What Head Start, High/Scope, the Nurse-Family Partnership, and Early Years in Sweden demonstrate so clearly is that if we have the courage to invest now in excellent Early Years provision it will yield exceptional results and in the long term it will be a cost-cutting exercise.

- Integrated Early Years practice needs to be rooted within a value-based approach which places the child and their developing sense of their own identity at the centre of our work. Children's centres need to develop a unique value-led approach in partnership with local agencies, children and families.

- What Reggio Emilia and the Swedish curriculum demonstrate so powerfully is that we need to provide early experiences for children based upon their natural inclinations for learning, on play and exploration. We need well-trained skilled practitioners who understand children's needs, who do not provide unnatural structure to the learning, but rather take the lead from the child. We need the Early Years curriculum to evolve and not create an imposed curriculum based upon ages and stages. Staff working with young children need excellent innovative training; they need high status and pay.

- We need to attract into the Early Years workforce a range of people who reflect the diversity of the world we live in. Children need both men and women working in children's centres and nurseries. They need people from a range of ethnic and cultural backgrounds. We need also adults working in children's centres and nurseries who have different capabilities and enable children to see that those people with additional needs have a great deal to contribute to all aspects of society.

- The role of the health visitor, midwife and community nursery nurse are central in supporting the young family and they have the relationships with the family which make all the difference in helping develop successful attachments and early communication. They are in there right at the beginning. This is well demonstrated by the work of the Nurse-Family Partnership. The fact that the health team are generally welcomed into the home in the early stages of life mean that they can help to signpost other services and opportunities for the family as well as pick up on specific concerns. Several research studies, such as the Early Head Start programme, demonstrate that it is important to be providing targeted sensitive needs-led services right from the start of life, or before.

- Children's centres and all Early Years settings are well placed to promote all aspects of the Every Child Matters vision, seeing the child in a holistic manner. Every area of their development is important and all are interwoven having an impact upon each other. In Sweden we see that diet and the preparation of food is part of the learning, that the use of the outside environment helps children to become confident in themselves and that challenging play promotes a sense of achievement and a trust in their developing abilities.

- Portage and Reggio Emilia show us how important it is to build upon what children can do, and work from there, using play as a central vehicle for learning.

- Regggio Emilia shows us how important it is to involve the wider community in developing children's centres, being proud of what is achieved and incorporating knowledge and expertise from the local area, through parents and families as well as town planners and architects, local businesses and colleges, churches and schools, and making use of local artists and storytellers to be part of ongoing projects and helping children to create their own learning spaces.

- What these different countries and different ways of working show us is that even though we might operate an informal open-ended way of working we are all accountable and must therefore use an evidence-based approach to assessing the impact of the work that we do with children, families and communities.

- What projects like Head Start, High/Scope and the Nurse–Family Partnership show us is that early support does make a difference to the life chances of young people and as a consequence to the nature and efficacy of communities, but that we must allow different ways of working to embed themselves before making judgements on short-term evaluations. This kind of change takes a long time; we must hold our breath and have confidence.

References

DCSF (2008) *Foundation Stage Curriculum*.

Early Head Start (2006) *Early Head Start Benefits Children and Families*.

Early Head Start National Resource Center (2009) *Quality Early Head Start Services: a Summary of Research-based Practices that Support Children, Families and Expectant Parents*.

Directorate for Education OECD (2004) *Starting Strong Curricula and Pedagogies in Early Childhood Education and Care. Five Curriculum Outlines*.

Eckenrode, J. (2008) *Nurse Family Partnership Program Demonstrates Results*. Ithaca, NY: Cornell University College of Human Ecology.

Malaguzzi, L. (1993) 'History, ideas and basic philosophy: an interview with Lella Gandini', in Edwards, C., Gandini, L. and Forman, G. (Eds) *The Hundred Languages of Children: the Reggio Emilia Approach – Advanced Reflections* (second edition). Greenwich, CT: Ablex Publishing.

Nurse, A. (2003) *Early Years Update*. London: Optimus Education.

Oberhuemer, P. and Ulich, M. (1997) *Working with Young Children in Europe*. London: Paul Chapman.

Further reading

Abbott, L. and Nutbrown, C. (2001) *Experiencing Reggio Emilia*. Buckingham: Open University Press.

Bully-Cummings, E., Gorcyca, D., Wrigglesworth, G., Schweinhart, L. and Pelleran, K. (2006) *High-Quality Pre-school: The Key to Crime Prevention and School Success in Michigan*. Report from Fight Crime: Invest in Kids Michigan.

Child Welfare League of America (2006) *Head Start*. CWLA.

Currie, J. (2005) 'Economic impact of Head Start', in *Encyclopaedia on Early Childhood Development* (online).

Krogh, S., Kristine, L. and Slentz, L. (2001) *Early Childhood Education*. London: Lawrence Erlbaum.

National Literacy Trust (2008) *Literacy Changes Lives*. www.literacytrust.org.uk/socialinclusion/earlyyears/headstattresearch.html

Oden, S., Schweinhart, L. and Weikart, D. with Marcus, S. and Xie, Y. *Into Adulthood: a Study of the Effects of Head Start*. Ypsilanti, MI: High/Scope Press.

Schweinhart, L., Barnes, H. and Weikart, D. (1993) *Significant Benefits, The High/Scope Perry Preschool Study Through Age 27*. Ypsilanti, MI: High/Scope Press.

Sharp, C. (2001) *Developing Young Children's Creativity Through the Arts: What Does Research Have to Offer?* London: NFER.

Websites

Administration for Children and Families:
www.acf.hhs.gov/

Brainy-Child:
www.brainy-child.com/article/reggioemilia.html

High/Scope UK:
www.high-scope.org.uk

Mathematica Policy Research, Inc.:
www.mathematica-mpr.com

Nurse–Family Partnership:
www.nursefamilypartnership.org

U.S. Department of Health and Human Services:
www.hhs.gov

Video material

Teacher's TV (2006) *Early Years – How do they do it in Sweden?*

CHAPTER 4

Education

Christine Blanshard and Jeannette Sax

A children's centre develops a culture 'that encourages children, parents and staff to become enthusiastic, independent and successful lifelong learners.' In the broadest sense of education Centres need to be a place where the learning is so embedded in the culture that it permeates 'every element and aspect of the centre.

(DCSF 2007a: 7, 8)

The vision to create a joined-up system of health, family support, childcare and education services so that all children get the best start possible in the vital early years remains high on the government's agenda. Evidence from recent reports, such as the 'Baby P. (Peter)' case where agencies caring for the baby, who died of neglect at 17 months old, were described as 'lacking urgency' (BBC News 2009a), highlighted serious failings among agencies working in child protection. The appalling facts of this case, coupled with the shocking outcomes from UNICEF (2008), which placed the United Kingdom bottom of a league table for child well-being across 21 industrialised countries, may suggest serious flaws in the effectiveness of 'joined-up' services.

UNICEF drew from its findings indicators such as poverty, family relationships and health, accusing it of failing its children (BBC News 2009b). Some of the key findings from the Baby P. case identified 'agencies acting in isolation from one another without effective co-ordination; poor gathering, recording and sharing of information' and more alarmingly 'failure to implement the recommendations of the Victoria Climbié inquiry, which heavily criticised it five years ago' (BBC News 2008). Significantly from both findings one could suggest the lessons that need to be learned place emphasis on better parenting. UNICEF UK calls on the government to set new standards for the early childhood workforce, bringing pay and conditions in line with those of Early Years teachers (UNICEF 2008). This suggestion is reinforced in the government's ten-year strategy where it acknowledges the challenges within the PVI (private, voluntary, independent) sector that has 'typically been viewed as a low pay sector with high turnover of staff, and relatively low levels of formal qualifications' (DCSF 2009:43).

With the UK's poor rate of child well-being in the industrialised world, which identifies one in three children as living in poverty and growing up with a poor quality of life, children's chances of achieving the same opportunities as those who are more advantaged are greatly reduced. Growing up in poverty is a serious issue which continues to shape strategy at all levels. In June 2007 a two-year development and research programme called 'Narrowing the Gap' was started. It was funded by the Department for Children and Schools Fund (DCSF) and the Local Government Association (LGA) working in partnership with other agencies. It aims to make a significant difference to the performance of Children's Trust arrangements and 'narrow the gaps' in outcomes between vulnerable children and the rest whilst continuing to improve outcomes for all children.

Background

Over the years the government has introduced many programmes to support children and families with the expectation of raising standards and narrowing the gap between those from areas of disadvantage and those of affluence. Many nursery schools that were set up by local education authorities post-war became Early Excellence Centres (EEC) at the end of the 1990s and early 2000 as 'part of the Government's broader strategy for raising standards, increasing opportunity, supporting families, reducing social exclusion, improving health of the nation and addressing child poverty' (Betram et al. 2002:5).

EECs were designed to offer access to high-quality integrated care and education services delivered by multi-agency partners within one centre or a network of centres. The national evaluation of the EEC pilot programme began in September 1999 and was completed in November 2002. It concluded that their integrated work made a valuable contribution to the government's broader strategy for improving outcomes for young children and their families. They also met many of the criteria for the children's centre core offer and identified valuable strategies to develop this work.

Following the Effective Pre-school Practice Evaluation (EPPE) study in 2001 the Neighbourhood Nurseries Initiative (NNI) was set up with one of the key objectives being to reduce child poverty by providing quality and affordable childcare to enable parents to return to work. A further two notable policy recommendations followed its evaluation in 2007 (Coxon *et al.* 2007). It firstly suggested that NNIs in the most disadvantaged areas may need longer subsidies until they were self-sustaining for parents adapting to moving from claiming benefits to earning and managing wages. Secondly, and of particular relevance to this chapter, the EPPE study established that the quality and qualifications of staff had a direct bearing on the outcomes for children.

In the most disadvantaged areas full-day childcare is an integral part of the children's centre's core offer, but education is not confined to the nursery environment.

The benefits of good-quality Early Years childcare are well evidenced in the EPPE project, but this chapter will look specifically at the role of education in children's centres that complements this provision.

The role of the teacher

The children's centre teacher's role is a relatively new role in most cases and one which is very different from classroom teaching. There are three strands:

1   supporting the childcare provision attached to the children's centre;

2   working within other services within the core offer;

3   supporting other childcare settings in the reach area.

It presents challenges that can either form the basis for an enjoyable, exciting and innovative role, or that seem insurmountable, leaving one feeling de-skilled and unclear of the value that one adds to the centre. Significant in the outcome is the value placed on early educational learning by the manager of the centre, who in most cases 'manages' the teacher.

The success of the role is very much dependent on the ability of the teacher to build good, strong, honest relationships with parents, some of whom are very vulnerable with previous negative experiences of school. With experience of this role, one needs to have broad shoulders to cope with the fragility of some relationships, be transparent within relationships at all times with a consistency and ability to communicate effectively with a diverse number of professionals and families. Above all it is crucial to remain professional at all times and to recognise and control professional boundaries with the ability to recognise the need for appropriate intervention and act accordingly.

Figure 4.1 Creating opportunities for experiential learning

The EPPE Project (2004)

> has emphasised the deployment of QTs [*qualified teachers*] into Children's
> Centre services in an effort to drive up cognitive development and close
> the gap between the most disadvantaged and other children.
>
> (Sylva et al. 2004, cited on 'Together for
Children' website)

It is therefore crucial that the provision of Early Years education and learning in children's centres and Early Years settings is excellent, providing equal
opportunities for less advantaged children so as to help improve outcomes
and close the gap between disadvantaged children and others.

Key skills

As the role will require the teacher to be confident and knowledgeable
enough to facilitate training for practitioners in observing, supporting and
planning for children's learning, the teacher must have a solid understanding

of child development from birth to five years and a willingness to lead confidently in this area.

Each centre will have its own specific needs and the skill of the teacher is to ensure a high level of childcare provision through a 'hands-on' approach, which will challenge and provoke discussion and reflection amongst practitioners. Being able to work effectively within a team and make the correct judgements that lead to positive outcomes requires considerable commitment. Having the ability and insight to be spontaneous, autonomous and expect little acknowledgement for hard work whilst hopefully working toward effective change is a prerequisite of the job.

The remit of the teacher working within a children's centre goes beyond what are perceived traditional educational activities. Having contact with families and professionals within the children's centre highlights the teacher's role as being significant to that community. It underlines the need for specialist Early Years qualifications and an understanding of and commitment to working in a holistic and diverse way with the local community. Most certainly an understanding of multi-agency working and of the roles and responsibilities of other professionals engaged within the children's centre community is imperative.

The role further requires sensitivity, patience and flexibility along with the ability to be autonomous in leading and modelling effective Early Years practice. What must translate from this role is a clear, concise understanding of child development from birth onwards and the implications of this for both parents and practitioners within the nursery and the delivery of children's centre services. It is a specialist role and one that requires a tight, thorough selection process directed by equally knowledgeable senior managers who themselves have the key skills and knowledge and experience of Early Years practice, underpinned with experience of the realities of working within children's centres, to ensure the successful selection of teacher's who will face up to the pressures and demands of what can be seen as a very challenging role. We must remember that to work closely with parents and to engage them in their children's learning whilst working alongside partners in health and social services is the core of this role and requires high-quality standards from practitioners if we are able to begin to make a difference to the lives of disadvantaged children and families.

Key workers

Links with multi-agencies is a strong theme which underpins the Early Years Foundation Stage (EYFS), which is statutory guidance for Early Years practitioners and became law for all settings to be working within it from September 2008. It has provided much needed uniform standard guidance for all Early Years providers; schools, nurseries, childminders and pre-schools alike are all required to meet the same criteria. To achieve good outcomes at the end of the reception year, all practitioners must work together with parents and the wider community to lay strong foundations. Key indicators that children's centres are measured by include children achieving at least six points in personal, social and emotional development and communication, language and literacy at the end of the reception year. Schools are increasingly noticing that children are struggling in these areas and not just those from 'disadvantaged' backgrounds: 'Increasing numbers of children are experiencing mental health problems. A recent ONS survey showed that 10 per cent of children aged between 5–15 experience clinically defined mental health problems' (DCSF 2001:5).

The rise of awareness of the value to a child's emotional, social and cognitive development of establishing healthy attachments in the first three years of life has to move someway to hopefully redressing this balance. Santos Pais, Director of UNICEF Innocenti Research Centre (IRC) suggests that

> high quality early childhood education and care has a huge potential to enhance children's cognitive, linguistic, emotional and social development. It can help boost educational achievement, limit early establishment of disadvantage, promote inclusion, be an investment in good citizenship, and advance progress for women.
>
> (UNICEF 2008:53)

The EYFS Statutory Framework further identifies the responsibility of Early Years providers and carers in supporting children's personal, social and emotional development by providing an environment that leads young children to feeling valued: 'being acknowledged and affirmed by important people in their lives leads to children gaining confidence and inner strength through secure attachments with these people' (EYFS 2007: Card 2.1).

The need to develop trust in a key person is an instinctive reaction for a baby. The baby's desire to attach to a trusted caregiver is a healthy development and one which begins at birth. This healthy attachment takes place with the primary carer, usually the mother, instantly and forms the foundation for a secure environment in which a baby will thrive and respond positively to external experiences. Conversely, babies who do not experience positive attachments from birth and whose emotional needs are neglected are less likely to thrive and respond positively to external experiences.

Children who grow up in areas which present external challenges and disadvantages, such as poverty, abuse or neglect are disadvantaged from an early age and at risk of developmental delay with the consequence of underachievement as the stress experienced can damage their brains.

Through a repeated cycle, parents themselves may often, and without realising, repeat the poor parenting which was passed down to them.

Creating such an environment, working within a multi-professional base, is complex and challenges the traditional teacher role. Characteristics of the role require warmth and empathy inherent in the individual. Essential in any relationship, the teacher must adopt a non-judgemental approach. Edgington believes that 'there is no place for the teacher who dismisses some parents as being the "ones" who don't care about their children' (2005:3). She further believes that to become 'specialists' in this area of Early Years, practitioners' must reflect on, and analyse, their practice if they are to achieve positive outcomes for children and families.

Early Years practitioners

Other Early Years practitioners that are linked with a children's centre are the childcare provision staff, childminders and crèche workers. Staff such as family outreach workers, toy library co-ordinators and playworkers may also be employed and contribute to a centre's offer, all of whom would be expected to have an underpinning knowledge of child development. The children's centre practice guidance builds on the EPPE project recommendations of employing highly qualified staff.

Continued professional development is good practice, and for staff in children's centres, joint and holistic training is of the utmost importance for staff to understand and appreciate individual professions' contributions. For example, where speech therapists are able to provide short courses to childcare practitioners it enables early intervention to occur on a daily basis and to be integrated into good practice. It also enables practitioners to identify more confidently when it is appropriate to refer to a specialist. A child's key worker is able to talk with parents and encourage them in ways to support their child from a basis of already having a relationship. This is not a substitute for speech and language therapy, but when practitioners are able to embed good practice such as commenting on play or knowing ways to access a child's level of understanding, more formal intervention at a later stage may be avoided.

It also has the advantage that children are working with their key worker and so will be more comfortable than having to attend a clinic in an unfamiliar place with unfamiliar people. As a nursery manager I found the Elklan training I received from the speech and language therapist working in the centre of key importance in providing strategies for supporting young children's early communication skills. For the nursery practitioners that also attended it gave them skills to improve children's communication.

> By investing in all those who work with children, and by building capacity to work across professional boundaries, we can ensure that joining up services is not just about providing a safety net for the vulnerable it is about unlocking the potential of every child.
>
> (DCSF 2007:13)

Case study: attachment training

Children's centres offer a central and neutral venue for training purposes.

They are accessible to the local community and a familiar venue for most. Revenue for the centre is provided when it is hired out for a training event.

Case study

A shared training event was held at a centre in Worthing, West Sussex. The management had recognised the need for integrated training. This was offered to the team of multi-disciplines engaged in work with children and families in the local community. The focus of the training, 'Attachment and the Key Person', was explored through sharing theory, good practice and discussion.

The value of understanding the topic and relating it to one's own practice was evaluated positively. A practitioner said, 'I feel more confident with new knowledge and feel better equipped to support families where attachment may be an issue. Knowing about baby massage complements this too' (24 March 2009). Furthermore, the opportunity to reflect on the theory and discuss the implications for joined-up work in this area, which would offer positive support to families and ultimately children, with a shared understanding by those working directly with them, and to learn from other practitioners' experiences, was seen as interesting.

The opportunity to share ideas to gain a better insight into other roles positively highlighted the need for interaction with other practitioners, hearing about different approaches and settings.

The outcome, a positive way forward for the desire of integrated working, would ultimately reflect the value of shared training that reflects a better understanding of other roles working with families. It resulted in participants promoting the need for more of the same being offered to a wider team of professionals and to parents.

A training centre

When a centre offers initial training to provide childcare qualifications it is also able to offer placements if there is onsite childcare. Students from a range of courses such as an early childhood studies degree, teaching degrees, and National Vocational Qualifications in childcare and health studies, as well as those on work experience from schools, are keen to have placements in children's centres. This provides valuable experience in early intervention and the opportunity to understand the government's commitment: 'The intention is that Children's Centre services become permanent mainstream community services, which are developed and delivered with the active involvement of parents/carers and the local community' (DfES 2005:2).

It also encourages practitioners to understand the importance and quality of parents' contributions in their child's development at an early stage in their careers. The presence of other professionals in the centre will provide valuable insights into other agencies' contributions and will hopefully give a valuable insight into the term 'integrated working'.

Where a centre is fortunate enough to have a range of professionals it is possible to be more adventurous in providing training such as hosting conferences for local childcare practitioners. The centre may have the links necessary to provide experts to deliver a conference and workshops in an environment which local practitioners may be able to access and feel comfortable to come to. Especially for those settings with limited budgets or childminders this is able to provide valuable training opportunities that may otherwise be beyond their reach.

Engaging with parents

A joined-up approach for agencies working together is undoubtedly challenging and carries with it a huge responsibility for practitioners. It also raises the importance of involving the parent so ensuring that change is long-term and breaks the cycle for future generations. For there to be a collaborative approach, which recognises and values the role of the parent, Athey (2006, cited in Whalley 2007) advises developing a shared language which will empower parents to engage in the learning environment relevant to their child's individual needs. Palmer (2006) believes that 'where the home and school work in harmony, children have a much better chance of success' (p. 211).

A parent as partner is not a new concept. The Pen Green Centre for under-fives and their families became a lead in exemplifying good, collaborative practice in which parents were empowered to make decisions in their children's learning. Pen Green was initially set up in an area where there was 'no tradition of working in an integrated way, with other agencies such as health and the Adult Education Services' (Whalley 2007:2) The aim to include parents as partners was an important factor of the research that led the centre to create a dialogue where parents, who had previously voiced hostile reactions based on their own negative experiences of education, were engaged in the decision-making and planning to transform the centre, which became a meeting place for the local community.

The subsequent five-year research project, the Parents Involvement in Their Children's Learning (PICL) Programme, highlighted the importance of extending the existing good practice to develop a 'rich and relevant dialogue between parents and nursery staff which could be sustained over a period of time' (Whalley 2007:9). It recognised that the tradition of teaching and learning, which had previously been 'the fairly uncontested domain of professional staff' (ibid.), needs to be opened up for discussion with parents and other professionals involved in the wider Early Years community.

The outcome of this research has impacted on many early childhood settings, resulting in them refining their practice to place more value on the home-setting partnership, recognising the role of parents as co-educators in their children's learning.

However, developing an integrated, shared language with parents remains an approach which needs time to embed and does not necessarily come naturally. The practice guidance states that 'all Early Years staff should receive basic training to work with parents' (DCSF 2006:26). Reinforcing

Figure 4.2 Sharing and learning together the importance of early literacy experiences

the point previously raised in this chapter, it requires practitioners to have a solid understanding of the theoretical aspects of how children develop and learn, which in turn can be shared with parents and related to the learning in the home environment. Early childhood services play a major role working with parents to offer advice and support for engaging their children in positive play and learning interaction.

Encouraging parents to actively engage with their children's learning

Ways in which parents can be encouraged to actively engage with their children's learning are varied and need to be tailored to the individual community and parents.

Typically toy libraries, 'Stay and Play' sessions, 'Well Baby' clinics, and 'Rhyme and Story' sessions are included in a children's centre's programme. Toy libraries provide an excellent starting point for many parents as they are able to borrow quality toys free of charge. Most beneficial to this service is the option to engage with professionals through informal discussions about the benefits of the different types of toys their children have access to. Providing parents with the opportunity to evaluate the benefits of individual toys to their children's cognitive development and evaluating what the children have gained from playing with them can deliver important messages about providing stimulating and valuable play experiences.

Enabling parents to feel able to ask for advice and access information that they might not otherwise seek has to be a valuable opportunity to engage with parents and empower them in their children's development. Providing an environment where parents feel supported and curious rather than judged is the key to effective early intervention.

Other ongoing activities such as a physical 'Rough and Tumble' play session may be available, providing opportunity to access larger play activities that facilitate physical development and lead to an understanding of the benefits of physical play as a means for young children to explore and take risks. For many children and families without access to a garden or safe play area, it was a welcome avenue to pursue.

A music-led 'Creatability' group, for both parent and child to share musical and creative activities and work together, enabled parents to engage in a variety of ways to support their children's development and interests in a more relaxed and rewarding context. Storytelling weeks focus on daily opportunities for children and parents to share quality time listening to stories and reading stories together. Practitioners joining in with the activities help to broaden both the child's knowledge and extend the parents' understanding of the value to the child's learning and development of such activities, as well as modelling different ways of enjoying stories together. This shared learning journey provides the basis for extending thinking and involvement for parents to feel more positive about intervening effectively in their child's play.

Significant to the success of engaging and empowering parents has been the children's centre café, or social area where it is suggested that some of the most successful early intervention work is carried out through conversations held between professionals and parents in an informal, non-threatening ambience. A parent who had casually mentioned that her two-year-old had little speech led to her being introduced to activities such as a music group to encourage language acquisition, Stay and Play to encourage socialising skills, and a family learning play and language course. In addition, through conversation it was possible to ascertain whether the health visitor had been involved and to encourage the parent to seek advice from the health professionals.

Who attends children's centres?

Parents will access children's centres for different reasons and in different ways. Some will actively seek out services and the parents are keen to take advantage of the opportunities available. They will benefit greatly from the services offered to their children. However, it may be fair to say that these children would probably reach government targets in terms of achievements without this early intervention. Although for children from these backgrounds there will be value-added outcomes, they are probably not the target audience from the government's funding perspective.

Some parents may come into a centre who would not traditionally access groups or libraries. They may not have the confidence to attend on their own or the literacy skills to see written publicity, possibly due to English being a second language. This raises the importance of how the centre is promoted within the community.

Some parents may not understand the value of providing stimulating play and learning opportunities for their children. Through attending ante- and post-natal services in the centre it affords them the opportunity to become familiar with the environment and key practitioners who may then be able to introduce them to appropriate services. For example, One Stop Baby Shop, with its integrated approach facilitates a health need (a health visitor to advise parents and a baby weigh point), whilst through the provision of play and learning resources allows for a seamless introduction for parents to the value and purpose of engaging in play activities with babies from birth onwards. For these families the benefits to their parenting role are enormous as they will be able to have firsthand experience and contact with professionals and resources that will engage their children in developmentally appropriate, playful activities.

Other parents may not come to services through choice but as a result of referral from other professionals. For all these parents it is hoped that the centre impacts positively on the outcomes for their children for as one parent commented recently 'having a baby can be very lonely and isolating'. How much difference it makes will vary with their concrete understanding of the connectedness of their attitude and behaviours to that of their children's overall development and well-being. This remains a challenging topic and one which will continue to demand much investment from professionals seeking to move some parents on to achieve better outcomes for their children. Being able to work alongside such diverse styles of parenting is part of the skill and challenge of the professional working in the centre.

The importance of relationships

In all of this a key challenge has to be the length of time it takes to develop positive relationships with parents who do not perceive the need to make changes in their parenting. Investing time to build positive relationships is a necessary and imperative process to engage in. One has to question the logistics and appropriateness in terms of time and funding to invest in a group of parents where only a small percentage of them will make a shift in their thinking and behaviour. There is a common belief that most parents want the best for their children but what is 'good enough' is often dictated by how much effort a parent is able to make. One can see 'good enough' care as when the 'care-giver is able to attune to, attend to and satisfy the basic needs of a child, adequately, the majority of the time'.

However, for a parent, key factors which may or may not determine their success at parenting will reflect their own understanding and experiences of parenting, as modelled to them by their own primary carer, finances, and often most significantly their own emotional reservoirs. In these circumstances parents will often make just enough change to move their situation from unbearable to bearable which may or may not be sustained. This in some cases, and sadly in the case of Baby P., gives a modicum of respite from the intervention of agencies such as social services but in fact still leaves the child at risk.

In terms of making a difference, coming to any one service rarely has significant impact but may be hugely important in being a key piece of the jigsaw or a starting point. A difference is seen when a family is able to build a relationship where trust is established between all parties. Engaging in various activities and discussions relating to the parent and child's needs empowers the parent to take ownership of their role and by doing so find a more positive way forward, secure in the support and advice of the professional. Developing a positive relationship with a key person is as significant to an adult as to a child.

One of the dichotomies of early intervention is that it is hard to quantitatively measure outcomes in the short term, given that a positive result is when children do not need to be referred on to specific services in future years. As discussed in Chapter 3, the Head Start programme, which has run in the United States for over 30 years, saw a positive impact in outcomes once the children reached adolescence. It is hoped in this country that this government and any future governments commit to the programme long enough to see positive outcomes regardless of politically changing agendas, which can obscure any measured impact.

Subsidised childcare places

Often the most notable short-term improvements in children's lives are for children who have subsidised places in the centre nursery, made possible under the generous funding of Sure Start local programmes. This is because the children usually accessed places younger than the free entitlement following a referral by practitioners such as health visitors. The fact that they were referred also meant that from the beginning, professionals were acting in a multi-agency manner, albeit that parents themselves were not always willing to access support. Significant improvements were observed in terms of the children's development, including social interaction, speech and language, and weight gain where the children stayed for meals. In these circumstances, although children will benefit from immediate early interventions, if parents are not offered or indeed are not accepting of appropriate support to enable them to make significant changes to their own parenting, the long-term benefits will be reduced.

Case study

A family was provided with a subsidised place two sessions a week for a nine-month-old baby and two-year-old child. The mother was suffering with post-natal depression, the children lacked stimulation and the two-year-old had speech delay. The family were referred by the health visitor. Although referred to speech and language service, there was a year's waiting list to be assessed. The aim of the placement was to

- provide stimulation for the children;
- provide opportunities for the two-year-old's communication skills to improve;
- provide respite for the mother.

Lunch was provided for the children during the sessions. Over the next two to six months, the children both ate an increasing variety of food and put on weight with the health visitor commenting on their improved well-being in terms of weight, pallor and energy levels. The nursery observed their increased involvement in activities and curiosity as well as the two-year-old's improved confidence and enthusiasm for joining in activities. Due to the training that nursery staff had in speech development they were able to work with the two-year-old in providing vocabulary and his speech improved. As his speech developed he became less frustrated as he was able to communicate his needs and wants. The mother benefited from having some time to herself and accessed the centre's café and social area, including the public access computers. As she became more confident she was willing to bring the children to some of the Stay and Play activities and she started to talk about joining one of the adult learning courses to improve her literacy skills.

In the case study above the role of the nursery was key in providing rich educational experiences to stimulate the children's emotional, physical and cognitive development. The location of the nursery as part of the children's centre enabled wider relationships to occur encouraging the family to become part of the learning community and access other services in a familiar and safe environment. This led to the mother improving her own emotional well-being, reducing her isolation and supporting her own learning that will improve her future employment chances.

Links with schools

Many adults themselves do not have positive recollections of school and their educational experience. As a result of this, they are fearful of engaging with teachers or activities that suggest 'school' or 'education'. One way children's centres are able to support parents is to help them overcome these fears. By finding creative ways of encouraging parents to partner in their child's education in the friendly and supportive environment of a children's centre the foundation may be laid for a positive relationship with preschool and school settings for years to come. Educators in the centre can provide a bridge of support and direct parents to the schools who can provide comfortable ways of encouraging parents to support their child.

One of the key indicators for children's centres is the improvement of scores at the end of the Early Years Foundation Stage, especially in the personal, social and emotional development and communication, language and literacy strands. The aim is to

> increase the percentage of children who achieve a total of at least 78 points across the Early Years Foundation Stage (EYFSP) with at least 6 points scored in each of the personal, social and emotional development (PSED) and communication, language and literacy (CLL) scales. And to reduce the percentage gap between the lowest achieving 205 in the EYFSP and the rest.
>
> (DCSF 2008 website)

It is therefore vital for us to engage with schools to achieve more positive outcomes. Schools are able to promote children's centre activities with their parents, especially those that might not come into contact with children's centres through childcare. If they have established good relationships with their parents the children's centre can engage in work with younger siblings from an early age. Work can also focus on enabling smoother transitions into school, encouraging parents to develop a better understanding of how to support their children appropriately. This may be done through family learning courses that the school and centre jointly agree on.

Case study: working with schools

Working in a centre with a less disadvantaged reach area, there is no childcare on site. However, this has encouraged the centre to work with local provision and in particular a First School with a nursery class.

Over the last year the children's centre has developed strong links with the school. The nursery classes have visited the centre for story time and in particular the school has run family learning courses at the centre due to the lack of space at the school. This has resulted in many of the parents engaging with other services and activities at the centre, such as stay and play, the toy library and the music group, which they may have been more resistant to accessing previously. At times the courses have not been full so it has enabled us to encourage other parents to attend. This joint working has enabled us to support each other and improve transitions by providing children with more opportunities to develop their social and communication skills so giving them more of the skills they will require for entry to school.

The school is also represented in the centre's centre partnership group so are able to contribute their perspective of the needs of the community and ideas for meeting those needs.

Schools have good statistical information about children's achievements at the end of the Early Years Foundation Stage which provides children's centres with good evidence for the support children require before starting school. By working together children's centres are able to be more effective in providing the specific activities and services that will enhance children's development and enable parents to engage at a much earlier stage with their child's learning. As parents have a fuller understanding of how vital their role is as an educator and not just a carer, outcomes for children will improve and transitions between home and school will become smoother. In the case study above, the parents have begun to access other activities at the centre and younger siblings have benefited from these. Wider relationships have been made with other parents and professionals and a stronger foundation is laid in the community for improved services for young families.

Key messages for the future

- The only effective way of changing parent's attitudes and behaviour arises out of a relationship which takes time to develop and the more resistant parents are to engagement, the longer it takes.

- Providing an environment where parents feel supported and safe is a prerequisite for effective early intervention.

- There is no line dividing education and care so the provision both in childcare and centre activities must reflect this.

- As parents are the first and key educators it is vital to engage them as early as possible to give children the best start in life.

- To provide good outcomes we must invest in providing highly qualified staff with a thorough understanding of child development.

- Transition times (birth of a baby, starting at a childcare setting, starting at school) are key events in families lives that require support.

- Creating a stimulating learning environment for children, parents and for staff is a crucial aspect of every children's centre.

- Working together with health, social care and voluntary sector staff enriches everyone's experience of using the children's centre.

- It is important to identify common goals in all sectors and work towards them in a systematic and co-ordinated fashion.

- Services must reflect local need and involve parents and families at every step of the way.

References

Athey, C. (2006) *Extending Thought in Young Children: a Parent–Teacher Partnership*, second edition. London: Paul Chapman.

Betram, T., Pascal, C., Bokhari, S. and Gasper, M. (2002) *Early Excellence Centre Pilot Programme, Second Evaluation Report 2001–2002, Research Report 2001–2002*. London: DfES.

BBC News (2008) 'Baby P report: key findings' (1/12/2008). Available from http://news.bbc.co.uk/1/hi/uk/7758897.stm [accessed 17 May 2009].

BBC News (2009a) 'Baby P's carers lacked urgency' (1/5/2009). Available from http://news.bbc.co.uk/1/hi/england/london/8029864.stm [accessed 17 May 2009].

BBC News (2009b) 'UK is accused of failing children' (14/2/2009). Available from http://news.bbc.co.uk/1/hi/uk/6359363.stm [accessed 17 May 2009].

Coxon, K., Dearden, L., La Valle, I., Mathers, S., Purdon, S., Sibieta, L., Sigala, M., Shaw, J., Smith, G., Smith, R., Smith, T. and Sylva, K. (2007) *Sure Start (2007) National Evaluation of the Neighbourhood Nurseries Initiative (NNI): Integrated Report*. London: DfES.

DCSF (2001) *Promoting Children's Mental Health Within Early Years and School Settings*. Nottingham: DfEE.

DCSF (2006) *Sure Start Children's Centre Practice Guidance*. Nottingham: DfES.

DCSF (2007a) *National Standards for Leaders of Sure Start Children's Centres*. Nottingham: DfES.

DCSF (2007b) *The Children's Plan: Building Brighter Futures*. Norwich: The Stationery Office.

DCSF (2008) *Self Evaluation for Sure Start Children's Centres*. Nottingham: DfES.

DCSF (2009) *Next Steps for Early Learning and Childcare: Building on the 10 year strategy*. Nottingham: DfES.

Edgington, E. (2005) *The Foundation Stage Teacher in Action: Teaching 3, 4 and 5 Year Olds* (third edition). London: Paul Chapman.

EYFS (2007) *Effective practice: Health & Well Being*. Department for Children, Schools and Families.

Palmer, S. (2006) *Toxic Childhood*. London: Orion.

Sylva, K., Melhuish, E., Sammons, P., Siraj-Blatchford, I. and Taggart, B. (1997–2004) EPPE (The Effective Provision of Pre-School Education Project).

UNICEF (2008) 'Reports of childcare double disadvantage for poorest' (11/12/2008). Available from www.childwellbeing.org.uk/pages.asp?page=53 [accessed 18 May 2009].

UNICEF (2008) Report Card 8, 11 December.

Whalley, M. and the Pen Green Team (2007) *Involving Parents in Their Children's Learning*. London: Paul Chapman.

Further reading

Anning, A. (2008) 'Early learning, play and childcare in Sure Start Local Programmes', in Ball, M. (Ed.) *Improving Services for Young Children from Sure Start to Children's Centre*. London: Sage.

Belsky, J. (1999) 'Interactional and contextual determinants of attachment security', in Cassidy, J. and Shayer, P.R. (Eds) *Handbook of Attachment: Theory, Research and Clinical Applications*. New York: Guildford.

BMA Board of Science (2006) *Child and Adolescent Mental Health: a Guide for Healthcare Professionals*. London: BMA Board of Science.

Child Poverty Action Group (2009) *Child Wellbeing and Child Poverty: Where the UK Stands in the European Table Spring 2009*. London: CPAG.

DCSF (2005) *A Sure Start Children's Centre for Every Community: Phase 2 Planning Guidance* (2006–8) [downloadable from www.surestart.gov.uk].

Duffy, A., Chambers, F., Croughan, S. and Stephens, J. (2006) *Working With Babies and Children Under Three*. Oxford: Heinemann.

Melhuish, E. (2004) *A Literature Review of the Impact of Early Provision upon Young Children, with Emphasis Given to Children from Disadvantaged Backgrounds: Report to the Controller and Auditor General*. London: National Audit Office.

Sunderland, M. (2007) *What Every Parent Needs to Know: the Incredible Effects of Love, Nurture and Play on Your Child's Development*. London: Dorling Kindersley.

Websites

Together for Children:
www.togetherforchildren.co.uk

CHAPTER 5

Health

Antonia Hopkins

Introduction

If you visit a children's centre you will see health professionals working alongside other agencies, childminders, teachers, nursery workers, staff from adult education and from the voluntary sector and many, many more, and always working in close partnership with parents. In most centres you will see a baby clinic – a time to meet with other parents, to see the health visitor and the midwife. A wonderful informal space in which to have time for yourself, but also ask questions and discuss issues as they arise. Maybe the toy-library co-ordinator is there to offer a range of toys to borrow, and there is a chance to find out about the next baby-massage session, or book onto a course. The health visitor will be on hand to answer questions about nutrition and breast-feeding. What children's centres can provide is that notion of a one-stop shop for families, for families with young children with a wide range of needs. Sure Start children's centres at their best enable practitioners to work together to support the needs of young children. They allow parents to feel confident to work with professionals, not to feel done to. Health must be central to promoting better life chances for all of our children and it must be central to the whole children's centre agenda. Many centres are led by a health professional and there is considerable evidence to suggest that such centres are extremely successful in meeting the needs of families.

This chapter will look at the role of health in tackling issues of poverty and of social exclusion and of providing truly integrated services for all. It will look at practice from different perspectives, explore some of the barriers to effective provision and consider some of the potential outcomes from health involvement, both for the individual child and for society as a whole. It will also consider a way forward in developing more comprehensive user-friendly services for children and families and enabling children's centres to really make that difference to every child.

Health inequalities

The population's health in the United Kingdom has improved considerably over the past 150 years (House of Commons Health Committee 2009:9). 'In 1841 life expectancy at birth for men was 40.2 years and for women 42.2. By 1948 it was 66.4 and 71.2 years respectively. In 2000 the figures were 75.6 and 80.3' (ibid.:9). Despite these changes in life expectancy there are marked differences depending upon gender, location and ethnic group. However perhaps the most significant difference in life expectancy relates to social class. 'In 2006 a girl born in Kensington and Chelsea has a life expectancy of 87.8 years, more than ten years higher than Glasgow City, the area in the United Kingdom with the lowest figure (77.1 years)' (ibid.). The causes of these health inequalities are highly complex and include such factors as smoking, diet and exercise, and will also include the wider issues of education and poverty. Access to appropriate health care will also make a considerable difference. There is also now evidence that lifestyle is impacting quite considerably upon the health of the nation and that the quite dramatic rise in such conditions as diabetes could be attributed to lack of exercise and some food choices. The last 30 years has seen a threefold increase in the number of cases of childhood diabetes. This is most specifically worrying in respect of the rising number of children and of teenagers with type-two diabetes. Type-two diabetes is usually only seen in older people and this reflects obesity levels in young people.

In 2002, infant mortality rates for families in managerial and professional occupations was 3.1 per 1,000 births, compared with 9.2 in routine/manual occupations. Risk factors affecting these inequalities were cited as low birth weight, prematurity, smoking, alcohol consumption, poor nutrition and stress. Accidents and injuries are also the main cause of death in childhood and are subject to class differences; children from the lowest social class are nine times more likely to die in a house fire than children from other social classes.

Other early health and development issues continue to make a significant difference for children's life chances. The early development of communication and language will significantly impact upon their later educational success; this is an area identified in the National Evaluation of Sure Start (NESS 2004/5) and will impact upon children's ability to make the most of their educational experiences.

A commitment to tackling health inequalities

The whole area of health inequalities has been studied for many decades. Key works include the Black Report (DHSS 1980), the Acheson Report (1998) and more recently the final study from the World Health Organisation (WHO) Commission on the Social Determinants of Health (2008). Successive governments have made efforts to address issues of health inequalities. Since the 1970s, more deprived areas of the country have received more funds per head than more affluent areas. The current government is committed to tackling health inequalities and the impact that these have on individual's lives. (House of Commons Health Committee 2009). In 2003 the first ever Public Service Agreement (PSA) was introduced that aimed to reduce inequalities in health outcomes. 'By 2010 to reduce inequalities in health outcomes by 10 per cent as measured by infant mortality and life expectancy at birth' (House of Commons Health Committee 2009).

Health Action Zones and children's centres form part of the raft of government initiatives that seek to address health inequalities. Poor health cripples children's life chances, impacts on the well-being of society and is costly financially. However, it sounds so simple in theory but the actuality of achieving such goals is highly complex. How might this target for change be addressed? Most importantly, children's centres have a core offer for all services; health has a particular responsibility to deliver the following in partnership with other agencies:

- ante-natal advice and support for parents/carers;

- delivery of the Healthy Child Programme (previously the Child Health Promotion Programme, CHPP);

- information and guidance on breast feeding, hygiene, nutrition and safety;

- promoting positive mental health and emotional well-being, including identification, support and care for those suffering from maternal depression, ante- and post-natally;

- speech and language and other specialist support;

- specialist services for children with additional needs;

- support for healthy lifestyles;

- help in stopping smoking.

Making it happen

The whole children's centre development is an expensive initiative with enormous potential. If it is to make a real, lasting difference then local agencies at every level need to be committed to the vision, to providing truly integrated services that see the child in a holistic manner at the centre of family and of community. Research into health inequalities needs to be translated into action by all those with power to do so. The local authorities are tasked with improving outcomes for all children under section 4 of the Childcare Act 2006. To do this they are required to work in partnership with both the NHS and with Jobcentre Plus (DoH 2007).

Children's centres are uniquely placed in addressing issues of health inequalities and of social exclusion. They are also so well placed in ensuring that health services are truly accessible in every sense of that word, that they are geographically just around the corner, but also they are offering services that are sensitive to the needs of the families whom they serve. They are able to consider how people access services and how they might provide outreach services as appropriate. They are also, if they are good at what they do, able to develop effective working relationships within their community to create the networks that support families day to day.

Children's centres can provide accessible health services which will help to meet specific objectives such as:

- reducing smoking in pregnancy;
- reducing infant mortality;
- increasing uptake and duration of breastfeeding;
- reducing incidence of low birth weight babies;
- improving physical activity;
- promoting healthy eating;
- promoting the early take-up of antenatal services;
- improving provision of postnatal services including parenting support;
- improving access to contraceptive services;
- a means of delivering integrated, multi-agency services;
- a means of improving choice for families; and
- a means of delivering key components of the National Service Framework for Children, Young People and Maternity Services such as the Child Health Promotion Programme.

(DoH 2007:6)

There is a strong imperative for health issues to be at the very core of the children's centre agenda, to improve health outcomes for all children, and most specifically for children in danger of social exclusion and of poverty.

The role of the health visitor

Central to effective community-based health is the key role of the health visitor in providing services that support the child from birth and working with the midwife before the baby is born. Health visitors and community nursery nurses who generally work with the health visitor provide a wonderful link with the local children's centre. Every family with a child under five will have a named health visitor, someone that families can meet with in their own home and that can provide ongoing care and support.

Health visitors can provide information and support on:

- children's growth and development;
- common skin problems;
- common childhood infections;
- behaviour, sleeping, eating, potty training, teething, temper tantrums;
- breastfeeding, weaning, eating, hygiene, safety and exercise;
- postnatal depression, bereavement and domestic violence.

An important aspect to their role will be organising and running baby clinics, an excellent way to welcome new families to a children's centre. Because health visitors are involved from the earliest stages of life they usually become trusted by the family and can help and encourage new parents. Integrated practice is central to the role of the health visitor as they will always work in close partnership with the local GP, social worker, school nurse, speech and language therapist, and local nurseries. Health visitors are there on the ground and provide a wonderful mechanism for affecting change within every community and supporting every child whatever their needs and background in achieving their individual potential. They continue to be pivotal in helping to make the children's centre vision a reality. Health visitors and their team are also aware of issues around early attachment. They are there to support the parents in those crucial early days to ensure that early attachments are made and to pick up on any potential problems. Critical to their role is their involvement in safeguarding children. This is an area that Laming emphasised in his 2009 report, the central role of health staff who visit children in their homes in picking up key indicators of distress, most specifically in the pre-verbal child.

The Family–Nurse Partnership

The programme known as Nurse-Family Partnership in the USA, explored in Chapter 3, sees the role of the health practitioner visiting families in their home in the early days of an infant's life as crucial, most particularly for vulnerable families. The establishing of that central bond of care and trust is central in making a difference. In England this intervention programme is called the Family–Nurse Partnership (FNP); the government has been running a pilot programme since March 2007, and early indications are promising. In the document 'Reaching out: an action plan on social exclusion' (Cabinet Office, Social Exclusion Task Force 2006) the government announced that it would test out the FNP for first-time vulnerable young mothers providing intensive home-visiting. Gordon Brown said in 2006 that 'because no child should ever be written off, for mothers of infants, we will expand the help of nurse-family partnerships'. This means an allocation of £30 million to support this programme over the period of the spending revue from 2008/09 to 2010/11. This will support the funding of additional sites across the country, with the intention that by 2011 there will be 70 pilot sites (Every Child Matters website, accessed 8/7/2009).

What is the Family–Nurse Partnership?

The FNP is:

- An intensive, preventative home visiting programme for vulnerable, first time parents that starts in early pregnancy and ends when the child is two
- The goals of this programme are to improve antenatal health, child health and to support parent's economic self-sufficiency
- This is a licensed, structured programme which was developed over 25 years in the US. It is delivered by specially trained family nurses drawn from health visiting, midwifery mental health or the school nursing team.

(Every Child Matters website, accessed 8/7/2009)

The programme is being evaluated to determine both short and long-term benefits.

Most recent research into the FNP suggests that:

- The FNP successfully engages and connects with hard to reach and vulnerable young parents
- Fathers are more engaged
- Clients value their family nurses highly
- The nurses are deeply committed and enthusiastic about the programme
- We seem to be able to meet the fidelity requirements, which are designed to help achieve similar outcomes to those in the US research trials
- Early Impacts look promising, such as reducing smoking in pregnancy and increasing breast feeding
- Hard to reach families are accessing centres through FNP.

(Every Child Matters website, accessed 8/7/2009)

The health element of the Children's Plan 'Healthy Lives, Brighter Futures' (DoH/DCSF 2009) demonstrates a strong commitment to the role of the health visitor in partnership with local children's centres: 'A strengthened role for Sure Start Children's Centres – both through additional health-based programmes, focusing on reducing obesity and smoking, and by ensuring that each centre has access to a named health visitor' (DoH/DCSF 2009:4).

Role of the midwife and midwifery services

Fundamental to all services within any children's centre is the midwifery service, working in clear partnership with all other health professionals. Working closely with the heath visitors, midwives based within centres or attached to them can provide timely and accessible services for all families, as well as enabling parents to have services on their doorstep such as antenatal and post-natal care. They can also provide more targeted services, for example helping to run groups for young parents, for parents of premature babies, providing advice on getting pregnant and on birth control. Being able to talk through concerns with a midwife that you know in the friendly, open environment of the children's centre can make all the difference to parents. Involving families in the children's centre early on in their child's life even before birth, perhaps even before conception, is so important for later outcomes.

The Children's Centre Practice Guidance (DfES/DoH 2006) states that centres should link with maternity services in order to:

- identify parents and babies at risk of poor outcomes;
- provide or arrange intervention when problems arise;

- provide relevant education and health promotion for the health of mother, father and baby: and

- provide social and emotional support to increase parenting competence of both mothers and fathers.

(DfES/DoH 2006:53)

The role of the speech and language therapist

Research has shown us the central importance of early communication when looking at children's later achievement:

> There is a very strong body of evidence to suggest that the foundations of communication development are laid in the very earliest of experiences. The early years are crucial for language acquisition and the first three years in particular contribute substantially to children developing key language skills by the time they reach early childhood.

(DfES/DoH 2006:60)

It is essential to recognise that children do not learn to read successfully if they have not developed sound language. Children's centres are about improving every child's life chances, if this is what we are about then we must focus on early language acquisition. The role of the speech and language therapist is pivotal to the work of a centre. Sure Start programmes often had their own speech and language therapists seconded from the primary care trust, offering a wide range of services directly to children and to families. However, with the move towards a more universal children's centres service, what is needed from the speech and language service is close collaboration with the childminders, nursery nurses, health visitors, midwives, portage workers, teachers, library co-ordinators, crèche workers and volunteers who work from the centre. This could be done through the appointment of a speech and language therapist with area-wide responsibility.

The speech and language service

Working with a speech and language therapist within the partnership work of the children's centre can support both informal and more formalised services for families. It can also provide much needed expertise for the children's centre team on early communication. The therapist needs to provide the following:

- a commitment to truly integrated practice that supports early attachment and early communication;

- opportunities to support parent and child interaction from birth, which can be done through direct work, or by offering training to all the above;

- being responsive to possible difficulties experienced in early communication and training children's centre staff to pick up on issues in this area;

- providing awareness raising on the language-rich context of play for all children's centre staff working in play-based settings, in the crèche, nursery, toy-library sessions, play and stay, library visits, childminder settings, health visitors and portage visits, all of which have an important role to play in promoting early language;

- providing materials such as play-bags and story-sacks that will stimulate language, and which could be part of the toy-library collection;

- helping to set up sing-along and story sessions for babies, children and carers;

- helping to provide an environment that stimulates interaction, which could be through providing a photo wall or a scribbling wall for children and adults or just lots of opportunities around the centre to get involved and have your say, whether you are an adult or a child;

- providing assessment and specific on-going therapy sessions within the children's centre;

- being part of the multi-disciplinary team that supports families day-to-day in the centre and within the community, enabling families to access expert services in their local area.

Oral health

Every children's centre will have access to the local oral health programme, and can provide excellent opportunities for joined-up working with local dentists. Oral health workers can be part of play and stay sessions or child health clinics and can be on hand to answer queries and offer advice. They can be particularly helpful when health practitioners run weaning sessions for families. Again what is so important is promoting early oral health habits and creating an environment that has at its core a common message on oral health that is exemplified in all the work of the centre, whether that is in the café, or out and about in play sessions in the local community.

Promoting positive mental health

Children's centres are in a unique position to promote positive mental health in their community. Right from the start the centre can offer a wide range of formal and informal services which will help to give children a good start in life. We have heard elsewhere in this book about the very crucial nature of those first years of the child's life in laying the foundations for learning and for secure attachments. Children's centres might address issues of positive mental health by providing the following:

- working closely with the Child and Adolescent Mental Health Services (CAMHS);
- activities that promote early attachment and the positive relationships between parents and child, such as baby massage courses, ensuring that some sessions are provided at times when working parents can access them;
- targeted services such as post-natal depression groups that are health visitor and parent facilitated, and introduce other elements of the integrated team, such as adult education;
- training for all of the children's centre team in being aware of mental health issues and what to look out for;
- a counselling service, where possible on site and in conjunction with the local GP surgery;
- play therapy sessions for children who have experienced trauma and emotional difficulties.

Responsibilities of NHS organisations

The key to successful integrated working lies in a clear sense of vision and commitment right from the top of each organisation, and that this sense of joined-up thinking permeates to every part of an organisation. Without this we are all spitting in the wind.

Statutory responsibilities

The Childcare Act 2006, Section 4 places a duty on local authorities to work in clear partnership with their partners in the NHS and Jobcentre Plus to improve the outcomes for all children and to reduce inequalities by the provision of integrated services for young children and their families

(DoH 2007:7). However, this sense of buy-in from the local primary care trusts has not always been swift in some areas, despite the clear benefits. The House of Commons Committee of Public Accounts report into the effectiveness of Sure Start children's centres commented:

> Partnerships with Primary Care Trusts have been slow to develop. Involving health closely in children's centres has a double benefit by providing a service most families need, and bringing more families into a centre, but pressure at Primary Care Trusts have contributed to difficulties in achieving more commitment from the health sector. All Trusts should establish agreements with local authorities to provide child and family health services through children's centres.
>
> (House of Commons Committee of
> Public Accounts 2006-07:7)

The commitment from the local primary care trust is crucial in the success of children's centres.

Some children's centres are led by health services and many have health staff co-located within one building. This clearly has enormous benefits for service-users and for other agencies all working together, able to share a common philosophy and a common agenda. However, even in the smaller centres where co-location is not a possibility there can be excellent provision offered by different agencies working together. Most importantly, they all need to develop a shared vision and they need to have a good understanding of what the local issues are and what services are already up and running.

The following services might be provided by the health team:

- baby clinics;
- baby massage often combined with baby sign to promote that all important early attachment, baby health and early communication;
- speech and language sessions;
- baby sign and baby communication classes;
- training programmes for health professionals and for parents such as the Elklan course;
- exercise programmes for adults and children, often working in partnership with parents (as in the rough-and-tumble group discussed in Chapter 8);
- parent craft classes;

- immunisation sessions;
- weaning programmes;
- continence service;
- targeted work for specific groups such as teenage parents;
- cook-and-eat sessions;
- dance workshops for adults and children;
- 'let's all eat together', lunch and tea groups for all the family, promoting healthy eating and getting people together;
- smoking cessation groups and individual sessions, for pregnant women and other family members;
- multi-professional meetings for children with additional needs;
- pre- and ante-natal classes;
- breast-feeding peer-support programmes;
- tongue-tie service;
- exercise groups for both adults and children;
- first-aid classes.

Information sharing

Of central importance is the whole area of information sharing in incorporating health services in the whole integrated approach to the design and delivery of children's services. This is a highly sensitive area and one that requires clear direction from senior managers and robust and transparent protocols that can be used effectively across different agencies.

Case study: information sharing, Willington Children's Centre, County Durham

Families using the Willington Children's Centre in County Durham are benefiting from the high level of integration and information sharing between health, local authority and other partners. Appropriate consent at each stage is a vital component to maintain the trust of parents using services. Clear policies and protocols give providers reassurance about how information will be used sensitively and kept confidentially, overcoming misunderstandings about what is legal and appropriate. This means that staff working across the full range of services – from GPs, midwives, health visitors, through to children's centre staff and schools, to specialists such as social care and domestic violence teams – are all confident in joining two-way exchanges of data and confidential records about individual families. This close working helps to identify families in need of services, and promote more effective targeting of action to encourage parents to become involved and use the services that can benefit their families. It also provides a secure context that supports and promotes the Common Assessment Framework.

(DoH/DCSF 2009:92)

Integrated working

Working with health in an integrated way is clearly essential if we are to ensure that services for children and parents meet their needs and are increasingly accessible. So what are the challenges and barriers to successful integrated practice identified from both local and national Sure Start programmes?

Barriers to the development of effective integrated practice

There is a clear commitment to integrated practice and a legal imperative to make it happen. However, there are a range of stumbling blocks that can impede effective joint working:

- *Staff.* Staff are often just covering caseloads, causing a considerable challenge with serious staff shortages leading to poor morale and an inability to take on different ways of working. There is a national and local shortage of health visitors and midwives and the government will need to train more in future if health staff with the required knowledge skills and competence are to be available to work effectively with partners in children's centres.

- *Desk space/storage space.* Co-location is the optimum way forward with health staff working alongside social care, education and voluntary sector colleagues based at a children's centre. Unfortunately there is limited space in most children's centres and as local authorities have strategic responsibility they often tend to use the available space for their own staff.

- *Design*. All new children's centres need to have storage space built in to accommodate the tools and equipment health staff require to provide services (weighing scales, examination couches, etc.) and also for the basic requirements to meet cross-infection policies (e.g. hand washing facilities). To date these have not always been considered or planned for. Health personnel need to be involved at the earliest opportunity in the design of children's centres and services. The current management of children's centres by the county council has militated against integrated working with health and other agencies, specifically with reference to the design of buildings and of services.

- *Information technology links, confidentiality issues of governance*. Sharing client/ patient information is a very difficult area to navigate at any time; however, rapid advances in IT developments regarding governance (e.g. Electronic Common Assessment Framework) are beginning to improve this situation.

- *Politics*. Clash of organisational cultures, with limited 'buy-in' from health can undermine the whole integrated services agenda. Funding streams are not always in place to ensure the sustainability of services. A sense of empire-building in different agencies can destroy a sense of shared commitment and erode the vision of partnership working.

- *Inclusivity*. The whole notion of integrated working is to ensure that all relevant and appropriate agencies are included and that there is some kind of balance of power. However, it can be that certain agencies are left out. This could be because of different organisational philosophies; maybe most particularly this can arise when a faith group is involved. However, to leave out certain sections of the community can be to miss out on the richness of experience and expertise that they can bring to truly integrated practice.

Key messages, developing new ways of working

- Health visitors and school nurses need to work in different ways, the National Service Framework (2004) advocates a change in the way we think about and deliver children's health services. Most particularly, services need to be designed and delivered around the needs of the child.

- There is a need to move away from paternalistic GP attachment – align health visitors and school nurses with children's centres geographical areas and integrated multi-professional teams.

- Skill mix in health teams needs to be increased in children's centres in order to work effectively and with partners. There needs to be an increased understanding of the roles and responsibilities of individuals within teams.

- The learning from local Sure Start programmes demonstrated that team working, particularly when health staff (i.e. health visitors and midwives) are co-located in children's centres, makes for better communication andimproved multi-disciplinary teamwork, and allows for a smoother handover of mother and babies at 10–14 days. This can enable more vulnerable women to have a more credible and seamless service, leading to a greater continuity of relationship and therefore a more enduring service for the family.

- However, by solely relocating children's health services to children's centres it must be acknowledged that with the current shortages of mainstream staff in midwifery and in health visiting it will be difficult to see significant improvements in services unless there considerable improvements in staffing levels.

- Eating habits are set early in life and there is a need to improve nutritional outcomes in pregnancy and from an early age. It is important to give mothers support and advice on nutrition and breast feeding through excellent midwifery services within the children's centre or as part of the wider umbrella of available services and to provide appropriate, sensitive peer-support programmes.

- The current focus on narrowly defined outcomes in respect of health inequalities is not always useful. Translating policy which has demonstrable positive effects on health inequalities into practice is the real challenge.

- There needs to be robust, comprehensive, safe, agreed methods of information sharing.

- We all need to be truly ambitious for the holistic development of each and every child and we all need to be open to learning from every other partner agency and from families.

Conclusion

Those who have worked in Sure Start programmes and children's centres are aware of the enormous impact that they can have on a local community,

Figure 5.1 Breast-feeding peer support creating a climate of empowerment

but it requires that we all rethink the way in which we work and that we are open to innovative ways of working. Those working in Sure Start children's centres have found it an exciting and challenging time, and families have appreciated the strength of the partnerships in their local programmes. This chapter concludes by recording some of these experiences.

Comments from a mother who experienced an integrated team approach

We all know what a wonderful place our children's centre is; we can have a coffee and chat with friends, old and new, and attend the many activities available daily. I'm sure all of you here have your own reasons for coming to the Centre either as a parent or as a professional, this is my story.

I started attending activities at the old Chapel when I was adopting my son. I made many new friends and received support as a new parent, which was also the start of important relationships being made. My marriage broke down before the formal adoption and I was terrified I was going to lose my son and our home but I had met people I trusted and could confide in and was given support to cope as a single parent.

I eventually met a wonderful man who became Daddy to my son and three years ago we decided to try for a baby but at 40 I needed all the help I could get. Rachel, who was the Sure Start midwife at the time, gave me parental advice and support. I also received counselling at the Centre to help put my past in perspective and enable me to look to the future positively.

Two years ago I found I was pregnant, after 15 years my dream had come true but sadly at 11 weeks I had a scare. Again I received understanding and support from the Sure Start team and was able to have all my ante natal care at the Centre where I felt at ease.

Last year my beautiful baby son was born, it was the most amazing experience in the world. Sadly the birth was traumatic and both baby and I were ill.

I attended groups but none of my close friends had babies and I began to feel lonely and isolate, the Sure Start team looked after me and I made new friends.

At three months old my baby was ill but doctors didn't believe me, after four months I asked a health visitor to call on us. Straightaway she made an appointment with a GP for that afternoon and ensured that that the doctor gave the correct medication.

This had taken its toll on me and a couple of days later I ended up at the health visitor's office at Fitzalan Medical Centre in desperation asking for help. I was only confident to do this because I knew the health visitor from their involvement with the Centre. They took me to the Doctor who checked my baby and assured me he was o.k., they told me they were more worried about me and made an appointment for me to see a GP the next day. I was diagnosed with severe Post Natal Depression (PND) and prescribed antidepressants.

I attended a PND support group run at the Centre by HVs. I met other mums who were suffering and we were able to support each other. Whilst at this group I was diagnosed with Post Traumatic Stress Disorder from the birth for which I am now receiving counselling from Catherine, one of the health visitors. I have been to some dark sad lonely places but with my GP Dr. Grant, Catherine and Ruth the Sure Start midwife, all working together to help me recover I will get well again.

Our Centre is much, much more than a fun place to be, for some of us it is the means of survival.

I hope my story can somehow convince partners and other agencies that multi-agency working is crucial and continue to help provide the services and funding vital to our families.

(Littlehampton Parent Board Member)

Comments from integrated team members

From the perspective of the health team leader

In order to develop effective interventions early and appropriately we can learn a great deal from the experiences of the local Sure Start programmes. Integrated, multi-professional, interagency working is not easy – it is very challenging and needs health professionals to think very differently about the way in which they work. Understanding partners, differing working cultures and sharing priorities – working to support agendas other than just health is an entirely new way of operating. Having a flexible attitude and a good sense of humour is essential. Translating national and local priorities into effective services which have meaning for parents and children and provide the required outcomes is exciting and frees professionals up to develop innovative needs-led services.

Providing integrated working environments for services to be delivered is like playing a game of 'Jenga' – if one piece is removed, there is a risk that the entire structure will weaken and even collapse, and makes the players involved anxious and stressed. It is difficult to describe how powerful, efficient and effective integrated working is when it works well – it is achievable.

Managing a health team as part of an integrated multi-agency, co-located team in a local Sure Start programme was one the highlights of my professional career as it enabled me to work in innovative ways I felt met the needs of the children, parents, families and the community. It enabled my team to use their considerable knowledge and skills and experience to provide a caring, approachable and accessible innovative and holistic service which met need as well as the targets set out locally and nationally to improve outcomes for children and families.

From the perspective of a midwife

After having the unique experience of working as a midwife in an integrated team, in my view the benefits are apparent. I was truly able to provide a holistic approach to the care of the women and families that I was caring for, having the support of and improved communication with other agencies. Working alongside other professionals from a variety of agencies enabled a better understanding of each other's roles, improved communication between us and promoted a prompt referral system between agencies. The women and families benefited from this with improved access to services, be it health, education or social issues. I also learnt so much more about the community I was working in and developed a great network of contacts from different agencies and resources within the community both of which benefited the family.

From the perspective of a nursery nurse

A diverse team, with all different types of personalities! That gave the team breadth – it meant you had more skills, resources, contacts, ideas, manpower, enthusiasum, knowledge, and patience, which made the team strong. It gave all members a chance to widen their skills and knowledge, and a chance to try out different ways to approach targets. A larger team than most were used to working with which took some to time adapt to, but this created bonds and friendships. A real fun time! It was great for the client, who had access to all services and personnel under one roof. The negatives – salaries were not necessarily compatible (i.e. team members in similar roles but from different agencies salaries were very different which sometimes caused problems) and it is soooo hard to go back! (To working in a uni-professional skill mix health visiting team.)

The holistic approach as applied by health practitioners was a key to success in Sure Start local programmes and thus health services need to be fully integrated into the transformation of the programmes into children's centres (Melhuish *et al.* 2007). There is much evidence to demonstrate that health-led services are better accepted and more successful than services led by other agencies (Halliday and Asthana 2007). The holistic approach is a basic principle of community development. It may also reflect the levels of trust and respect enjoyed by health professionals, due in part to the universal nature of the provision of health services, therefore there is no stigma attached, and often initiatives are better received as they are not specifically targeted at 'vulnerable groups'.

If we are to make a difference in addressing issues of poverty and social exclusion through the children's centre movement then we must combine the tremendous groundswell of good work and positive practice in the community with a true commitment through lasting policies, not 'here today, gone tomorrow' initiatives that are not given time to bed down and have an opportunity to make a difference.

References

Acheson, D. (1998) *Independent Inquiry into Inequalities in Health.* London: The Stationery Office.

DfES/DoH (2006) *Sure Start Children's Centre Practice Guidance.*

DHSS (1980) *The Black Report, Inequalities in Health.*

DoH (2007) *Delivering Health Services Through Sure Start Children's Centres.*

DoH/DCSF (2009) *Healthy Lives, Brighter Futures: the Strategy for Children and Young People's Health.*

Halliday, J. and Asthana, S. (2007) 'From evidence to practice: addressing health inequalities through Sure Start the Policy Press', *Evidence and Policy,* Vol. 3, No. 1, p. 41.

House of Commons Committee of Public Accounts 2006–07.

House of Commons Health Committee (2009) *Health Inequalities.*

Laming (2009) *The Protection of Children in England: a Progress Report.* House of Commons.

Melhuish, E. *et al.* (2007) *National Evaluation of Sure Start.* London: Birbeck College.

NESS (2004/5) *National Evaluation of Sure Start 2004 and 2005.* London: Birbeck University of London.

WHO, World Health Organisation, Commission on Social Determinants of Health (2008) *Closing the Gap in a Generation, Health Equity Through Action on the Social Determinants of Health.*

Further reading

Briant, J. (2006) *National Children's Bureau Littlehampton Sure Start Survey Registered Non Users.* NCB.

Briant, J. (2006) *National Children's Bureau Littlehampton Sure Start Children's Centre Impact Survey Report.* NCB.

Briant, J. (2006) *National Children's Bureau Crawley Children's Centre Impact Survey Report.* NCB.

Cabinet Office, Social Exclusion Task Force (2006) *Reaching Out: an Action Plan on Social Exclusion.*

DoH/DfES (2003) *Every Child Matters – Change for Children.*

DoH (2004) *Choosing Health.*

DoH (2007) *Maternity Matters.*

DoH/DCSF (2007) *Children's Plan.*

DoH/DCSF (2007) *The Child Health Promotion Programme.*

Marmont, M. and Wilkinson, R. (2006) *Social Determinants of Health.* Oxford: Oxford University Press.

NICE Clinical Guideline (2007) *45: Ante and Postnatal Mental Health*, April.

CHAPTER 6

Social services

Carole Beaty

There are approximately 11 million children in England. Of these . . .

- 200,000 children live in households where there is a known high risk case of domestic abuse and violence
- 235,000 are 'children in need' and in receipt of support from a local authority
- 60,000 are looked after by a local authority
- 37,000 are subject to a care order
- 29,000 are subject of a Child Protection Plan
- 1,300 are privately fostered
- 300 are in secure children's homes

(There is overlap in these categories, for example, a child who is living in a household with domestic violence may also be subject to a child protection plan)

(Laming 2009:13)

The scale of need outlined above, the immense cost in terms of the social and emotional consequences of not improving the well-being and the safety of our children at the early stages of their life, must dictate that addressing the above issues must be of the highest priority for both national and local government. To begin to effect this step change in services and to transform outcomes for all our children and young people the priority given to safeguarding must be brought about through 'strong and effective leadership, early intervention, adequate resources, and quality performance management, inspection and support' (Laming 2009:13). Children's centres as the key arm for the delivery of services for children must stand at the very heart of reform for children and must be pivotal in creating services and opportunities that help prevent young children from becoming one of the above statistics.

Children's centres are charged with helping local communities to become more sustainable, to become better places to live in. By helping the development of a local community they must be supporting the building blocks of any community, families, and at the centre of those families, children, each and every one. So they need to link right across the board with schools, colleges, voluntary sector organisations, faith groups, Jobcentre Plus, and so on, developing that ever expanding web of contact, making excellent links so that families and children can use those links.

Families will use their centre at different times for different things. Sometimes their need will be very explicit: advice and care from the community midwife when a new baby is expected, childcare in the centre nursery, running a cookery group with other parents, going to baby massage with the community nursery nurse and baby sign with the speech therapist. However, the 'open door' policy of every children's centre means that families with a range of needs will access services, and some of those families will have more specific needs, more acute problems that may be very obvious or may be hidden. This is one of the complexities of early support, user-friendly intervention that at times it will have a very different flavour and it will require astute, well-trained staff working in strong clear partnership to pick up on the particular needs of the family and act according to the best interests of the child. This of course is the complexity and the challenge of the work, and where it is essential to have the support of a senior social worker either working on site or with clear links with the children's centre.

The continuum of need

Children's centres are charged with providing universal services for children and families as well as early support and early intervention. Children's centres offer open access to all families living in the locality and apparently are set up without an agenda, but of course that is not entirely the case. They should offer a welcome to everyone, and anyone who has visited some of our excellent centres will have experienced that sense that here is a place into which they could bring their children and find support, help, advice and fun. However, the children's centre is charged also with working with children and families with specific needs. It is charged with supporting the process that makes a difference in terms of narrowing the gap between those children who fail to achieve their potential and those who do.

> Social services play a central role in trying to improve outcomes for the most vulnerable and a key measure of success will be achieving change through closing the gap between their outcomes and those of the majority of children and young people.
>
> (Every Child Matters website, accessed 26/5/2009)

When you work in a children's centre you are aware that people come through the door at all sorts of times and for diverse reasons and if the centre is working well then it will offer a very wide range of sources of information, training and care. Centres should all work closely with social services, which may mean that social workers are located on site; they may have a peripatetic role, offering an overview and supervision. Or, as in West Sussex, there may be a children and family centre model adopted with key centres having combined family centre and children centre staff with outreach to other smaller centres. All these have their strengths and their limitations.

Staff in children's centres know, whether they are a speech therapist, a portage worker, or a crèche co-ordinator, that families and children who they see every day will experience difficulties. They will experience problems, maybe with their parenting, or with post-natal depression, with domestic violence or with debt, with lack of self-esteem or with housing. Sometimes those problems or issues will be very obvious to the person themselves and to those they talk with, and they will seek out help. Sometimes those issues are hidden or covered up, not known, or denied by the individual themselves and their families, perhaps surfacing here and there once in a while. Sometimes those issues are apparently unknown to the individual, but obvious to the bystander. The children's centre staff are uniquely placed to pick up on those issues, both those that are overt and ones that come in a rather more covert form.

The children's centre by its very nature is a warm, open, loving and caring place that provides opportunities for all, but must be aware and watchful, questioning and vigilant. It takes skilled, confident and well-trained staff from all areas of work to assess a level of need and to act upon it. It takes experience and it takes judgement. Working across professions and across agencies can have its dangers and its drawbacks because it may be that we see something that we are uncomfortable with, but we think someone else will pick up on this and someone else will take that forward. Maybe also if we are used to working with families in different ways, for example as a teacher in centre, then we do not pick up on a more specific health issue, maybe an issue to do with mental health. Sometimes we just don't want to look foolish, to show our ignorance in an area that is not our own. However, all of us are on a continuum of need and we move along it back and forth; sometimes our needs are very clear, very specific, we seek help for our debt problem or for the fact that we are not coping at work; at other times they are hidden, but may be no less acute. So it is with families in children's centres.

Maybe a child within a family has just come off the child protection register; they still have a most specific need. They may not be on the social services' radar in the same way, but they need help and support. How vital then that with the support of the social worker the children's centre offers that ongoing care and monitoring. It is vital also that every member of the team is supported through supervision and through training and that the ideas and views from every member of the team are given credence and validity.

Case study

A family with four young children under the age of five had recently been taken off the child protection register with the support of their social worker and family support worker. At the final case-conference signing off this family, there was recognition of the progress this family had made. Charlie, a little boy of two, had been the subject of emotional and social abuse from both of his parents. With counselling and home visiting from the family support worker this was seen to cease and Charlie was growing into a confident and happy little boy. A CAF (Common Assessment Framework) meeting followed the case conference and an action plan was put in place. Attending this conference along with the family's social worker was the social worker permanently attached at the local children's centre, along with the manager of the nursery which was part of the centre, along with a nursery nurse with a health background who worked three days a week in the nursery and two days in the centre running baby massage groups and offering outreach services to families. It was agreed that Charlie would be offered a subsidised place in the nursery for two days a week while his mother could spend time with her younger children. The nursery nurse was asked to take on the role of lead professional, and to be Charlie's key worker in the nursery. Charlie quickly settled into the nursery and at the next CAF meeting everyone could report good progress, Charlie was enjoying the freedom he experienced in the large nursery and the family were more settled. However, two months later the nursery nurse noticed that there was a change in Charlie's demeanour; he was not so keen to come to nursery, was often brought in late or did not come at all, and he had become withdrawn and tearful. This in itself might not have been significant, but the nursery nurse was on the lookout for other signs that might confirm or challenge her growing concerns. She talked with the social worker based at the centre and they decided to consult with other members of the CAF team involved with the family. The health visitor made a visit to the family and found Charlie's mum very distressed, and the younger children in a poor condition. One of the children had a bruise on his head that his mother could not explain. The health visitor reported the bruise to the duty social worker, and a case conference was convened where the family went back on the child protection register and ongoing monitoring and appropriate support was provided for all the family.

This case study demonstrates the importance of having the expertise and experience of all members of the children's centre team and ensuring that their viewpoint is listened to by all practitioners involved. It is the front-line staff who are likely to notice changes and patterns of behaviour that might be a cause for concern.

Within the children's centre the strength and, of course, sometimes the danger of the work is that it is relationship based. Families and children build up strong bonds with children's centre workers; often they have been through a great deal together. They may have worked on committees and on management groups together fighting for the proper development of their centre. They may well have worked with other agencies to ensure that the parent voice is heard. They may have worked to ensure that a family with a child with additional needs has the home that they need. So when a child in a family is in trouble or a parent is crying out for help, maybe we do not see the situation as objectively as we should. We are seeing different families in different contexts and just maybe we are not being alert to the danger signs. This is when the presence of a social worker with the background and the training in assessment and identification is so important for children's centre work. There needs to be a sense of managing those boundaries in co-working to ensure consistency. It also provides a great sense of confidence and reassurance to the staff and volunteers.

But of course, most importantly, the social worker based at the centre or affiliated to it must share the common vision of the children's centre and must be attuned to the way in which the different members of the children's centre team work, whatever their background. They must be willing and able to seek that common ground.

The social worker will have a good understanding of 'thresholds' in terms of understanding where the child is in relation to safeguarding children procedures and will have the knowledge and the experience to know how and when to intervene to prevent the escalation of need.

Sometimes families are just there at the centre, they arrive first thing in the morning and do not leave until the last member of the team has gone home, and it seems that they just move in and by their very continuing presence alert the team to that unspoken cry for help. Is it that they are telling us loud and clear that they are in distress and need? We need to consider that just maybe we are creating a culture of dependency which is not useful or appropriate to this person; it is a time to challenge motivation. Here is a role for the skilful family support worker, the health visitor or teacher to engage them in conversation on an ongoing basis and help to get to the bottom of their current issue. However, the children's centre is a whole team and the caretaker and the café manger, if the centre are fortunate enough to have one, are part of the team and it may well be that a parent or child will talk more freely to them. It is important then that they are a valued member of the team with appropriate supervision and a clear understanding of what support is appropriate and who to go to with their concerns. Children's centres offer a relational support, but must also be watchful and accountable. It is not just bouncy castles and smoothies, it must be clearly focused upon the best interests of the child.

The Common Assessment Framework

The development and the use of the CAF has been discussed elsewhere in this book, but it is important to explore its uses in the context of the children's centre in relation to the continuum of need and the way in which social services might support its effective implementation into children's centre practice.

Generally the child's family is the best place for a child to grow up. However, there are times when that child and that family need extra support over and above normal services and informal support and contact offered by a local children's centres. When more than one practitioner is involved in meeting a child's needs then the CAF will be used as a framework for assessing need and designing an action plan. It is a tool at the earlier stages of intervention and support, but with that aspect of formalisation. It is very early stages for the CAF, but in terms of partnership working it has certain advantages for the children's centre:

- It brings together a wide group of professionals with the child and the family.

- It has an air of informality and sharing about it that helps to mitigate any sense of stigmatisation.

- Where the children's centre is involved, parents and children feel more confident and comfortable because they have an ongoing relationship.

- Staff from children's centre feel that something is being done and there are clearly stated outcomes in terms of who does what when, and what the family hopes for from the situation.

- Social services may not do the assessment themselves, but can support the whole process and are aware of those all important thresholds of need.

- The role of the lead professional is vital for the family as they have just one source of contact, and this is usually someone that they know well.

However, views about its use are varied as the Laming Report (2009) found out:

'The CAF has made a huge difference in this area to the early identification of children and young people in need.'

Local authority managers during a fieldwork visit

'The CAF can be very effective in building bridges and shared understanding between different professional groups.'

Police organisation in written evidence

'The CAF has caused a lot of confusion and is burdensome to complete, not least because not all agencies know how to feed their information into it.'

Voluntary organisation in written evidence

(Laming 2009:42)

The CAF has made a difference to integrated working and has helped to enhance this process. However, there are specific areas that need to be addressed further:

- Danger of the CAF becoming 'process-focussed' (Laming 2009:42).

- Becoming a 'barrier to services for children' where access to particular relevant services might depend upon a completed CAF (Laming 2009:42).

- All agencies need help in completing the CAF appropriately and then using it 'consistently' (Laming 2009:42). Social services providing CAF mentors and CAF surgeries can be of immense value here.

- The role of the lead professional is vital for the family and of course for the whole success of the process. It is often the case that the health visitor or community nursery nurse will take on the role of the lead professional where the child is under five. There is a considerable danger of overload with this role. There needs to be clear management from all agencies to ensure both consistency in the delivery of this role and viability in terms of workload.

- The CAF as a process needs to dovetail with other mechanisms for the identification and support of children with particular needs such as early support materials for children with additional needs, and portage and health visitors serious case files.

Safeguarding children and care procedures

Some children will come at the end of the continuum of need and be at risk of significant harm. Here is where much of the social worker's time is involved. It will be that children's centres will meet with children in this category and staff at centres will be part of this necessary process. A social worker on site will be of primary importance or at the least an attachment to the centre. Because the centre has information from across the local area and links to services it is well placed to pick up concerns and therefore needs to have in place clear lines of reporting and accountability. This is where the social worker's role is so vital for their knowledge of the law and of procedures.

So that image of a continuum of need is important, as we offer multi-faceted universal services to families, as is the clear awareness that families and children move up and down that continuum and of our responsibility to them.

Listening to children

Early intervention for the child under five is the remit for many children's centres; however, in some areas this has changed, with a remit of 9 months to 19 years. Many in the childhood workforce are skilled at tuning into children. Picking up from the young child their need and their possible distress is an essential role within the children's centre environment. The child may be too young to tell us directly but the skilled worker in all areas of practice with supervision and support can identify important signs of abuse and neglect. The social worker attached to a children's centre can offer invaluable support in this area.

A value-based way of working

All of us bring to our work a set of values that inform our practice and our judgement day to day, moment to moment. We have values that are bred in the bone, they come from our upbringing from our parents from our life experiences, they are informed by our beliefs, and sometimes we are not aware of them until they bring us up short in a situation. They are also framed by our professional background if we have one. As we work with children and families we challenge and test those values and we use them to form judgements about courses of action. Sometimes those values are at variance with others from other areas of work and of course the whole area of parenting is a really hot potato when it comes to making and acting upon our judgements. You put together in a children's centre a whole range of people working in different ways and with different professional heritages and of course you will have different views on parenting. There will be the view of 'good enough parenting', where the love is clearly there, but where some parts of the delivery make you feel uneasy. It may cause tension in the centre between members of the team, a feeling that we are not acting when we should or acting when it is perceived to be heavy handed and inappropriate. Integrated working needs to address the whole thorny subject of parenting, it is not in itself good enough to be working together if we are not observing and challenging.

There is a clear role for the social work team as well as the health team, who have a more global understanding of the needs of the child and usually the home situation. The experienced social worker's grasp of legislation and procedure, as well as a clear professional understanding of how to intervene and how to offer support, can help the team to clarify issues which are of concern. This will prove to be invaluable in reassuring all concerned that we are working in an objective and appropriate manner. The social work team needs to be there to offer ongoing training and supervision, a time to observe our own value systems and consider how we meet in that overlap with our team members. Working from a value base that is informed by a faith-based profession may be very different from the midwife or the portage worker; it may have a specific and sometimes different agenda. Nevertheless unless we want to turn integrated working into a tower of Babel, all talking different professional languages, we need to find that common area to stand together and a skilled social worker can help to achieve this.

Professional identities

The shift is to have a more co-ordinated approach to the development of the children's workforce. The integration of services around the child is not just a fanciful hope, it is an imperative.

However, although there is this push to work more closely together, it does not always work; this integration and that failure can lead to poor communication and a lack of understanding of roles and responsibilities, and families being let down. One reason that multi-professional working fails is the strength of professional identities, which of course are important and constructive yet can lead to a rigid way of working and a sense of exclusivity. It is important to reframe aspects of our professions so that boundaries become more open to a greater sense of inclusivity and understanding.

> The size of the professional groups within the [*children's*] workforce has led to the existence of strong professional identities in many parts of the workforce. For example, teachers, social workers and health professionals are well-established professions with very strong and in some respects very different 'professional identities' and approaches to 'the client'.
>
> (Hartle *et al.* 2008:10)

The idea that different professions have different approaches to the families they work with is an important one and something that needs constant revisiting within the children's centre arena.

It may also be, as we are dealing with human nature, that one area of work or a profession will take the ascendancy within a children's centre, or of course within the local authority and this may lead to the dumbing-down or the dismissal of another way of being or a profession, causing that person or those people to lose their status and their voice within the centre. This may mean that others are not listening when they are expressing concerns about a family. Important then that those rivalries are addressed in training and by managers who must themselves be modelling appropriate integrated behaviours and challenging mono-professional cultures.

The NPQICL (National Professional Qualification in Integrated Centre Leadership) (NCSL 2007) identifies four responses to multi-agency working:

Protester
Sabotaging
Withholding information
Withholding resources
Building silos
Claiming exclusivity
Pessimism
Cynicism

Prisoner
Uncommitted
Discontented
Claims has no resources
Remains in comfort zone
Professionally insecure
Apathy

Passenger
Observer
Shares when required
Fence-sitter
Jobs-worth behaviour
Lip service

Participant
Taking initiative
Sharing information
Pooling resources
Building partnerships

Networking
Inclusivity
Passion

(NCSL 2007:15)

Getting back to core business

While social workers may well be committed to the whole vision of integrated working and early intervention and delivery through children's centres, the truth is that in the current climate they are being pulled back a great deal of the time to their 'core business' which is work on the sharp end of the continuum of need. They struggle with large caseloads and often with bureaucratic systems. Staff shortages in key areas can make the whole business of early support frankly a pipedream.

Other professions recognise the constraints that social workers contend with:

> NAHT has the greatest respect for colleagues in social services and we recognise that they are often working in highly-charged situations and may have impossible workloads. They are too busy 'fire-fighting' difficult cases and often find themselves caught up in highly bureaucratic administration that prevents the essential early intervention work that can avoid later crisis.'
>
> (NAHT 2009:1)

This must be an issue of funding and of intent; if we are to address issues of poverty and of the statistics offered at the beginning of this chapter then the rhetoric is not enough. All the Power Point presentations in the world will make no difference at all if both central government and local government are not committed to early intervention. We need experienced family support workers and social workers working in clear partnership with children's centres if we are to ensure the strongest delivery of early intervention programmes.

> A recent report co-authored by MPs Graham Allen and Iain Duncan Smith highlights the need for early intervention, noting that 'child poverty and income are only part of the picture. Building human capabilities is at least as important and rewarding. Capable, competent human beings will almost always find their way in life, find work and raise happy families.' The report also highlights the importance of the first years of a child's life and how they lay the foundation for that child's growth and development; the author's believe that 'medical evidence points overwhelmingly in favour of

a shift to Early Intervention. It highlights the essential importance of years 0–3 in human development, and the vital influence on years 0–3 of their primary caregivers. That in turn makes it essential to prepare children of 0–18 for their future role as parents. Skills that for generations were passed on, almost unconsciously, now have to be taught: if they are not, we will reap the consequences.' (Graham Allen MP and Rt. Hon. Iain Duncan Smith MP, Early Intervention: Good Parents, Great Kids, Better Citizens (Centre for Social Justice/Smith Institute, 2008))

(Laming 2009:24)

Early support, early intervention, call it what you will, is just so important in so many circumstances, but it is not always easy to define, and families and practitioners will keep the debate alive. What practitioners and researchers know is that it is essential; sometimes it is very light touch, a piece of signposting to certain services, at other times it is offering a range of services for a family in time of need.

Because it is not at the sharp end of practice, maybe because it is not so visible and it is difficult to assess what you might have prevented, there is always the tendency in time of need to draw services back, but early intervention needs to be embedded in both training and practice. It can save lives, benefit the economy and support the development of the community.

Information sharing

Children's centres need clear record-keeping and clear lines of accountability. Record-keeping on contact with families will often be managed in line with other partner agencies such as health visitors. The whole area of sharing information, always a difficult issue, is highly complex in such a multi-faceted animal as a children's centre. There are rightly sensitivities about sharing information, most particularly in the health sector. However, assessment of need and achieving safety for children must never be hampered by rigid and mindless adherence to the laws governing data protection. The safety and the welfare of the child is always of paramount importance; agencies may lawfully share specific confidential information about a parent or about a child, without consent where there is a specific public interest. It will always be a matter of proportionality:

> The key factors in deciding whether or not to share confidential information are necessity and proportionality, i.e. whether the proposed sharing is likely to make an effective contribution to preventing the risk and whether

the public interest in sharing information overrides the interest in maintaining confidentiality. In making the decision you must weigh up what might happen if the information is shared against what might happen if it is not and make a decision based on professional judgement.

Information sharing: guidance for practitioners and managers

HM Government 2008

(Laming 2009:41)

Family support

Children's centres need to provide a wide range of family support services from parenting classes to outreach services. They need to do this in clear and effective partnership with other agencies. It may well be that when a children's centre is opened in a community there will already be family support work happening, and while there is no point in reinventing the wheel it is important to find ways of incorporating these into the ongoing vision of the centre. Often the local Home-Start programme will offer excellent visiting services for families with young children.

Home-Start

Home-Start offers a confidential service without judgement to families who may be experiencing difficulties. It is interesting that 25 per cent of families refer themselves to this service, which helps to support a family's confidence and independence by (Home-Start website):

- seeing families in their own homes to provide friendship and practical assistance;
- reassuring parents that their issues are not unique;
- helping to build upon parents' strengths and supporting emotional well-being;
- supporting parents in getting the fun back in family life.

Volunteers who have parenting experience themselves can offer (Home-Start website):

- time to listen;
- a break for parents;

- the support to make good use of local services;
- reassurance and practical help;
- support with the children.

Planning services to meet local needs

The Family and Parenting Institute carried out a study of the planning and the delivery of family support services in children's centres in 2006. This study aimed to explore the planning, commissioning and delivery of family support services from both the fourth and the fifth wave of development of Sure Start local programmes and highlight good practice.

This study emphasised the importance of using parents to engage other parents and to elicit their views. Most particularly the study emphasised the importance of:

- Starting consultation processes as early as possible
- Using local community partners to access parents
- Using a variety of techniques to engage different parents – such as face to face dialogue; questionnaires, focus groups, suggestion boxes
- Asking parents about location, format and content of services
- Involving parents on management boards, planning committees and through their own groups, to plan and deliver some services
- Training and preparation for parents and professionals to work together
- Input being seen to be acted upon and input mechanisms developed which are reviewed regularly for effectiveness and acceptability.

(Ashby *et al.* 2006:4)

Reaching hard-to-reach families

The idea is to have a children's centre in every community, yet if these centres are just used by families who might well access services anyway they are not really addressing the possible families who are sometimes referred to as 'hard to reach'. However, this could be a misnomer as it just may be the services which are hard to reach by families. It is always worth considering the way in which services are offered to families. I am sure that we have all experienced services that are almost impenetrable in nature; is this deliberate or is it just that those people offering them have stopped thinking about the service user? It is worth considering our own experiences and how it can make us feel when we are designing services for children's centres, and look at issues of accessibility.

Children's centres are for everyone and we want to make sure that the people using them feel that the services they receive meet their needs. Sometimes it seems that central and local government feel that a children's centre will open and somehow that will meet the needs of the local community.

The National Audit Office in their study on Sure Start children's centres for the House of Commons Public Accounts committee commented:

> While most of the early centres are in relatively disadvantaged areas, only one third of those visited by the National Audit Office were proactively seeking out the most disadvantaged families in their area. Parents are generally happy with the services that are provided, but smaller ethnic minority communities, single fathers and children with special needs are less well served. Families with children with disabilities in particular need better information on what services are available for them, and advice on accessing services not provided from the children's centre.
>
> (House of Commons Committee of Public Accounts 2007:1)

It takes a good knowledge of the local area and of the particular needs of individuals to ensure that services are designed and delivered to start to meet the highly diverse concerns of individual families. The rather simplistic notion of hoping that just opening a children's centre might make a difference is not going to be enough for local children.

Outreach home-visiting services can make a great deal of difference in terms of supporting vulnerable families, families who are going through a particularly difficult time. However, this is easy to say, but difficult and complex to deliver; it takes sensitive and attuned staff. 'They are on the parent's home territory and must be sensitive to the context in which they are working. They will need to be able to offer practical help and support' (DfES 2005:32).

Some children's centres will make use of volunteers from the local community to do home visiting; in others it is carried out by community nursery nurses and family support workers or there is a link with organisations such as Home-Start. All these can make a tremendous difference to families who are isolated and have particular needs. What is of paramount importance is that staff who are undertaking this highly complex and vital work are adequately supported, trained and supervised and that social work staff have full involvement in this programme.

Making a difference through outreach programmes

For many families it is the outreach programmes that will make a real difference to the quality of their lives. Some families will not wish to access the centre, but will find individual contact and support from a home visitor invaluable. For this to happen there needs to be:

- clear lines of accountability and responsibility;
- excellent supervision offered through health/social services staff;
- plenty of informal ongoing contact to build confidence and trust;
- excellent ongoing information, through contact with the centre, newsletters, flyers etc. (always ensuring that these are accessible to families through translation, etc.);
- clear procedures for home visiting;
- assessment of need carried out by relevant agencies, health and social services;
- ongoing targeted work that clearly relates to the families need;
- consistent staff working with families;
- a true value placed upon the work of the home-visiting staff by every section of organisations running children's centres.

Barriers to effective working

- Poor understanding of how different agencies work and about their procedures and protocols;
- lack of a common vision;
- staff being pulled back to their core business and management seeing integrated early intervention as an extra;
- staff shortages leading to a lack of commitment to early intervention;
- professional rivalry between agencies;
- lack of clarity on roles and responsibilities.

Key messages

- The need to establish clear shared aims and objectives;
- the need for a strong and apparent buy-in to integrated early intervention work from all levels of organisations: health, local authority and the voluntary sector;
- an open way of working that enables the development of innovative working at every level of an organisation;

- strong partnership working with the local area and with local families;
- adequate resources in terms of staffing and funding, a notion of a sustainable budget and where possible pooled budgets;
- fostering an ethos of trust through joint planning, training and delivery;
- the co-location of services where possible so that children's centre staff have access to qualified and experienced social workers;
- excellent lines of communication that are open, flexible and foster positive working relations and do not solely depend on interfaces with machines.

Laming's recommendations for social workers in his 2009 report are important for all those working to support the needs of all children and families:

The Social Work Task Force should:

- Develop the basis for a national children's social worker supply strategy that will address recruitment and retention difficulties, to be implemented by the Department for Children, Schools and Families. This should have particular emphasis on child protection social workers;
- Work with the Children's Workforce Development Council and other partners to implement, on a national basis, clear progression routes for children's social workers;
- Develop national guidelines setting out maximum case-loads of children in need and child protection cases, supported by a weighting mechanism to reflect the complexity of cases, that will help plan the workloads of children's social workers; and
- Develop a strategy for remodelling children's social work which delivers shared ownership of cases, administrative support and multi-disciplinary support to be delivered nationally.

Children's Trusts should ensure a named, and preferably co-located, representative from the police service; community paediatric specialist and health visitor are active partners within each children's social work department.

(Laming 2009:50)

References

DfES (2005) *Sure Start Children's Centres Practice Guidance.*

Hartle, F., Snook, P., Apsey, H. and Browton, R. (2008) *The Training and Development of Middle Managers in the Children's Workforce.* London: Hay Group.

House of Commons Committee of Public Accounts (2007) *Sure Start Children's Centres*.

Laming, H. (2009) *The Protection of Children in England: a Progress Report*. House of Commons.

NAHT (2009) *Laming Report: Joined up Thinking, but not Joined up Working*. Conference, National Association of Head Teachers.

NCSL (2007) NPQICL (National Professional Qualification in Integrated Centre Leadership) *Training Materials: Multi-agency Working Collaboration Matters*. Nottingham: NCSL.

Further reading

Ashby, V., Apps, J., Hussain, F. and Reynolds, J. (2006) *Family Support in Children's Centres: Planning Commissioning and Delivery*. Family and Parenting Institute.

Atkinson, M., Jones, M. and Lamont, E. (2007) *Multi-agency Working and Its Implications*. London: NFER.

Laming, H. (2003) *The Victoria Climbié Inquiry, Report of an Inquiry by Lord Laming*. Norwich: The Stationery Office.

Quinton, D. (2004) *Supporting Parents: Messages from Research*. London: Jessica Kingsley.

Websites

Every Child Matters:
www.everychildmatters.gov.uk/socialcare/

Home-Start:
www.home-start.org.uk/about/what-we-do

CHAPTER 7

The voluntary sector

Sim Dendy

Introduction

Right at the beginning of this chapter I need to be honest (for that is part of my job as you will see) and explain what I do and why I have been asked to write this element of the book. I work as a leader of a church (which is why I need to be honest – although you might not agree that has always been your experience!) now based in Southampton where I specialise in developing partnership projects with government agencies and other charities and churches.

I have been working in community development on behalf of the church for over 15 years, but it is especially over the last five years as the various government programmes, such as children's centres, have emerged that I have become more and more involved in connecting various agencies together. This has included encouraging churches to work with the statutory bodies, as much as encouraging the statutory bodies that working with local churches will be beneficial and that they won't preach at any warm body that comes through the door!

So although I am writing about the voluntary sector I do so with a background of church work and a bias towards it for which I do not apologise and am not embarrassed about, but want you to be aware of my personal stance to understand where I am coming from as we dive into this chapter.

Background

Volunteers will find the discussion about integrated working, joined-up thinking and any other modern phrase we can think of a little strange, as volunteers have often tried to work in an integrated way for years. The voluntary sector or 'third sector' as it is often called has always prided itself on keeping the needs of the person that they are supporting as central to the way of working rather than the result of the work (i.e. finance or statistics) being more important than the individual's needs. In fact many volunteers and charities prefer to work in this way to allow them to operate in the way that they see fit for the individual, rather than being dictated to by the government of the day that is trying to gather statistics for a particular area of concern, or the business that is trying to make a financial return rather than thinking about the needs of the person who is sitting right in front of them.

Arguably many of our existing statutory agencies such as health, education and social care came from the third sector before it even knew it was called that. In the United Kingdom many of these early initiatives had their roots within the traditional parish church at that time.

Before the National Health Service began in 1948 there were many hospitals and health centres already in existence, largely initiated and developed by local churches (which is why so many hospitals carry the name of a saint, such as St Richard's or St Mary's, as this was the name of the church that started or supported it). All hospitals began as voluntary establishments for the 'sick poor' as wealthy people would have a doctor come and visit them in their home. Eventually some of the hospitals became 'endowed hospitals' supported by estates that had been repossessed, but many were still totally reliant on charity and volunteers for hundreds of years before they were nationalised.

Probably one of the most famous nurses of all time, Florence Nightingale, was inspired by a divine Christian calling to become a nurse even though it was considered by her family as beneath her status, which caused many problems, especially with her mother. Against all family and societal odds she studied the world of medicine and started providing medicine for those in poverty in 1844, and began appealing for improvements in the Poor Law, especially in the areas of health care, and challenging it to provide help beyond the boundaries of medical care. During the Crimean War, while desperately trying to care for the needs of those wounded during the fighting, she made the observation that the high fatality rate in her care was not due to poor medicines or lack of skilled nurses but due to poor diet and ineffective sanitation. Once these issues were resolved by a special commission sent by Queen Victoria the fatality rate fell to around 2 per cent, which was incredible for that era. She wasn't forced to go as part of her job, she got no pension from supporting the soldiers, no pay (although her father provided some finances for her), no overtime and certainly no holiday allowance, but she and many others like her decided to volunteer their time and their skills to help those in need. As she famously said herself 'I think one's feelings waste themselves in words; they ought all to be distilled into actions which bring results'. Volunteering is an active word and the best volunteers are those who get involved regardless of the need or the lack of resources to help that need, recognising that the need of the individual is more important than any programme or institution.

In the area of education the church also played a large part in the setting up of schools within the local community. From as early as medieval times the church, chapel or monastery was a place of learning, often with the intention of the child gaining Christian knowledge and eventually becoming a minister. Robert Raikes of Gloucester, who is traditionally seen as the founder of the Sunday school in the 1780s, started by collecting the children who worked with chimney sweeps together and teaching them to read from the Bible and to write verses of scripture. This concept spread rapidly amongst churches until thousands of children (and many adults) were attending Sunday schools, mainly in the North of England and in Wales. By 1831, some 1,250,000 children attended Sunday schools (around 25 per cent of the population at the time). In the nineteenth century there were still not many formal schools, and those that existed were run by the Church of England with a high proportion of the teaching on religious education. In 1833 the UK parliament agreed to start funding the construction of schools and so the nationalisation of schools began (although this had been the case in Scotland since the sixteenth century). Although most schools are now nationalised there are many private and church schools that exist (sometimes only on a technicality) as charities as that is how they originally began with volunteers simply recognising the need.

The establishing of health and education through hospitals and schools can be clearly seen as having its roots in voluntary work, but the other key statutory area of social care could arguably still be seen largely as a voluntary sector.

William Wilberforce was well known for his fight against slavery, which became law in 1833, one month after he died and 50 years after he had begun to highlight the cause to parliament. Wilberforce, without recognition, did much more than abolish slavery in his lifetime. Due to an encounter with God and the Methodist preacher, George Whitfield, Wilberforce decided to commit his life to serving others and was well known for his charitable deeds and generosity. Wilberforce set up numerous charities including the Royal Society for the Prevention of Cruelty to Animals (RSPCA) as well as supporting the factory workers' rights, prison reform and financially supporting the early Sunday school movement, recognising the benefit education would bring in alleviating poverty.

Before the Charity Act in 2006 (which now includes, amongst other things, amateur sports!) the only areas a charity could engage in would be the relief of poverty, the advancement of education, the advancement of religion, and other purposes considered beneficial to the community.

The concept of charity and social care goes back to ancient times when the practice of providing for the poor had its roots in all major religions. Many British churchgoers in the middle ages would give to charity, as it would be a sign of their piety and generosity. The parish church would often have a diaconium (office of the deacon), which would administer to the needs of the poor.

Historically there have always been volunteers helping provide for the needs of society, either through a church or charity, doing whatever it can to help support the needs of the individual, setting up many projects and institutions such as universities and hospitals along the way. This whole arena has now become formalised in recent times, becoming known as the 'third sector'.

Unless you are already working for a government agency you will probably be asking 'What is the third sector?' The theory is that there are different areas that make up our society that contribute to the way that we operate. The key areas are the market (i.e. businesses), the state (i.e. the government) and the community (i.e. family). The third sector is the element that sits between all these, providing for all and serving all as shown in Figure 7.1. As you can see, the third sector has a significant role to play, and many social writers are stating that the third sector has more power than any of the three areas that it connects due to the unique position that it holds and the impact that its work has on society.

The third sector is desperately needed as it does many things that the government, business or communities are either unable to do or unwilling to do. As mentioned above, this puts it in a strong position when it comes to integrated working as it is *integral* to the various areas of society working together.

Although this puts the third sector and volunteers in a very strong position when it comes to working in partnership, there is widespread suspicion in the

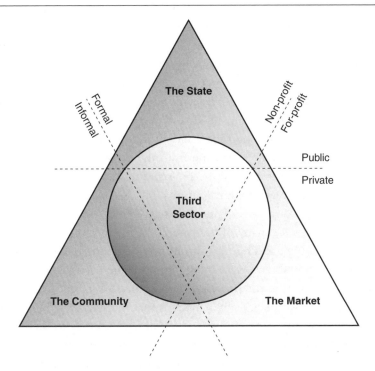

Figure 7.1 The third sector

third sector that it is often used by the government (but can also be by businesses and communities as well) to take on areas of responsibility that they are not ultimately responsible for and may be seen as a cheap and quick result for achieving the government's targets. For instance when a charity is raising money for a new health clinic for children with a specific disease such as muscular dystrophy, is that not the responsibility of the National Health Service? Or when a charity provides free parenting skills for teenage mums is that not the responsibility of their families, their communities? Or when a business utilises adults with special needs from a back-to-work charity programme but pays them nothing, or worse below minimum wage for their contribution, are they misusing the charity while gaining the benefit?

The third sector is often happy to help, seeing the person with the need as central and keen to work in partnership if that person and their need can be helped more effectively, but sometimes the third sector needs to realise that although it may not have the finances of a big business or the resources of government it holds a very pivotal role in the concept of integrated working.

My earliest recollection of the Sure Start programme (which later developed into children's centres) was back in 2000 in an old church hall when a random collection of town councillors, business leaders, church leaders, charity workers and members of the community were invited to get together and discuss the possibilities of applying for the Sure Start programme to rolled out into our needy estate on the edge of Littlehampton, one of the most deprived housing estates in the South.

One of the things that struck me from the early conversations that we had was that one of the aims of the programme was that it would encourage a grass roots approach with parents making up a *minimum* of 50 per cent of the managing committee. I immediately thought that it would never work – I worked with many of the parents on the local housing estate and knew this was a big ask. This had also never been done before in this way; local charities and projects were often set up for the needy community but rarely involved them in the process. I must confess I thought it was all a bit of spin and what would actually happen is that the statutory bodies would end up running the programme and paying lip service to any parental involvement. After all we were talking about a ten-year programme with millions of pounds of government funding! (I need to apologise for having such doubts – for someone who passionately believes in people changing radically I am ashamed to admit that they were my initial thoughts.)

The outcome in Littlehampton was that the old church hall that we met in (which was owned by Arun Community Church that I worked for at the time) was demolished and a £1.3 million community centre entitled Wickbourne Centre was built in its place. The parents were totally involved throughout and became very inspiring as they grew in confidence. Their involvement meant that the local community owned the project from the outset, and since it opened in February 2005 it has become a real hub of the community and an excellent example of the effectiveness of integrated working. Many of the parents who were part of the initial managing committee have gone into further education or taken on voluntary or paid roles within the new centre.

Working with the parents was not always easy; many of them came with years of emotional baggage, but as the Sure Start programme developed into children's centres the transformation of many of the parents was incredible, having a very positive effect on them, their families and the community as a whole.

The policy of partnership working that was being mooted in 2000 was a reality and now a proven successful reality. Many non-believers were converted along the way.

It wasn't just working with parents that was an issue; for some the idea of working with a local church was a problem and there were some within the church who were not sure about partnering with a government agency either. The local community were very comfortable working with the church and couldn't see the problem, as we were well known in the area for working in the community. The old church hall had been used for years by ourselves and organisations such as the Wire Project for running various community activities. Although the national agenda was to encourage partnership working there was a lot of suspicion from Government Office of the South East (GOSE) and Department for Education (now Department for Children, Schools and Families) that working with a church would exclude people from accessing the programme. The parents on the other hand couldn't understand the problem and even keenly suggested that we should have a stained glass window at the front of the building to show its connection with the church!

Fortunately the partnership between the local church and government did happen (the stained glass window didn't, which I was personally quite glad about!) and became a very successful model that has been used since by a number of churches that have developed similar programmes along the south coast in partnership with children's centres.

Arun Community Church, as well as taking responsibility for the running of the centre, also connected into the Neighbourhood Nurseries Initiative and developed a successful nursery for up to 64 children as part of the children's centres programme.

Where we are now

Historically, volunteering has often been a group of well-meaning individuals who try to help people by providing a service with very little resources, finances or training. Today, more often than not, volunteering is seen as a positive contribution to society. I now live in Southampton and work for a church based in the city centre, and the community development and opportunities for volunteering are continuing at a pace. When we run our annual Christmas café, which feeds around 500 local homeless people for the Christmas week, we often get 50 volunteers coming to help each day. Each month our double-decker red bus visits ten housing estates to engage with young people with nothing to do, utilising dozens of volunteers. Every week our churches around the city provide positive activities for elderly, parents, unemployed, homeless, refugees, addicts, children and young people, and every group is led by volunteers. Debt advice is given, parents and toddlers groups are run, coffee shops are open and teenage mums are supported.

But these volunteers and many others like them are a new breed. The volunteers are properly checked and have to sign a 'job description' to ensure that they know what is expected of them. They are properly trained in food hygiene, first aid and child protection. They get supervision, support and a place that they can grow. Some go to college to improve the quality of their voluntary work; maybe one day they may get paid for what they love to do voluntarily.

It's not good enough for volunteers and the third sector to think that any well-meaning help is alright. If we want to be taken seriously by potential partners we need to ensure that we are trained appropriately and that we work in a safe manner. But at the same time we must not lose the values that make us unique or we will just become a subset of the government, business or community rather than holding the place of tension in the middle of the triangle. We have a responsibility to ensure that as we commit to good practice guidelines we must not forget the needs of the individual, for that is why we started volunteering in the first place. It is our place to remind businesses that are trying to ensure a financial success on a project that that is not the reason for our existence. It is our place to remind the health professionals when they talk about statistics that we are there to care for the well-being of the individual and not to ensure that our quota is up to government targets.

Many of the old-style drop-in playgroups run by mums have gone and been subsumed by pre-schools and nurseries with Ofsted-inspected facilities and NVQ-trained staff. However, if the Early Years establishment provides perfect care following Every Child Matters principles, but the practitioners are always under a mountain of paperwork assessing two-year-olds and ensuring staff competency and become so busy practising childcare that they forget to care for the child, what good will it be for the child? ('If I speak with human eloquence and angelic ecstasy but don't love, I'm nothing but the creaking of a rusty gate' (1 Corinthians 13 verse 1 – sorry couldn't resist!).)

Maybe the third sector needs to remember and help other agencies that it works in partnership with to understand that the person that we are caring for comes first, and although standards must always be maintained and if possible improved it must always be with a double check that this is really for the benefit of the one we are trying to provide the service for, not the service provider!

Outcomes

We can call them case stories or anecdotal evidence or we can just call them what they are – great stories about lives that have benefitted from agencies working together. I love a story with a happy ending ...

Marsha is a single mum with a five-year-old boy and is an asylum seeker. Due to political involvement in Zimbabwe she had to leave behind her good job, home and family and move to England. On arrival she was scared and lonely with no idea how to access help or how to find friendship and support. Having a cousin in Southampton she moved there and after walking around the neighbourhood came across a children's centre in a tiny church hall with a drop-in for parents. Shy at first, Marsha is now accessing a number of services provided for the local community at the centre for her and her child and even getting involved with some of the administration of the centre on a voluntary basis.

Michelle is a single mum with three very needy children. All three of the children had medical and educational needs, and Michelle was struggling with being a parent, unable to write and severely lacking in self-esteem. Although she had enjoyed school she had dropped out early due to getting pregnant with her first, and struggled for a number of years by herself in a small flat. Local friends suggested that the children may enjoy an after-school club run at the local children's centre. Nervous about her children's behaviour, Michelle took her children along and stayed with them and quite enjoyed the club herself. Over many months the team in the centre befriended Michelle and started to offer different programmes for her and her children. The health visitor was able to make recommendations for the children to access specialist help, the educational psychologist was able to assess some of the learning needs of the children, and the educational lead, a qualified teacher, encouraged Michelle to learn to write. Now, a number of years later, the children are regularly attending school and clubs, Michelle is leading one of the after-school clubs and is about to start on a college course.

Keys to successful integrated working

For me there are four keys to successful partnership working. Although there may be other specifics depending on the partners involved, these four keys will go a long way to ensuring success as you encourage integrated working between agencies whether voluntary, statutory, business, or a combination.

Key one: understand your partners

There is a proverb that says 'before you criticize someone walk a mile in their shoes'. (The joker in me says, 'then you will be a mile away, have their shoes and can say what you like!') But the purpose of the original proverb without my addition is to encourage us to understand one another's perspective before we criticise each other.

We need to take time to understand each another. If you are developing a health project with a local GP surgery, find out what their needs are, spend a day in the surgery, offer to help answer the phones, ask questions rather than assume the answers. One of the best things I ever did while developing the children's centre in Littlehampton was to sit with all paid staff who were employed by health, education and the local district council, ask questions of their work and allow them to ask questions of myself and my colleague. Many of their assumptions about the church were raised that day and hopefully clarified.

Often as we take the time to understand one another we can then appreciate others' needs and gain knowledge of why they have to work that way. Taking the time to understand others is also a way of humbling ourselves and showing that we are not assuming knowledge of others' needs – this act in itself can break down many assumed barriers.

Key two: finding the overlap

Straight away when you work in partnership there will always be obvious differences. The perceived lack of skills, organisation, experience, resources that the other organisation may have could become a focus for your concerns when it comes to working together. Rather than concentrating on the things that your two organisations do differently it is important instead to find the areas of your work that overlap and complement one another.

Many partnerships fall apart due to fighting about small things that don't matter in the bigger picture but become the focus of disagreement. Instead of

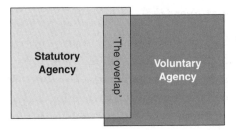

Figure 7.2 The overlap

wasting valuable time arguing your differences and creating fights that don't need to be won or lost, find the areas of overlap that you both agree on and work on those areas (Figure 7.2).

Obviously if the Vegetarian Society tries to work with the local chicken farmer on a healthy eating project they may have to work quite hard at finding the overlap; it is not impossible, although it may seem to be at the outset. As a church working with children's centres we had to agree that we had different agendas but we could agree that we both wanted children to have a great start in life and that we were keen to support families. Once that was agreed upon we found many ways to develop partnership projects such as running a breakfast club and a walking bus.

Key three: building strong relationships

The long-term success of the partnership will never be based on any terms of reference, contracts, service level agreements or any other pieces of paper – it will be based on the strength of your relationship. As with two celebrities getting married the length of their marriage does not depend on the strength of the pre-nuptial legal document but on their relationship with each other.

It is imperative that there is a good relationship and trust between partner organisations, because when relationships get stretched and difficulties come (and they always will!) it is only the foundation of a strong relationship that will see past the suspicion of the other and be able to overcome the hurdles, gaining strength in the process.

Practically, this may mean building a relationship between the key decision makers initially, but I have discovered that although that is appropriate initially the web of relationship needs to be widened as soon as possible as those key decision makers may move on and the relationship has to be started again, which can really damage any momentum achieved.

Key four: don't fight over labels

I remember when we were about to open the children's centre in Littlehampton and there developed a discussion over who should have prominence on the front of the building. The money had come from the government but the building was still owned by the local church. We had conversations about whether the names should be side by side at the top of the building or whether all partners should be listed alphabetically (which was fine by me as we started with the letter 'A'!). In the end I felt it was more important that the building opened on time, on budget with the community it was serving as the focus of attention, and the conversation soon disappeared.

It is so easy to fight over labels and prominence that it can get silly. I worked on a local project once where everyone insisted that they *must* have their logo on the bottom of the headed paper, so there was hardly any room left to write anything! I also worked on a vocational skills centre project with a number of schools and colleges providing practical training for young people in the community. The team was so focused on the task of opening the college on time that when it came to sorting out the sign we left it to the design company to decide. We won a local partnership award for that project ...

Don't fight over labels; there are more important things to worry about such as will the project be successful and will it be beneficial for the group that it has been set up for. At the end of the day the labels do not matter to the people who attend the project, they only matter to those organisations that need to boast about their work due to their personal insecurities.

The future

So where is the future for integrated working for volunteers? Now that it has been proven that it can and does work by numerous projects around the country, and that volunteers have a very important and vital role to play, there is no limit to what can be achieved as we work together. Our nation and the various communities that make up today's Britain desperately need some help and no one organisation can do it by themselves, we need each other.

I believe that together we *can* make a difference.

CHAPTER 8

Training, education and employment

Carole Beaty

The interesting aspect of the whole area of training, education and employment within the children's centre development is that it has the potential to bring together the whole range of issues that underlie the Every Child Matters agenda. It can create the 'glue' for enabling services to look more closely at their fundamental vision. It can be a way to more closely promote partnership across all agencies. We need centres that facilitate in each and every way, empowerment and aspiration for staff for partner agencies, but most essentially for children and for parents. Aspiration, a 'can do' approach, must be pivotal to all that we do in the new world of children's centres. The whole training and possibly employment aspect of the children's centre agenda can bring together exciting opportunities for parents which can raise the status of individuals while ensuring that communities also experience a boost. It can have enormous benefits for children through the provision of good quality childcare, through excellent nursery, crèche, or childminding facilities. If the training and employment offered through the centre is an aspect of childcare or learning about children's development this would make a great difference in terms of positive parenting.

A key focus of the government's drive to address the issue of child poverty has been to look at the whole area of workless households and how this might impact upon a child's life chances. The Sure Start Children's Centre Practice Guidance (DfES 2005) states a clear case for the involvement of children's centres in supporting parents in going to work:

> Living in a household where nobody is working is a significant indicator of poor outcomes for children. Research shows that they are less likely to achieve their potential. Employment helps lift families from poverty. It also has a positive effect on children's mental health, behaviour, social integration and educational performance.

Children's Centres are well placed to contribute to the employability agenda and achieving the *Every Child Matters* outcomes of achieving economic well-being by helping address and reach the following key Government Targets:

- Increasing the take up of formal childcare by lower income working families by 50%;

- Helping 70% of lone parents back to work and halving child poverty by 2010; and

- Improving the literacy, numeracy and language skills of 1.5 million adults by 2007 and a further 750,000 by 2010.

(DfES 2005:38)

While there may be a clear correlation between workless households and child poverty and the inability for individuals to attain their potential, this drive towards employment at all costs maybe misses out on the subtleties that underline the research and the problematic nature of employment when put alongside the other aspirations of Sure Start children's centres, most specifically the drive to ensure effective attachment in the early years. Sometimes it seems that children's centres are asked to pursue different agendas and this can lead to a feeling of discontinuity and lack of a coherent focus.

Lack of employment: contributing factors

The press likes to highlight the whole area of families and of communities where worklessness is the norm and where children might well be born into that mindset. However, the sensational nature of headlines often belies the subtle interweaving of issues that might make worklessness likely, or even inevitable. Social isolation and the lack of self-esteem for some people is a real disincentive for seeking employment and training. Poor experiences at school might also make a significant difference to returning to formal training. Most significant for many households, particularly single-parent households is the availability and cost of childcare, as is the quality of childcare provision. While this government is committed to eradicating child poverty and is apparently committed to providing affordable, quality childcare the situation on the ground presents a far from ideal picture:

The government has tried to create a universal childcare network without providing anything like the money needed. Its decision to fund this network through credits instead of biting the bullet and subsidising nurseries needs an urgent review. The Daycare Trust says only half a million children receive the credits to get them a nursery place. But there are 3.5 million children living below the poverty line, most of whose families would jump at the chance.

(Toynbee 2005:1)

The expense and availability of childcare places is only one issue when it comes to returning to work or to training. There is also the very important issue of the quality of childcare places on offer. If the children's centre movement is to make a real difference then children need to experience positive relationships with trained adults who really want to work with children and who see their work as a career. Parents need to feel confidence in the childcare provision on offer. As Polly Toynbee remarks later in her article, we still lag a long way behind some of our European colleagues in terms of the way in which we value the staff who work with children and by association the children themselves.

In Denmark every childcare worker has a three-year degree; it is well paid, high-status work and there are long waiting lists for jobs. Britain pledges one staff member with a degree in each day nursery by some unspecified date. High-status training and good pay could transform this into a popular profession: when the government upgraded and enthused about teaching, applications for teacher training rose sharply (90% in the last five years). Nurseries need that too, because bad nurseries do harm, while the best do wonderful good.

(Toynbee 2005:2)

High-quality childcare is essential if we are to meet the challenges of the Every Child Matters agenda, but this does not have to only be in a nursery. Through children's centres, parents should be able to access good-quality places in crèches and with childminders. Children's centres have a key role in supporting practice in all these areas. This might come about by offering high-quality training for practitioners, or providing a venue for childminders to meet. Having a good-quality crèche on site is always a great incentive for parents to engage in training and in governance. A high-quality Ofsted-regulated crèche can also be a wonderful place to exemplify good practice and to engage parents in ongoing discussion about their children's development. Skilled crèche practitioners are invaluable in a children's centre, however large or small. If they have a good understanding of what the centre offers they can talk with parents and carers about their options; it doesn't need to be formal, it can be a chat at the beginning or end of a session. Crèche workers, childminders and nursery workers can provide a wonderful resource for the centre in terms of signposting activities and events and in picking up on issues that concern parents.

For many practitioners working in all areas there will always be the ongoing debate about encouraging parents back to work, when a key principle of the children's centre agenda is to ensure positive attachments in the early years. However, maybe what is important to bear in mind is that we need to provide parents with choice and with opportunities, and children always with excellent high-quality experiences and adults with whom they can make genuine robust attachments.

The NESS evaluation picked up on this concern:

> Many SSLP's expressed some ambivalence about the appropriateness of an employability target. Parents themselves are often reluctant, for both cultural and financial reasons, to take paid work before their children at primary school. Yet paid work is the main route out of poverty and its disadvantages.

> By emphasising confidence building, raising aspirations, and helping parents to improve their skills, Sure Start children's centres can reconcile any potential conflict between promoting good parenting and promoting employability. They can provide parents with greater control over their own lives and greater choice about how and when to engage with paid work.

> (Anning and Ball 2008:132)

Life-long learning: creating opportunities for training and education

The great thing about children's centres is that whatever form they take, whether they are a virtual centre with flexible venues or part of a school or health centre or part of a library, or whether they are purpose built, or maybe a mobile venue, they are there. They are on the doorstep or they are just around the corner, and can provide easily accessible education for all. Education can support a wide range of needs and aspirations; it can be a way of getting people together around a common topic, and it can be a way of exploring potential. It can be an avenue to acquire new skills and to make new friends. Children's centres are uniquely placed to bring education out of colleges and universities and into the community. What is important is that everyone working within a centre has a 'can do' approach to learning. Whether they are childminders, health visitors, portage workers, caters or caretakers they know what is on offer and how individuals might access courses appropriate to them. A children's centre vision must be about life-long learning for all. Literally a degree on your doorstep, not in the hallowed halls of a university. So what kind of training and education might a children's centre provide?

Ways into education

Volunteering

A central tenet of the Sure Start programme was the power of volunteering as a way into education and employment (see also Chapter 7). With the current downturn in the economy and with the numbers of unemployed rising there has been increased recognition of the role of volunteering in all sections of the community. In a children's centre working within a local community there are plenty of opportunities to deploy volunteers in a wide range of different roles, across different sectors.

- providing peer support within the community, working to increase individual's confidence and self-esteem;
- peer support for breast-feeding, working with community midwife and breast-feeding co-ordinator to help new mothers;
- play work for play-and-stay activities, or working in the crèche or the nursery;
- helping with cookery classes;
- supporting a community café;
- helping with the toy library;
- supporting the process of governance and evaluation;
- delivering introductory packs to new parents, or families new to the local area;
- storytelling, helping with the library;
- helping out with children's activities within the centre, such as dance and physical activity;
- helping with information points.

All the above and many more can make an enormous difference to individual's. Having someone to talk to who understands how you feel can have a real impact in terms of change. It is so reassuring to talk with someone who has the same or similar experiences. Volunteering can be the basis of future employment and can provide a sense of empowerment and of aspiration.

Case study: volunteering into employment

Hi there,

I should like to start by thanking Sure Start Littlehampton for the greatest opportunity I have ever been given in my entire working life.

Almost seven years ago I was a new mum. I lived in what is known 'statistically' as a 'depressed' area. Thank God is all I can say because if I hadn't I wouldn't have received the Sure Start newsletter through my door. I read through whilst feeding my newborn and saw so many good things that Sure Start had to offer.

For example a crèche, a pleasant and private place to feed my child if I went into town, the opportunity for a friendly face to talk to, but most important a way into a new career.

My son was approximately 9 months old when I decided I wanted to get out of the house and do something of use as I was feeling a bit low and useless, so I remembered that Sure Start were looking for Home Visiting Volunteers and so put my name forward. Great decision as I was from that moment ensconced into helping other parents in my community who were in greater need than me for whatever reason.

I had a journey to go through and some demons of my own to face before I was ready to help others and boy did I face some demons. Fortunately I passed the volunteers course and am glad to say that I had the opportunity to help someone who was in desperate need of a little company and to escape her four walls every now and then. Well while on my volunteer's course I was asked if I would like to join the Sure Start stakeholder's board and support other parents on the board. I said yes and once on the board realised just how valuable parents are to these organisations.

Most of us had no professional training at public speaking and were just humble homemakers so it was even more rewarding when I was asked to be chairperson for the board. The programme manager at that time was very dedicated to including parents and wanted us to experience as much as we were comfortable with, and I must say although I was nervous beforehand I had a great time. And I am so proud of myself for being able to undertake such an important task. Whilst on the board I was also privileged to be given the chance to further education and so completed a 12 month course with the PLA (Pre-School Learning Alliance) and passed with a level 2 certificate in Pre-School Practice. All of this because a group of people in a small community all working together to make people's lives that little bit more bearable.

Now almost seven years on and another child who was privileged to be a part of Sure Start, I now work in a school which is what I wanted to do and I have so much praise and thanks to give to so many people who just cared about what they were doing.

(Sure Start parent Board Member Littlehampton, West Sussex)

Volunteering brings many rewards for a children's centre as well as for individuals. However, it also brings with it a range of responsibilities and it is important that volunteers are fully integrated into the whole staffing structure of the organisation and that they are fully trained and valued. It is important that all volunteers get something significant back for the important work that they do.

When arranging volunteering opportunities it is essential to:

- Provide appropriate checks (Criminal Records Bureau, etc.).
- Consider the type of work that the volunteers will be undertaking and provide appropriate training, including first-aid, child protection, equal opportunities and listening skills.
- Ensure that volunteers are well matched to their task.
- Provide ongoing supervision within the appropriate team.
- Make sure that volunteers developing career prospects are considered and matched to the work that they undertake for the centre.
- Ensure that other members of the team are aware of the role of volunteers.
- Where possible provide childcare for volunteers undertaking training, through nursery, crèche or childminding facilities.

Family learning

A central feature of Sure Start children's centres is to promote early communication skills, and start to develop an enthusiasm for literacy. Inspiring learning for the whole family can be a wonderful way to start this process. Children's centres run book events and book weeks often with their local schools, nurseries and libraries.

Family learning is a good way back into education. West Sussex Grid for Learning links their courses specifically to the Every Child Matters agenda.

- *Being healthy:* cookery; first-aid; staying safe.

- *Staying safe:* early learning; playing with language; learning together at home and at school; story sacks; learning with grandparents.

- *Enjoying and achieving:* research shows that achievement in school relates to the level of parental involvement. Many family learning courses help parents and carers to support their children's learning:

  – all family literacy, language and numeracy courses;

  – learning together at home and at school/learning with grandparents;

  – art, science, language, and information and communication technology courses.

- *Making a positive contribution to the local community and to society:* helping in school; family art courses which create group pieces for school (e.g. murals); looking after ourselves.

- *Economic well-being:* supporting people to address issues of socio-economic disadvantage to achieve their potential. Family learning can provide that first step back into education.

(Adapted from West Sussex Grid for Learning, accessed 5/5/2009)

In my experience, family learning courses provide a very valuable way into education and learning. Courses like 'story sacks' offer an informal feel which is fun and unthreatening. It provides an opportunity to discuss other opportunities that people might wish to explore. Tutors are enthusiastic about the courses they are offering, and knowledgeable about what further courses are available.

Links with Jobcentre Plus

Children's centres at their best offer a lively mix of fun and serious opportunities. The government has always been clear that employment opportunities should be part of that mix. Links with Jobcentre Plus have not always been easy or entirely successful. Jobcentre Plus should help facilitate parents' and carers' opportunities into training and employment. However, while partnership working with the job centre is fundamental to the children's centre vision there are no specific requirements for the level of its involvement.

Aston *et al.*'s (2008) Institute for Employment Studies research for the Department of Work and Pensions provided some valuable insights into what works in this partnership and what has proved more challenging. The aim of this project was to present information on what might be seen as good practice to support the future development of sound partnership working between Jobcentre Plus and children's centres. The survey began in the autumn of 2006 by sending questionnaires to all the Jobcentre Plus areas, to ascertain the nature of involvement with children's centres. This was followed up with a case-study approach to explore in greater depth the nature and experience of partnership working and what elements really did make a difference to partners and to service users:

> The research identified a number of factors that have contributed to the success of Jobcentre Plus in working effectively through Children's Centres. These included using Childcare Partnership Managers (CPMs) as Jobcentre Plus ambassadors; getting involved early; promoting reasonable expectations and delivering against them; and having clear working arrangements.
>
> (Aston *et al.* 2008:2)

This piece of research identified a wide range of different types of involvement. This went from a children's centre displaying leaflets to an outreach adviser delivering services within the centre. However, the full-time involvement of an adviser was seen as a very costly alternative. One way to bridge the gap is to provide a 'linked adviser' responsible for co-ordinating the contact between Jobcntre Plus offices and children's centres (Aston *et al.* 2008:2).

Service users who made use of the Jobcentre Plus opportunities offered at children's centres found it convenient to have the advice and support so close by. There was also a sense that they could meet with someone from Jobcentre Plus in a 'non-stigmatising' environment, which was seen as a strong advantage. The accessibility factor was certainly of central importance in this piece of research.

The researchers felt that gradually Jobcentre Plus was becoming a stronger presence within children's centres, with increasingly better communication between partner agencies. They felt that there needed to be a strong commitment on both sides to make this work. Staff within the children's centre needed to be open to the opportunities presented by Jobcentre Plus.

The crucial 'success factors' here seem to be:

- Being prepared for the long haul with perhaps only modest overt returns in the early years;
- The projection of a helpful and supportive image, as an offset to different, widely held and less engaging perceptions of Jobcentre Plus;
- The delivery of practical, useful and relevant help and support to individual Centre users, through whom others may be drawn in;
- The use of experienced, empathetic and knowledgeable staff, with time to work on long-term cases.

(Aston *et al.* 2008:106)

Job centres can be intimidating and frustrating places to visit. The children's centre option can be an inspired choice for some service users. It often depends on how material is presented and how representatives set up their stall so that people feel that they can pop in for a chat on a regular basis and feel that they are being listened to. In my experience it is important that all partner agencies are aware of Jobcentre Plus's presence and how and when service users might be able to access advice and support. It is also essential that representatives from Jobcentre Plus are aware of the whole ethos of a children's centre and that they become fully involved in the ongoing work of each centre.

Linking with training organisations

Children's centre links with training organisations such as local further-education colleges and higher-education institutions can prove a very productive partnership both for staff and for parents. Offering validated courses for parents and for staff can provide a rich source of learning for all involved. Working with organisations like the Pre-School Learning Alliance can be a very effective way of promoting the central vision of the children's centre. Promoting that essential child-centred approach for parents and practitioners is just so important. It is also a way of keeping at the very forefront of our thinking the Every Child Matters agenda.

Developing a physical activity group for the under-fives: 'Rough and Tumble'

I originally got involved with running a group at Littlehampton Children's Centre in 2004, because there was nothing really on offer for young children to do. There was a lot in the press about new government initiatives targeting childhood obesity, but as a programme I felt we were doing very little in terms of large movement exercise. The whole thing about healthy eating and getting hooked on exercise early in life is just so important. My son was two then and he just loved anything exciting with a bit of a challenge. So I decided to set up a group, 'Rough and Tumble' in the fantastic hall at the centre. I did quite a bit of background research, went to visit other mobile groups, got lots of ideas, but found many of these groups were just so expensive. I knew that local parents would not want to pay this much, I wanted to keep the costs as low as possible. Then I worked with the teacher at the centre, Chris, and the local occupational therapists to choose the equipment that Sure Start had agreed to pay for. The occupational therapists gave me some ideas for getting started. There was a PLA (Pre-School Learning Alliance) level three course starting at the centre, so I began this at about the same time. This helped me with planning the sessions linking them into the Foundation Stage Curriculum. It helped me when talking to other parents and carers about how they might carry some of this physical activity on at home or when they went out. When we started we did blocks of five sessions, and after the first few sessions which were very quiet, we had people queuing around the block, it was such fun. Often we had to turn people away, so now we run two sessions in a morning.

They run like this:

- Arrive and welcome, making sure someone is around to make newcomers feel at home.
- Warm-up exercises.
- Using the equipment, this is always set up in a different way to give children a challenge, sometimes we work towards a theme. (It is really important to get all the adults, parents and volunteer helpers involved here so that children are supported and encouraged.)
- Music and movement slot, I take the lead here and everyone, yes everyone, follows. We have such a laugh (I like to use music from different

cultures and that really goes down well, especially as we come from a culturally mixed community here).

- Snack time, this is a time to wind down and also to enjoy some water and fruit together. It's an opportunity to try out different fruit too, that can be quite a challenge for some children, who say they never eat fruit. They soon find they love it.

- End of session.

We run sessions as a drop-in so people can just come along when they like, so there is no pressure and no paying up front. I have been doing it for four years now and our numbers are growing all the time, with some children being referred through the local health visitor. It's great that they know we are here, a great example of multi-agency working. It has proved a wonderful resource, and a very good way to get people through the door, once they are here they find out about all the other things that are going on. I am learning all the time too and now I am doing a CACHE (Council for Awards in Children's Care and Education) Certificate in Play Work with two other mothers. This is really challenging, but it helps me every day when I am observing the children and supporting them in making that next step in their learning.

Now we have taken 'Rough and Tumble' out into the community. With a couple of other mothers I run a before school group at my local primary school called 'Wake Up and Shake', just twenty minutes, but it's such a good way to start the day and a great link with the local school. We play lots of games like the Beetle Game and What's the Time Mr. Woolf, all those favourites that children can also play in the playground. It really is amazing where one good idea can take you! It really shows you that if nobody is going to provide it you have to do it yourself and what fun that can be.

(Parent Board Member)

Every children's centre a learning community

A central theme of the NPQICL (National Professional Qualification in Integrated Leadership) is that each and every children's centre is a learning community that, like a pebble dropped into a pond, radiates out in its sphere of influence. At the centre of those circles of influence lies the child, and those leading practice and learning within centres need to be pedagogical leaders, attuned to the needs of the child. Centres need to be communities in which developing debate about our shared values is part and parcel of our work.

> The learning community is a key methodological concept in the NPQICL programme. Not only does it respond to a basic human need to connect and engage with others, but it can also provide the sort of psychological environment in which it is safe for participants to be themselves, to reach out with and to others, and take responsibility for their own learning needs.
>
> (NCSL 2009:24)

From volunteers to crèche and nursery workers

The wonderful thing about children's centres is that the whole area of shared working and of providing new opportunities throws up possibilities for getting people involved and making use of their skills, then of course enhancing those skills through training and through employment chances. So it is with developing crèche facilities in and around the children's centre.

The development of crèche services can often be highly complex and can be fraught with difficulties. However, providing a fully Ofsted-regulated crèche makes a great deal of difference in terms of creating an atmosphere of trust and reliability. It is essential that the children's needs come first and that where crèche services are offered they are of high quality, and that those working within them are given excellent training and supervision.

Many of the crèche workers at Littlehampton children's centre started off bringing their children to events at the centre, and then became involved in the volunteer training programme; this often happened from a chance remark, which the attuned practitioner picked up. From volunteer training many parents then went on to take their level one CACHE (Council for Awards in Children's Care and Education) training and from there their levels two and three. All courses were offered at the centre, which makes a great difference for busy parents and carers wanting to develop their training and their employability, but unable to travel too far. Having an onsite crèche makes all the difference for parents wanting to really engage in their own personal and professional development. Their children are just a minute away in a happy, well-regulated environment. Many parents then went on to get employment in local schools and in nurseries. This was an enormous achievement for these crèche workers, and just exemplifies the holistic nature of the children's centre work and the importance of involving everyone in that clear vision.

Key messages for developing training, education and employment in children's centres

- Creating a positive learning environment for all children, staff and parents.

- Providing courses from basic cookery to degree level where possible on site or in an accessible venue.

- Ensuring all staff and volunteers are ready and able to discuss options with parents; they all need to be well trained and part of the planning process.

- Working closely with partner agencies to make learning and employment opportunities available and fully accessible. A person in a suit sitting by a display doesn't often work. Somebody coming to a play-and-stay activity to chat to parents might.

- Look at the links between agencies, rather than what separates us, keep talking about a common vision for a community.

- Be open to all possibilities; there are a lot of people and organisations out there offering great training opportunities. It all helps with the CV.

- Keep learning yourself!

References

Anning, A. and Ball, M. (2008) *Improving Services for Young Children: From Sure Start to Children's Centres*. London: Sage.

Aston, J., Dench, S., James, L., with Foster, R. (2008) *Jobcentre Plus and Children's Centres*. Department for Work and Pensions.

DfES (2005) *Sure Start Children's Centres: Practice Guidance*.

NCSL (2009) *The Impact of the National Professional Qualification in Integrated Centre Leadership (NPQICL) on Children's Centre Leaders and Their Centre*. National College of School Leadership.

Toynbee, P. (2005) 'Dig deep to make Sure Start just as brilliant as it can be', *Guardian*, 13 July.

Further reading

NPQICL (National Professional Qualification in Integrated Leadership) (2007) *Pedagogical Leadership*. NCSL.

Websites

West Sussex Grid for Learning:
wsgfl.westsussex.gov.uk

National College of School Leadership:
www.ncsl.org.uk

CHAPTER 9

Parental involvement

Carole Beaty

This book has emphasised throughout the role of parents and families in the work of Sure Start children's centres. What this chapter seeks to do is first to look at the essential elements of involving parents in the development of centres and the design of services. Second, it looks at different ways to engage parents and families in this process. Parents are our greatest resource within a children's centre; they need to set the agenda for services, and they need to be pivotal in everything that we do. From the outset, Sure Start programmes were expected to engage with families to help create a sense of uniqueness for each programme in response to local needs. A key element of these early programmes was the idea that the empowerment of parents would help to enrich the local community and help it to become more sustainable. The significance of parental empowerment lay also and most crucially in its impact upon adult–child relationships. Helping parents to feel that they had a greater say over their own futures would support their confidence in parenting. The very kernel of Sure Start programmes has and will also be that dynamic between adult and child. However, this approach required an entirely new way of modelling services a radical approach which would seek to move away from a more hierarchical way of working to one that was more user-led in nature. With the move away from the Sure Start model in areas of specific deprivation to the more universal and more poorly funded model of the children's centre, sometimes it can seem that that parent voice has been lost.

> Engaging with parents was seen as a way of combating social exclusion by developing community cohesion. Such an approach marked a significant break with past professional practices, which were characterised by a more individualised, hierarchical, formal and expert approach to the relationship with users.
>
> (Anning and Ball 2008:63)

Figure 9.1 At the heart of all communities and all societies is the bond of early attachment

The idea of parental power and of parental involvement always sounds just right, just what we want, but this edict to involve parents belies the complexity of this way of working and the sometimes highly entrenched views on the part of some agencies.

Consultation

When Sure Start programmes were first set up at the end of the 1990s the central tenet of all programmes was that parents should be there from the outset, helping to identify sites for the centres, helping to design buildings, and having a definite say in what services should be offered and how they should be delivered. Clearly this is entirely sensible, as people know what they want, what they need and how they would like it delivered. It has always been essential that staff working from a centre are familiar with their local area and are familiar with the services that are offered and how they are used. Consultation with local providers of services and with families is fundamental to the start of any new children's centre. However, it can take practitioners right outside their comfort zone.

Fathers as well as mothers need to be part of the consultation process and centres need to be imaginative about how they will set up consultation events, ensuring that timings for these events are possible for local families.

For some men the very female environment of the children's centre can be off-putting. Holding a family fun day or setting up an outing can be a good way of attracting parents. Maybe using an already existing venue or activity could prove a useful way in. Some families will need specialist support and particular information. Parents of children with complex needs will have their own very particular needs and will have considerable experience of using services which will aid the process of service design. Children also need to be part of this ongoing process of consultation; this might be done through art days and storytelling activities, or being asked to reflect on their experiences of living in the local area, what they like what they might like.

The Lambeth programme is keen to develop a culture of listening to children and is pioneering various approaches to consult with children and young people including:

- Our Lives in Lambeth – children up to the age of six have been asked to send in pictures, words and photographs that illustrate their lives in Lambeth, to be used in a touring exhibition.
- The Listening Group – parents and carers are the experts at listening to children, the Group brings them together with early years professionals to devise approaches to consulting with children.

(DfES, DoH 2006:21)

This ongoing consultation process is so important not just when the programme is set up, but as it rolls out and develops, it is important to check back, to adapt and change in response to changing need. But how do you get it right for everyone? Clearly it is not possible to have an individual centre for each family, and in the end those running centres have to hold the line in terms of interpreting the needs of local families in the best and most comprehensive manner they can. It will not suit everyone and there is always the danger that services will start to be shaped by the most vocal and vociferous parents, that maybe cliques will form and that some people will feel pushed out. This requires skilful and vigilant management to ensure that everyone as far as possible has a voice. It also requires excellent informed supervision for centre managers and all those working front-line with families. Centres need a co-ordinated approach to parents, so that everyone is receiving clear and consistent messages, making sure that the centre provides a lively parent forum and good representation by parents on the management board, whatever form this takes. Also vital is the use of outreach workers to gather the views of parents in their homes; this might be part of the role of health visitors and community nursery nurses.

Ownership

So who owns the centre, who ensures that what happens day to day is relevant, accessible and really does make a difference? Polly Toynbee and David Walker describe Bellingham Children's Centre in south-west London and the way in which parents are fully involved in all aspects of the service:

> Sure Start's success rests on the involvement of parents. They take a third of seats on the board, which administers a budget of £875,000 a year. From the earliest days Shirley and the other mothers made a ritual of a free community lunch once a month, cooked by the parents together. The mothers now exert a political muscle that this ward certainly never had before. They have persuaded the council to build a leisure centre nearby with sports activities for older children and adults. A new tent-shaped youth centre has just opened in the grounds, with an extra nursery attached. You get the picture – here are stunning new buildings, an area transformed, streets reclaimed, neighbourhood wardens on patrol and a community of parents who know each other well and will work together as their children progress through local schools. Parents who used to be isolated strangers come together, bringing their babies and small children, and find here life-changing experiences they never imagined.
>
> (Toynbee and Walker 2008:137)

That wonderful sense of ownership of a 'co-construction' of meaning and of intent that Reggio Emilia provides in its work with children and with adults must be the foundation stone of a children's centre. Sometimes practitioners in all fields may be resistant to this way of working and maybe they are not really listening. Local authorities may find parents setting the agenda uncomfortable when they might look for a more universal way of delivering children's centres providing a standard, one-size-fits-all model. Here of course lies the danger with the move from the gloriously open and innovative and often frankly overfunded model of Sure Start to possibly a more proscribed local-authority-led model; maybe parents will have less of a say. What remains a concern is that despite the apparent success of the Sure Start children's centre programme you hardly ever hear it mentioned by politicians, and people not directly working with it rarely know what a children's centre is. This hardly bodes well for the future of the programme and for parental involvement in its development.

Management and governance

An important way that parents would be part of the running of Sure Start programmes was through their involvement in the governance of programmes.

However, since the whole children's centre development moved to the local authority there seems to be less emphasis on this aspect of parental involvement and a far greater concern with parents' involvement in their children's learning, no less important, but these elements need to be seen as a complementary whole.

It is essential that parents are part of the strategic process for children's centres as they develop in clear partnership with agencies. Sure Start programmes have generally proved very successful at engaging with parents.

> Governance arrangements for Sure Start Children's Centres should bring together all the parties needed to facilitate a multi-agency approach and should challenge the centre to constantly improve its performance. Parents should be included in formal governance arrangements. Sure Start Local Programmes were particularly good at engaging parents and it is important that this is carried forward into Sure Start Children's Centres, and that al parents have the chance to be involved.
>
> (DCSF 2008:30)

Having parents on the advisory board or whatever form of governance the centre adopts is a great advantage to any centre. It is an opportunity to tune into local needs, and their immense enthusiasm for supporting their children's development helps to move the agenda forward. It is essential that everyone from whatever organisation they come should be aware of the parent's views and ideas. It is also essential that different groups are represented on the board, so that each area has a voice. This will mean that individual groups, say for example the young parents group, will need to find someone to represent their ideas and experiences. Effective parent representation on the board takes careful planning and needs a sense of engagement from practitioners. There must be a real buy-in from centre staff and from the management structure across all the different agencies. This is highly complex work and requires a great deal of thought and patience. It requires a clear sense of how an open and inclusive approach alongside the necessary boundaries will keep the process of parental involvement safe and sustainable. Anning and Ball, when discussing the findings of the 2007 NESS evaluation, highlight this dilemma: 'There was sometimes a tension between informal relationships between staff and users, and the need for staff to be objectively impartial in their work' (2008:73).

Parents need to feel that their views are listened and responded to; they need to see themselves and their families reflected in the work of the centre. We need to be able to translate their vision and amalgamate this with the local and national requirements. Parents can easily feel patronised by busy professionals who are not used to working in this way and even if they are, can get it so wrong. We need to keep checking back and evaluating our work all the time. We need to want and to expect parents and families to challenge us, to push us right outside our comfort zone. It can be scary work this but it is never less than exciting.

Training and induction programmes for parents working on the governance programmes of children's centres are vital; here is one parent talking about the experience of a weekend away for parents on the board for existing board members and new members, both parents and practitioners for which Excellence in Cities funding had been secured.

> Being a parent on the Board sounds quite scary, but it's just trying to explain to them [*new parents*] that actually, it's not that scary. It just means that, if you do want to talk to somebody, then you can speak to one of us [*existing board members*]. That we can take it that step higher if you don't feel that you want to. So things like the weekend boost your confidence a bit more to go out and say that to people. Before I wouldn't have done.
>
> (Briant 2007:8)

Setting up clear procedures for governance is most important if parents are to feel that they really can make a difference. Parents also need to feel confident in different forums.

Case study: aiding parental involvement within advisory board structures

A centre has established an induction procedure for all parents involved with the board in order to increase their confidence and involvement. The induction includes a number of development days which cover issues like breaking down barriers, getting rid of jargon, how to take minutes and understanding the format of meetings.

Before each board meeting, the centre holds a 'pre-board meeting' for parents only, to provide an opportunity to look at the agenda and minutes, and talk them through. The chair of the board is a local parent, which provides further reassurance for the other parents. Having gained confidence from the experience, the chair has now trained to be a childminder.

(Adapted from 'Improving the Employability of Parents in Sure Start Local Programmes – NESS' (June 2004) in DCSF 2008)

Barriers to effective working with parents, carers and families

- Specific process-led barriers such as jargon can create a real sense of inclusivity that can shut people out;

- agencies that have never had a culture of working with parents as partners in designing services and how they are offered can find this very difficult;

- having a very strong agenda that offers a top down model, that reverts back to how services have traditionally been offered to families;

- paying lip-service to parental involvement, dipping toes in but not really allowing parents to take a lead in service reform, design and delivery;

- hierarchical nature of some agencies making them impenetrable to families;

- professional attitudes that problematise particular social groups or family forms (Balloch and Taylor 2001, Ball 2002 in Anning and Ball 2008:65);

- lack of a truly participatory model of working;

- promoting unrealistic expectations in local community groups, leading to a feeling of being let down and disengagement;

- uncertainty about future funding leading to lack of engagement, a kind of seen-it-all-before attitude and sense of broken promises;

- attitude of doing unto families in a service-led model.

Key messages for parental and family involvement

- Most importantly, there must be an intention to make true family participation a reality from all agencies and organisations involved.

- Respect for families and their circumstances.

- An openness to new ideas, even if these seem quite radical in nature.

- A sense of openness and engagement with the community.

- Knowing the local community its ethnic and cultural mix, its opportunities and its challenges.

- Commitment from national and local government for ongoing funding for children's centres.

- A welcoming approach from all staff and volunteers who work at the centre and undertake outreach services.

- Parents having a genuine voice at all levels of the children's centre, its management and its service delivery, and seeing the results of their participation.

- Joint parent/practitioner training both formal and informal.

- Ongoing evaluation of services by families.

- Making sure that parents' knowledge and skills are put to effective use throughout the centre both in service planning and delivery, and that parents are members of the partnership board, running an activity group for children and parents.

- Informal spaces for parents, families and practitioners to meet together, breaking down barriers to effective communication.

- All voluntary activities that parents and families engage with need to be seen as an end in themselves, but also need to form part of parents' ongoing personal and professional development. Each element needs to feed into this ongoing climate of change and empowerment.

- Just doing it, working together on a project or activity, and getting to know each other in real contexts.

- Developing the vision with families and revisiting it over and over again.

- Getting out there and talking with parents where they are.

Working with families is our core business. If this gets lost in the need to tick boxes and meet targets then we are nowhere; we are lost in an initiative wilderness. We need to get out there and offer well-run innovative services, working hand-in-hand with our most important partners, the parents.

References

Anning, A. and Ball, M. (2008) *Improving Services for Young Children from Sure Start to Children's Centres*. London: Sage.
Briant, J. (2007) *Littlehampton Children's Centre: an Evaluation of an Early Excellence Project: Parent Training*. London: National Children's Bureau.
DCSF (2008) *The Sure Start Journey: a Summary of Evidence*.
DfES, DoH (2006) *Sure Start Children's Centres Practice Guidance*.
Toynbee, P. and Walker, D. (2008) *Unjust Rewards*. London: Granta.

Further reading

Meadows, P. and Garbers, C. (2004) *Improving the Employability of Parents in Sure Start Local Programmes*. NESS Research Report. DfES.

CHAPTER 10

Children's centre leadership

Carole Beaty

Background

Leadership within children's centres is a highly complex and challenging task, most particularly because the very role itself demands individuals who will cause disequilibrium by challenging the status quo to bring about change. Both local and national government purport to wish for a change in the way in which services are offered to families; however, it is often left to those working on the ground to initiate and manage that change. This can cause considerable tension and stress. Central to the role of the children's centre leader is the understanding of a vision that inspires practice and is the momentum to move practice forward in all areas of integrated working. If we refer back to Bronfenbrenner and his concept of the child within the context of family, community, culture and media, and the ongoing affect of all those contexts upon a child's perceptions of themselves and their possible life chances, then we need a leader with the will and capability to affect change in all those spheres of influence.

When Sure Start centres were set up originally in 1999, the emphasis was on young children's development and the way in which we might create services and opportunities that will support families and the developmental needs of every child. However, the emphasis evolved over time. What remains at the heart of the children's centre philosophy is a capacity to unsettle existing practice and move the agenda forward, keeping the child at the heart of that process.

Defining leadership within children's services

As practices in service design and delivery are challenged, so is a concept of leadership within integrated children's centres. We are evolving a new way of moving forward in Early Years practice, away from a more hierarchical way of being in which individuals are defined by their status to a more open way of leading together, so that while adhering to a clear set of professional principles and training there is an eager sense of shared learning.

This style of leadership suggests a good deal of risk-taking and support for others. It must also take a degree of both humility and confidence if such high-risk strategies are to be put in place. Leaders within centres and those who are responsible for their work at the more strategic end of practice need to be aware of what the issues are day to day in the lives of families as Lord Laming reminded us so powerfully. Leadership must not get subverted by the rhetoric and by bureaucracy, but must remain clearly grounded in the everyday life of children.

The ELEYS (Effective Leadership in the Early Years) study found that effective leadership in Early Years settings was characterised by:

- Identifying and articulating a collective vision
- Ensuring shared understandings, meanings and goals
- Effective communication
- Encouraging reflection
- Commitment to on-going, professional development
- Monitoring and assessing practice
- Distributed leadership
- Building a learning community and team culture
- Encouraging and facilitating parent and community partnerships
- Leading and Managing: striking the balance

(Siraj-Blatchford and Manni 2006:3)

Early Years practice as revolution and change

The whole context of Early Years practice is political and in some ways this has been seen as a dangerous agenda, not for the faint hearted. The aim is for empowered adults and children in local communities with agency over their own lives. For a leader of a children's centre to coalesce the health, education, care, community and voluntary sector requires a strong understanding of local community needs, child development and different professional contexts. That area of professional literacy is central to the role of leaders in Sure Start children's centres, that deep understanding of different professional heritages and different working practices.

With the start of the Sure Start programme came a vision to involve the local community and to allow parents and families to have ownership over their own services; however, there was always an agenda. Sure Start leaders had to bridge that unstable gap between the dreams and aspirations of a local community, individual parents, what was realistic and possible and the targets and feelings of the professionals involved. At times that has appeared to be an enormous task. Leadership within Sure Start children's centres is usually shared between different professionals who come to children's centre work from a variety of heritages and who need to meld these experiences into a seamless whole. These individuals need to evolve a shared vision and an ethos that will ensure that service-users are powerful and competent users of their own services with a clear sense of their own agency.

Within the Reggio Emilia approach there was a sense of 'co-construction' of meaning, that is, adult and child working alongside each other to create a sense of wholeness, completeness in bringing about a new way of seeing that might not have been achieved in isolation. So it is in the development and creation of children's centres; it needs a new co-construction of meaning in the way in which services are created and are accessed. We need parents, families, communities and professionals working alongside each other as they create a new way of seeing and learning from each other. For leaders this is a risky, yet exhilarating experience. It cannot be done in isolation and needs at its very core the establishment and maintenance of trusting, strong relationships. Like all community-based work this takes a long time to establish, but it is really worth the effort. Central to the evolving relationships in integrated children's centres is the capacity to try out new ways of working across the different sectors, offering services with a lighter touch that might encourage that co-construction of meaning and of intent; for example, putting on a fun day that also provides opportunities for parents to become involved in parent/child exercise classes, a post-natal depression group, or a play session that facilitates parent's involvement in their children's learning. Comments and evaluations can inform that sense of co-construction. Leaders within children's centres need to be on the lookout all of the time for opportunities to weave into the whole yet another strand of partnership working that will support the whole spider's web of services from all sectors and that can provide an excellent pattern of integrated working.

What is integrated working and how do leaders support its evolution?

What this book has sought to address is why integrated working is so important for children and families and for the professionals from all sectors who work with them. However, integrated working is hard to define and be explicit about, yet we all know when it is not working. Families are also clear when services are not sufficiently integrated to meet their needs; how many of us have heard from parents about the number of services, in different places, speaking different professional languages their children have attended and at times the lack of communication between those services. Fully integrated practice takes a long time to achieve and a great deal of resistance can be met along the way. Even the language surrounding the word 'integration' can lead to confusion, with different organisations using it in very different ways. There can be wide organisational cultural differences that need to be challenged.

The government believes that a less complicated, user-friendly system is needed, and integration is seen as a way of making this happen. A children's centre can act as a service hub for the community by bringing together a range of practitioners working together in a multi-agency manner to support the needs of families. At times this will involve the co-location of services, at others the hub will be more virtual in nature.

The Care Services Improved Partnership (CSIP) sees the road to integrated practice as a continuum:

A Continuum of Partnership

A certain degree of co-operation between autonomous bodies, they have a relationship but there is no transparency or sense of coherence, nor shared point of contact with services users.

A co-ordinated user-centred network embodying some alignment of policy making, service commissioning management and practice.

A coherent relationship between integrated bodies – the point of connection is a clear focus on the needs of the user.

(CSIP 2006:25)

Individuals and organisations will be somewhere upon this continuum, both in their thinking and in the practical realisation of the work that they do, and how they include others day to day in their practice. For leaders in children's centres the important thing is to establish where on this journey individuals see themselves and how they conceptualise their own journey. It can be a useful exercise to provide a visual representation of the journey, during a meeting or workshop, and ask individuals to place themselves upon this visual continuum and at the same time for them to place the organisations for which they work on the same continuum. Looking at shared barriers can also be valuable in that shared journey towards a greater sense of integrated practice. Creating that sense of a community of practitioners having a shared vision is a vital role for the children's centre leader. It is also important to take a lead from service users.

The role of the centre manager

Having worked in education both with young children and with adults I came into managing a centre with an educational perspective. It was the most confusing, the most exciting and the most challenging job I have ever had. I have always been committed to parental involvement, but this was on a different scale, this was asking parents to take a lead. I was doubtful at first, but what came across so powerfully as I began this job was how obvious it is that service users should be there making it happen. They know what they want, what they need, it all has to be facilitated and managed and of course that is where the challenge comes. Managing sometimes conflicting interests, but being as fair and open as possible. People asked me what I did day to day, each day was so different, it could involve working in a play and stay session, getting covered in glitter, or running a meeting for parents, attending a CAF meeting or visiting a family. A truly diverse post. Getting it wrong much of the time, learning from that experience and starting again. Coming up with what seemed like insurmountable obstacles, working with others to find a way round.

Most important to this role is getting to know your area, what is going on, who is providing it and where the gaps are. Just keep asking, talking engaging.

(Children's centre manager)

Pedagogical leadership

The whole Sure Start children's centre movement focuses upon the notion of supporting the family in giving the child the very best start in life. This means that some of the work of the centre will focus upon the needs of the adults; however, those of child remain paramount. Therefore it is essential for children's centre leaders to have a sound understanding of the developmental needs of young children and the way in which early experiences will affect later life. The idea of pedagogical practice is important in the whole area of understanding children's learning needs. The term pedagogy is closely associated with the practice of teaching and learning.

Pedagogy needs to be seen as a far wider term that recognises the child as a social and spiritual being, operating within and influenced by a whole range of diverse yet intersecting contexts. Those working with children within those contexts need a diverse and relevant range of knowledge and skills. Research carried out at the Thomas Coram Institute has been of importance:

> As used in continental Europe, the word 'pedagogy' can relate to the overall support for children's development. In pedagogy, care and education meet. To put it another way, pedagogy is about bringing up children, it is 'education' in its broadest sense of the word . . .. Parents are sometimes referred to as the first pedagogues, but pedagogy is also a foundational concept that informs many sorts of services, providing a distinctive approach to practice, training and policy.
>
> (Petrie *et al.* 2008:4)

Pedagogical leadership within the context of integrated children's centres has a specific meaning relating to the way in which children's developmental needs are supported and encapsulated within the whole ethos of a centre. This takes the term into a wider, more inclusive context, away from the teacher's role, to encompass everyone working with and for children in the centre. This idea of pedagogical leadership is closely linked to the Scandinavian model of the pedagogue. Leaders of children's centres need to be leading the learning within the centre, and this will include the whole area of reflective practice in every aspect of work. Effective leaders need to keep the following at the centre of their practice:

- understanding the importance of early experiences in creating a dynamic environment for young children;
- seeing the child in a holistic way;
- being mindful of the way in which young children learn most successfully;
- creating situations in which parents are involved in many different ways in their children's learning;
- engaging other professionals in the process of supporting children's learning;

Importantly, children's centre leaders need to be aware of the way in which each and every person working with families might most effectively engage parents in their children's learning and promote an understanding of educational opportunities in the multi–professional staff with whom they work. For example, work with health visitors on early speech and language will produce great benefits for every child. This could come in the form of informal discussions on early communication with the teacher within the centre or could involve more formal qualifications being offered such as the Elklan course. Such programmes offered within a centre have the benefit of bringing together parents and practitioners to debate the issues around early communication.

The pedagogical environment

The way in which the environment is set up to promote learning will also be an essential part of the pedagogical leader's role. For example the following might form the basis of any centre and might help to create a climate in which learning and the exploration of learning is part of everyone's experience:

* ensuring that all staff and volunteers use observations of children's learning to inform service planning and delivery;
* providing a visually exciting environment in which adult's and children's art work is on show;
* providing a wide range of courses for parents, practitioners and members of the community;
* creating a climate in which the development of learning is always part of the ongoing discussion;
* having a cyber-café available that enables a free-flowing exchange of ideas.

National standards for children's centre leaders

With the move towards a more universal model of children's centres based upon the Sure Start model, the government introduced a set of national standards for the leaders of integrated children's centres. This provides a framework for training and for evaluation. It also enables a more sustainable dialogue for children's centre leaders when working with their supervisor and line manager.

> The leaders of children's centres have a responsibility to ensure that their centre really makes a difference to the individual children and families it serves. How well are those services managed? How well integrated and

how effective are they in reducing the gap between the most disadvantaged children and their peers? Is every child and their family better off? Are they healthy more resilient, better able to enjoy new opportunities?'

(DfES 2007:3)

The 'National Standards for Leaders of Sure Start Children's Centres' document makes it very clear what leaders of centres need to achieve:

- Establishing and sustaining an environment of challenge and support where children are safe can flourish and learn.

- Providing the vision, direction and leadership vital to the creation of integrated and comprehensive services for children, mothers, fathers and families.

- Leading the work of the centre to secure its success, its accountability and its continuous improvement. Central to such success is the quality and level of collaboration, with other services and the whole community.

- Working with and through others to design and shape flexible, responsive services to meet the changing needs of children and families.

- Ensuring that all staff understand children's developmental needs within the context of the family and provide appropriate services that respond to those needs.

- Ensuring that the centre collects and uses all available data to gain a better understanding of the nature and complexity of the local community served by the children's centre.

- Using such knowledge and understanding to inform how services are organised and how to offer differentiated services that are responsive to all groups including fathers, children or parents with disabilities or additional needs, and black and minority ethnic communities.

(DfES 2007:5)

The leadership standards are based upon a range of legislation designed to ensure more comprehensive, more clearly integrated services for children and their families. These include: 'The Children Act 1989', 'The Children Act 2004', 'The Childcare Act 2006', 'Every Child Matters' and 'Championing Children' (DfES 2007:6). The standards are organised into six specific, yet complementary areas (DfES 2007: 6):

- leading learning and development;

- building and strengthening teams;

- managing the organisation;

- stronger families and communities;
- being accountable and responsible;
- shaping the present and creating the future.

The National Professional Qualification in Integrated Centre Leadership

The NPQICL was introduced in 2005 to support the development of integrated practice in Sure Start children's centres. The original programme was written and designed by the Pen Green Centre in Corby in the West Midlands. This famous Early Years centre had already carried out innovative work in the whole area of integrated community-based practice. Leaders of children's centres are likely to come from a very wide range of different backgrounds and the programme reflected this level of diversity. It was based upon a therapeutic model which required participants to engage in a process of personal and professional reflection as a means of developing confidence and skills in creating a dynamic learning community within their centres, and within their local community. Participants and tutors were encouraged to engage in a collaborative journey of discovery and enquiry that would enable all members of the learning community to establish a new understanding of what was meant by leadership. Participants and tutors together engage in a sense of reflection about not only their own leadership style and experience, but also the leadership that they have experienced, and how this has impacted upon them. Children's centres offer a very new way of thinking about services for families and require a very new type of leader. Two of the central pillars of the NPQICL programme are:

- co-construction of meaning and ideas between participants and tutors;
- the creation of a dynamic learning community both within the course and within the participants' centre.

The Purposes of the NPQICL are to:

- Provide for Early Years integrated centre leaders a programme and qualification equivalent to the National Professional Qualification for Headship.

- Create opportunities for integrated centre leaders to consider the leadership implications of their roles.

- Examine the nature of multi-professional services and their implications for integrated centre leadership.

- Create a forum for reflection, dialogue and discussion about leadership practice in integrated centres.

- Examine how leadership is defined and described in the literature of leadership and to relate theory to practice.

- Guide and support practitioner research into the leadership issues in participants' own centres.

- Develop leadership capacity.

(NCSL 2006:5)

A central challenge of leading a children's centre is establishing a trusting environment in which to create a real sense of effective multi-agency working.

Getting connected

The NPQICL programme was designed in such a way as to support the development of connectivity across the whole community and with different agencies. The programme encourages both participants and tutors to engage with a range of different concepts and as far as possible be honest and open in analysing the way in which different activities and different members of the group impact upon each of them. This can seem like a risky and at times uncertain process, yet it can yield quite considerable dividends in terms of developing understanding of the process involved when working within a multi-agency team and helping them to move their thinking and their practice forward. The great joy of the NPQICL programme is that it brings together leaders or aspiring leaders from a range of different backgrounds with such a rich range of experiences. Working together on specific activities within the course brings up many of the issues, conflicts and concerns that are often evident within an integrated setting out there in the real world. This surfacing of feelings and ideas is a powerful means of learning and supports the process of personal reflection. It provides an opportunity to address those issues and feelings in the comparatively safe environment of the group, in which the tutors are 'holding' the group and can provide potentially appropriate support. However, the course requires both participants and tutors to dig deep in terms of accessing their own personal and professional resources.

Michael Schratz and Rob Walker (1995) suggest that much information required for people to connect effectively is hidden by each of the individuals concerned: '. . . Since it is the invisible part of ourselves where change must take place, it is important that we find ways of doing research that touch it.'

(Schratz and Walker 1995:172)

For many of the staff in most organisations, the real business of relation-ships is below the surface. Dislikes, fear, resentment, mistrust, envy, jealousy and anger and frustration remain submerged.

(NCSL 2006:12)

It requires tutors to work in a quite different manner with participants and to enable each member to feel connected to the sense of shared enquiry, but also to feel connected as a group and as a community. This feeling of creating a sense of partnership is an important foundation of the children's centre movement. Working back in the centre requires us all to be as clear with each other, to be focused upon our shared sense of endeavour and to break through barriers of hierarchy that can often stand in the way of true and open communication. This can be a very daunting challenge when working within large public organisations such as a local authority; it requires that we all challenge long-held perceptions about power and where in the organisations individuals find themselves. The shift away from the innovative Sure Start model to the more universal children's centre model means that centres and more specifically leaders of centres lack the autonomy that they once enjoyed to respond to the individual needs of the community. However, the children's centre leader is in a unique position of knowledge and understanding about the local community and should be very well connected.

Transforming practice

The development of integrated children's centres is a key arm of the gov-ernment's policy on transforming practice in children's services; standing perceptions of practice on their heads requires fortitude and courage. It also requires quite a degree of resilience and of self-knowledge. This idea of 'leadership consciousness' (NCSL 2006) is an essential ingredient in the NPQICL programme mix. When leaders are enabled to transform the way in which services are run, then they need to develop a community of 'reflective practitioners' in which each and every member of that commu-nity examines the way in which they work with children and with families and makes conscious their deliberations.

> It is his (Donald Schon's) contention that in most occupational groups, significant developments in working practice were unlikely to be achieved unless professionals deliberately and consistently submitted their professional experience to rigorous examination and exploration so that the insights and understandings gained could be incorporated into an individual's practice wisdom and applied in new situations as they unfold. This type of learning, through insight accumulation, is at the heart of the NPQICL leadership learning methodology.
>
> (NCSL 2006:6)

Many of the NPQICL programme activities require participants to reflect upon their own leadership style, their own practice and develop an honest assessment as to how it impacts upon their day-to-day work.

Andragogical and pedagogical leadership

Key tenets of the NPQICL programme are notions of both andragogicial and pedagogical leadership. These form valuable and at times controversial foundations of the course.

Andragogy

Andragogy is the term related to the way in which adults might learn. It requires both tutors and participants to consider the unique way in which adults might respond to the content and to the process of a course.

Malcolm Knowles considered that adults learn in quite specific ways and that we need to ensure that we differentiate learning accordingly. He believed that andragogy was premised upon the following assumptions about the characteristics of adult learners:

1   Self-Concept: As a person matures his self-concept moves from one of being a dependent personality toward one of being a self-directed human being

2   Experience: As a person matures he accumulates a growing reservoir of experience that becomes an increasing resource for learning

3   Readiness to learn: As a person matures his readiness to learn becomes orientated increasingly to the developmental task of his social roles

4   Orientation to learning: As a person matures his time perspective changes from one of postponed application of knowledge to immediacy of application, and accordingly his orientation toward learning shifts from one of subject-centeredness to one of problem centeredness.

5   Motivation to learn: As a person matures the motivation to learn is internal.

(Knowles 1984:12)

Within the NPQICL programme this idea of the empowerment and the liberation of the adult learner is a very exciting concept and one that informs the whole course. However, this concept at the start of the programme can be a bemusing and at times frustrating idea. Sometimes it feels that the tutors are abdicating responsibility and this can feel uncomfortable. As the programme develops and a real sense of a learning community is achieved then the participants tend to take hold of this notion of andragogical practice and also begin to look at it more closely within their own unique settings.

Evaluation of the NPQICL programme

What is essential about this programme is that it has a genuine and lasting impact upon the quality of leadership within children's centres and that this will have a corresponding affect upon children and families. It would be easy for children's centres to be become yet another government initiative that fails to meet its potential. Leaders of centres have the opportunity to create quite a dynamic change for children. The NCSL evaluation of the NPQICL programme revealed very positive results, although their research highlighted the complexity of the programme and the challenges of facilitating all aspects of the course. The study showed that participants appreciated the empowering nature of the programme, and that it supported their work back in their children's centres.

Impact of programme on participants

- More confidence in oneself as a leader
- More self-awareness
- Better understanding of what motivates colleagues
- Better ability to communicate with other professionals
- New ways of relating to senior management teams
- Greater knowledge about other professions
- Insight into, and in some cases transformation of, one's leadership style
- Ability to identify the most appropriate leadership interventions for particular circumstances
- The skill to use different leadership strategies effectively

(NCSL 2008:7)

While the programme does present some aspect of theory on leadership, it does this within a context of enabling participants to explore their own leadership style and their developing strengths when providing clear and dynamic leadership in uncertain times. Participants, although often very uncertain about the experiential nature of the programme, often seeking a much more structured and teacher-led form of learning come to value this free flow of ideas and feelings, this co-construction of meaning. This sense of self-reflection and analysis in partnership with others is such a key element of the whole children's centres agenda that the course helps to replicate that feeling both of exhilaration and of insecurity. That participants do it together and face dilemmas in the virtual space of the seminar room that they face in reality every day, provides a great sense of personal authority and leads to growing awareness and confidence. Leading a children's centre is an enormous challenge, but the potential for personal and professional growth is immense and the NPQICL programme reflects the energy and ethical nature of children's centre development.

Case study

I started the NPQICL course whilst a nursery manager in a children's centre as it looked like it could give me some practical skills and knowledge whilst incorporating some theory at an appropriate academic level. It did not disappoint.

A small group of fourteen of us were able to form a supportive learning community. We came from different counties and different disciplines, although heavily weighted towards education. During the teaching times we were able to explore different theoretical models, but were also given plenty of time to reflect on how that related to our everyday experience. A fundamental part of the course was to write a journal about our experiences which proved a good discipline and encouraged reflective practice. To support this process we had a mentor who visited us three times throughout the year. An independent listening ear was very helpful to keep me focused and rise above some of the challenges of the job and the course. It was assessed through two assignments and a setting visit. The assignment had a clear structure and enabled me to consolidate much of my learning.

By studying different leadership styles and theories I was able to reflect on my style and how helpful it was in the work context. It also gave me the opportunity to develop new styles. The assignments gave me the opportunity to gain useful feedback from colleagues about my leadership. By having to meet the standards for integrated centre leaders it prompted me to explore all areas of leadership and not just those I was comfortable with.

The course had a profound and favourable impact on my leadership due to its reflective nature and academic challenge. I still use many of the skills I learnt during the year and the learning community has continued beyond the course, albeit in a smaller group. Like all of us, I have much to learn, but the NPQICL gave an excellent boost to my leadership journey and set me in a very positive direction.

(Children's centre manager, West Sussex)

The future of the NPQICL programme

While the changing nature of the political landscape continues to shape the whole children's centre movement, the NPQICL programme is developing to accommodate this change. There is also a sense that the unique attributes that this programme provides in supporting self-evaluation and reflection through experiential learning need to be maintained for future programmes.

> The evidence . . . suggests that the key elements of the programme, in particular its experiential nature and personalised approach, can be a real force for change. Given the challenges facing children's centre leaders in seeking to reduce inequity and give every child good life chances, it remains of key importance that competent leaders are being developed and will be available to run the children's centres of the future. NPQICL can play a key role in this endeavour.
>
> (NCSL 2008:48)

Key issues for children's centre leadership

Creating the ethos

Central to the whole area of successful leadership of children's centres is the creation of an atmosphere or mood that inspires change and innovative experimental practice, but also helps to create a sense of security in shared endeavour. Leaders create a climate in which colleagues, partners and service-users work, and learn daily. That climate is the water in which we all operate and within which we have the power to bring about change. Change can be fractional in a children's centre, one child finding their feet in a play session, a parent who has felt isolated receiving a warm welcome and finding out more about an exercise programme. Change can be vast, offering services that are genuinely joined-up, and service-user led. Daniel Goleman talks of the 'Leadership Repertoire' (Goleman *et al.* 2002:67) and the importance of developing a 'resonant' style of leadership.

> Resonance stems not just from leaders' good moods or ability to say the right thing, but also from whole sets of coordinated activities that comprise particular leadership styles. Typically the best, most effective leaders act according to one or more distinct approaches to leadership and skilfully switch between the various styles depending on the situation.

> Four of these styles – visionary, coaching, affliative, and democratic – create the kind of resonance that boosts performance, while two others-pacesetting and commanding – although useful in some very specific situations, should be applied with caution . . .
> (Goleman *et al.* 2002:67)

Developing an atmosphere of trust

Supervision

An essential element of good practice within the children's centre leadership role is that of sound supervision of all areas of work. Depending upon which background a leader has come from this may not be a professional concept with which they are familiar. For many it is a new concept, but vital for achieving that sense of 'resonance' and flow within an organisation. It is likely that a children's centre leader will be expected to offer supervision across professional boundaries and to colleagues who have different training and a different knowledge base. However, if the leader is to keep momentum in moving the whole agenda forward, as well as ensuring the effective day-to-day running of the centre, then regular, fruitful and challenging supervision is essential.

Effective leadership and supervision

- First and foremost a leader of a centre needs excellent supervision from their line manger, and possibly if their line manger is not working locally then they need someone in a professional capacity who has a sound grasp of local trends. The leader of a centre is the hub of the wheel and as such needs excellent, informed, consistent support as they bring about change.

- Leaders of centres need to be fully aware of professional boundaries, but need to see how these might become permeable to enable a real sense of co-construction of meaning and intention. This requires that leaders are 'leaderful' and work at creating excellent relationships in every area of work.

- Every leader of an integrated centre needs an understanding of how other organisations and disciplines work; this might be achieved through work shadowing and through joint training.

- Shared supervision or matrix management needs to form an essential of practice in children's centres; this can lead to valuable cross-fertilisation of ideas and a clearer sense of partnership.

Having the power to effect change

If leaders of integrated children's centres, whatever their background are to support the whole change agenda in children's services then they must be given the power and the authority to achieve this. They need to have status within the children's centre community and must work together right from the beginning with other partners to create a local vision and to set about commissioning services. However, this whole issue of power is often a problematic one, where the children's centre manager is seen as in a subordinate position; this can lead to considerable loss of creativity, and can force a centre leader into a role of responding to new initiatives rather than being proactive. The whole area of Early Years is highly political and radical in nature. Children's centre managers need to be given the power, status and confidence to challenge existing practice and help in a positive way to shape the future.

Working with families in the leadership role

Perhaps most important in the whole area of the leadership role is the alliance between the centre and the children and families which it serves; if leaders are to make a difference to the local community then they need to share their leadership role with the parents. This may take the form of a parent forum or partnership board on which parents' views and ideas are listened to and incorporated in the planning and development of the centre. This was always the fundamental ethos of Sure Start centres, but has not always translated successfully into the children's centre development. If children's centres really are going to be community led and respond to local needs then it is essential that parents and families are the driving force in the management of each centre. A central tenet of the children's centre movement is not to do unto parents for their good, but to work alongside them to make positive and lasting change. It is important to build upon the Sure Start model if we are to enhance children's services and to affect social change.

Key messages

- Children's centre managers need appropriate support through knowledgeable and challenging supervision from well qualified and experienced line managers.

- Centre managers need to work together with parents and carers to create a climate of shared endeavour.

- Integrated working depends for its success on shared understanding of different forms of professional practice and bringing together shared agendas. Children's centre managers are uniquely placed to help develop a mutually inclusive way of working.

- Developing a full understanding of the local community, existing services for children and looking at what needs changing is fundamental to the role of the manager.

- Children's centre managers need to be able and willing to challenge hierarchal and bureaucratic ways of working that might impede the delivery of services for children and families. They need to keep in mind that they will, as Whalley says, cause 'disequilibrium'.

- Central to the work of a children's centre is the way children learn and develop and this must inform how centre managers design and deliver services.

- Children's centre managers need the power and the support to bring about change.

References

CSIP (2006) *Bringing the NHS and Local Government Together: a Practical Guide to Integrated Working*. Care Services Improved Partnerships.

DfES (2007) *National Standards for Leaders of Sure Start Children's Centres*.

Goleman, D., Boyatiz, R. and McKee, A. (2002) *The New Leaders: Transforming the Art of Leadership into the Science of Results*. London: Time Warner Books.

Knowles, M.S. *et al.* (1984) *Andragogy in Action: Applying Modern Principles of Adult Education*. San Francisco, CA: Jossey Bass.

NCSL (2006) *National Professional Qualification in Integrated Centre Leadership: NPQICL*. National College of School Leadership.

NCSL (2008) *The Impact of the National Professional Qualification in Integrated Centre Leadership (NPQICL) on Children's Centre Leaders and Their Centre.* National College of School Leadership.

Petrie, P., Boddy, J., Cameron, C., Heptinstall, S., McQuail, S., Simon, V. and Wigfall, V. (2008) *Pedagogy: a Holistic, Personal Approach to Work with Children and Young People, Across Services.* London: Thomas Coram, Institute of Education.

Schratz, M. and Walker, R. (1995) *Research as Social Change.* London: Routledge.

Siraj-Blatchford, I. and Manni, L. (2006) *Effective Leadership in the Early Years Sector.* London: Institute of Education, University of London.

Smith, M.K. (2002) *Malcolm Knowles, Informal Adult Education, Self-direction and Andgragogy.* Encyclopaedia of Informal Education.

Whalley, M. (2006a) 'Children's Centres: the New Frontier for the Welfare State and the Education System? Engaging with the Struggle', Presented at the Early Interventions for Small Children in Families at Risk Conference, Oslo, Norway.

Whalley, M. (2006b) *Leadership in Integrated Centres and Services for Children and Families: a Community Development Approach – Engaging in the Struggle.* Corby: Pen Green Research Centre.

Further reading

DCSF (2008) *Every Child Matters: Change for Children.*

DfES (2005) *Sure Start Children's Centres: Practice Guidance.*

DoH (2007) *Delivering Health Services Through Sure Start Children's Centres.*

Williams, S. (2006) *Evaluation of National Professional Qualification for Integrated Leadership.* Henley Management College.

High-quality leadership and the Early Years Professional Status award

Steven Popper

Introduction

This chapter explores how several key factors of the historical evolution of British Early Years services have led to the development of a new, specific, degree-level professional award, that of Early Years Professional Status (EYPS). The chapter considers the nature of this award and the role and responsibility of the new Early Years professional. The chapter compares EYPS with its closest professional relative, Qualified Teacher Status (QTS), and raises several issues about the impact of EYPS on the successful leadership and integration of children's services, particularly within children's centres. It concludes with some suggestions of a way forward.

Key factors affecting the evolution of Early Years policy

Before looking at the EYPS award in detail, we need to consider the context that it has emerged in. Early Years services in Britain currently receive more funding and more professional and political attention than at any time in their history. Regular statements are made by politicians (e.g. the Secretary of State for Children, Schools and Families), professional organisations (e.g. the British Association for Early Childhood Education) and employment unions (e.g. UNISON) about the range, quality, accessibility and benefits of such services, which now seem to be a key focus of government policy.

Such a focus does not come without strings. With the increase of funding and political attention comes accountability, and the accountability of Early Years services for the delivery of good quality and increasingly integrated educare provision has reached new levels, with more deeply ingrained statutory requirements, regulations and expectations than ever before.

One such (and relatively new) expectation is that those who lead the running and development of Early Years services – whether within children's centres or not – should be educated to at least graduate level, and should, in addition, hold the award of EYPS.

But how did this situation come about? There seem to be three particular factors that have driven the evolution of childcare to its current situation. These are:

1   the need to re-organise and rationalise the vast range of Early Years childcare services available;

2   the establishment of a duty of care and a developing notion of children's 'entitlement' to childcare services;

3   the increasing concern about the quality of Early Years education and care.

Key factor 1. The need to re-organise and rationalise

The 'Start Right' report

Back in March 1994 the Royal Society of Arts published Sir Christopher Ball's influential report 'Start Right: The Importance of Early Learning'. This document drew attention to the widespread variance and lack of coherence of pre-school provision available at that time, concluding:

> The existing diverse pattern of provision lacks coherence, co-ordination or direction. It fails to meet the needs of either children or parents. It is unevenly and inequitably distributed. It does not provide an assurance of high quality.... Governments have failed over many years to establish a local framework within which local developments could take place.
>
> (Ball 1994:31)

The 'Start Right' report identified the existence of 'seven major types of provision' (Ball 1994:33), which consisted of nursery education, reception classes, local-authority day nurseries, private and voluntary day nurseries, private nursery schools, playgroups, childminders, and what it called 'Combined Nursery Centres' (Ball, 1994:34), which were precursor of the integrated children's centres now being invested in nationally. It was this last form of provision that the report most admired and recommended, particularly for the diverse ways in which they combined education and day-care services along with facilities designed to be accessible by parents on a drop-in basis.

While commending these precursors to today's children's centres, however, the 'Start Right' report cautioned that in order to perform well and meet children's needs systematically such integrated and co-ordinated services would need to be professionally led. Leaders of these services, as well as being competent managers and organisers, would have to have a clear understanding of factors such as early child development, the importance of good record keeping and the areas of learning that should be engaged with in any good Early Years curriculum.

Consequences of the 'Start Right' report

The 'Start Right' report was to have two major consequences. The first of these was the government's publication, in 1998, of its National Childcare Strategy. This was a public confirmation of the government's official commitment to developing the quality of childcare. Its two major strategies were (1) an increase of funding for such services, and (2) the promotion of better integration of education and childcare services. Such integration was to be planned for and monitored by the new Early Years Development Partnerships (later termed Early Years Development and Childcare Partnerships) set up in every local authority. Integration and co-ordination between services were now expected to take place in a structured manner.

This developing concern for integration of services would eventually lead to the Childcare Act of 2006, which established 'A new Early Years Foundation Stage (EYFS), which establishes a framework to support providers in all sectors in delivering *consistently high quality integrated care and learning* to support the development of all children from birth to five' (DfES 2006a:6, my italics).

The second consequence, eventually, was that the 'Start Right' report's advice that all Early Years services should be professionally led would be taken up by the subsequently established Children's Workforce Development Council. The establishment of degree-level EYPS would finally become the vehicle for ensuring that, wherever possible, children's centres and other forms of pre-school provision were led and managed by highly trained and professional staff.

Key factor 2. Duty of care and children's 'entitlement' to services

The establishment of a duty of care

The key piece of legislation that opened the door for everything that has followed was the Children Act of 1989. While greatly concerned with child protection, it also set out to determine the responsibilities of local authorities towards children living within their boundaries; or, in other words, local authorities' responsibilities to provide services for such children. In section 17, the Children Act (1989) set out a definition of a child 'in need' (i.e. in need of local authority services):

a) The child is unlikely to achieve or maintain, or have the opportunity to achieve or maintain, a reasonable standard of health or development if services are not provided;

b) The child's health or development is likely to be significantly impaired, or further impaired if services are not provided; or

c) The child is disabled.

(The Children Act 1989, 17:10)

In other words, each local authority now had a duty to monitor whether or not any children were 'in need' of supportive services in the first place, and, if they were, to provide relevant and appropriate services for them. It is worth noting, however, that the Children Act (1989) itself did not define what these services might be. 'Health and development' remain huge areas, and relevant services provided by local authorities subsequent to the Children Act (1989) included anything from schools and hospitals to speech therapy and playgrounds for deprived environments. In other words, the existence of the new duties emanating from the Children Act (1989) did not, in themselves, lead to the kinds of integration and co-ordination of Early Years services so heavily promoted by the 'Start Right' report of 1994.

Targeted services or universal services?

In addition, the notion of the existence of specific children being 'in need' of services was not completely problem-free. In the first instance it immediately suggested that there also existed children who were *not* in need of services. The impact of such categorisation of children meant that the first wave of local-authority-supported services developed as a result of the Children Act (1989) were targeted towards those children understood as being 'in need', rather than being designed to be universally accessible by all children and their families. Such accessibility was not yet considered desirable or necessary, as at the time it seemed most sensible to target the services that were available to the children identified as being in most need of them. In other words, there was no guarantee of universally available services. This caused many problems for many parents who felt a need for children's services, but were not identified as within the targeted groups that local authority services were available to.

Even so, for the first time on such a national scale, local authorities now had *statutory duties* towards the provision or support of specific services other than schools for children. This was to be of crucial significance.

The establishment of children's rights

Also approved in 1989 (and signed up to by the UK government in 1991) was the United Nations Convention on the Rights of the Child (UNCRC). This was an international agreement of two things: firstly, the principle that children had specific human rights, as identified by the UNCRC; and second, the undertaking of a commitment to ensure that these rights were recognised and supported by the policies and legislation of the countries that signed up to the UNCRC.

The UNCRC categorised the children's rights it had identified into four groups: rights to survival; rights to protection; rights to development; and rights to participation. The first of these three categories have often been classified as welfare rights; those rights that seek to cement children's entitlement to things such as access to certain standards of education, nutrition, health services, and so on, and it was these types of rights that were focused on by the British government once the UNCRC came into force. Initiatives such as Every Child Matters (2003), the Children Act (2004) and the Children's Plan (2007) can all be understood, at least in part, as vehicles for ensuring that children's welfare rights are met. For example, the Children Act of 2004 laid down the duty for all local authorities to appoint a Director of Children's Services by 2008 who would be 'accountable for (as a minimum) the delivery of education, social services and delegated health services for children'.

Consequences of the establishment of children's rights

It can be argued that a key difference that the notion of children having rights made to childcare policy was the growing realisation that, since *all* children have the same rights in law, then *all* children have an equal entitlement to education, social services and health services. In other words, any targeting of such services towards children identified as being 'in need' (as done initially by the Sure Start project, for example) needed to be complemented by the *universal* availability of these services. This strengthening realisation can be seen in the UK government's 'Choice for Parents, the Best Start for Children: a Ten Year Strategy for Childcare' (H.M. Treasury 2004). This document set out the general aim that 'childcare should be available to [*all*] parents when they need it' (2004:2.60), as well as the desirability of adopting 'an approach that integrates children's services' (2004:3.23).

Such a universal availability would be planned for and co-ordinated by leadership from central government in the first instance (i.e. from the Secretary of State for Children, Schools and Families), then by leadership at local-authority level (i.e. from local-authority Directors of Children's Services) and, finally, from individual Early Years professionals holding EYPS, who would be tasked with the leadership of units of integrated and co-ordinated childcare services.

Key factor 3. Increasing concern about quality

Integrated and co-ordinated childcare services would not be sufficient in themselves without some concern for their quality. The 'Start Right' report (Ball 1994) noted that children's services had been subject to much local variance and national inconsistency in terms of their quality, and had suggested that better national co-ordination of childcare services would be likely to lead to better quality outcomes for children than the rather arbitrary and disconnected provision that had seemed to be 'a long tradition' (Sylva *et al.* 2004:2) in childcare provision for young children.

The EPPE Project

It had long been acknowledged that Early Years provision has the potential for having considerable short-term and long-term benefits for young children. Such benefits (as identified by Woods 2005) range from improvements in academic achievement and positive personal development in the short term to enhanced and better-paid employability and greater social inclusion in the long term. However, in order for Early Years provision to make a positive difference towards such outcomes, it would have to be of consistently high quality. This was one of the conclusions of the influential 'Effective Provision of Pre-School Education' (EPPE) Report (1997–2004), which stated that the quality of Early Years services made all the difference to the potential benefits for children who attended and used them. The

EPPE Project concluded that 'high quality pre-schooling is related to better intellectual and social/behavioural development for children' (Sylva *et al.* 2004:ii), that 'pre-school quality was significantly related to children's scores on standardised tests of reading and mathematics at age 6' (2004:ii), that 'pre-school was particularly beneficial to children who are more disadvantaged ... [*and*] good quality pre-school can be seen as an effective means of achieving targets concerning social exclusion and breaking cycles of disadvantage' (2004:iii). Overall, consistently, there was 'a significant relationship between the quality of a pre-school centre and improved child outcomes' (2004:iv).

The government's response

These findings were of great interest to the government, which had already (a) in 1999 set itself the target to halve child poverty by 2010, and (b) in 2003 published its 'Every Child Matters' green paper, which stated its intention to have all children's services work towards a common set of five 'improved child outcomes':

- be healthy;
- stay safe;
- enjoy and achieve;
- make a positive contribution;
- achieve economic well-being.

All the evidence available seemed to confirm that high-quality pre-school provision held substantial potential benefits for almost every area of a child's life, not just in the short term, but in the long term too. Investment in such provision, therefore, seemed to be highly desirable, as it would seem to pay dividends in key areas – education, social behaviour, employability, combating social exclusion, combating poverty, and so on – in the long run.

The ten-year strategy

The government made this explicit by publishing its new long-term child-care strategy: 'Choice for Parents, the Best Start for Children: a Ten Year Strategy for Childcare' (H.M. Treasury 2004). This document engaged with the issue of quality in two significant ways.

First of all, it confirmed the importance of offering high-quality provision and suggested that such provision had a range of possible benefits, including helping children overcome disadvantaged backgrounds, increasing the chances of higher educational achievements later in life and enhancing the quality of children's emotional, cognitive and social development.

Second, the document summed up the government's strategy for ensuring such high-quality provision. This strategy had two key components: a high-quality workforce to deliver a good standard of service, and a regulation and inspection regime to monitor Early Years provision and ensure that certain standards were maintained.

The Office for Standards in Education (Ofsted) had been responsible for inspecting the quality of all funded Early Years services since 2001, and would continue to be the body responsible for assessing and reporting their quality. But the most crucial element of ensuring quality would be the quality of the Early Years workforce itself. As 'Choice for Parents' makes clear:

> Research shows that settings with well-trained and appropriately qualified staff offering the right learning and development opportunities lead to the best outcomes for children. *In particular, the quality of the leadership of a childcare setting has an important influence on the overall quality of care provided, with evidence showing the settings led by a teacher or another graduate are particularly effective.*
>
> (H.M. Treasury 2004:25, my italics)

This conclusion was to lead directly to a two-pronged strategy for developing quality in Early Years services. The first of these would be the identification of 'Key Elements of Effective Practice' (DfES 2005), which was to be both a training and assessment tool for local authorities to enhance the quality of their childcare workforce. The second would be the simultaneous establishment of graduate-level Early Years professionals and the Early Years Professional Standards (2006).

Key Elements of Effective Practice (KEEP)

As identified by the 'Start Right' report (1994) Early Years childcare services had been (and remained) staffed by personnel who had received widely differing levels of training, ranging from no training whatsoever to degree-level training. Addressing this unhelpful variation in expertise and quality would become one of the first initiatives of the Primary National Strategy's Foundation Stage Team (established as a result of 'Change for Children', 2004). In February 2005, after a period of sustained consultation with local authorities, the Primary National Strategy published its 'Key Elements of Effective Practice' document. This recommended guidance was promoted 'for use by local authorities in their work with settings providing government-funded early education' (DfES 2005:1) – in other words, *all* funded Early Years services, whether schools, playgroups, integrated children's centres, private nurseries and so on. The KEEP guidance attempted to (a) identify features of good quality Early Years practice common to all types of Early Years provision, and (b) give local authorities a possible structure and range of content for their Early Years in-service training and internal quality assurance processes. The document itself makes this clear:

> KEEP is an evaluation tool for local authorities. KEEP provides a way of evaluating and then strengthening the impact of training. It should be used at a strategic level to develop programmes of continuing professional development, to inform job descriptions and service level agreements and to strengthen evaluation processes.
>
> (DfES 2005:7)

The significance of KEEP

The potential importance of KEEP towards the promotion of Early Years integration and high quality cannot be underestimated. KEEP was the first attempt to define generic central features of high-quality Early Years practice and provide a common language for Early Years practitioners of all sorts (including, importantly, both those who worked in schools and those who worked in all other settings) to discuss, share and reflect upon such practice. Not only this, but KEEP was a national initiative, not just a local one. For the first time, therefore, Early Years professionals across the country had a common set of Early-Years-focused quality criteria to measure and enhance their practice and provision by. KEEP can also be understood as a direct precursor of the Early Years Professional Standards that would emerge in 2006 (see below).

The six 'key elements'

There were six 'key elements' of high-quality Early Years provision identified by KEEP, and it is worth noting how closely these compare with the

Table 11.1 Comparison of KEEP and 'Start Right' key indicators of quality

'Key Elements of Effective Practice' (DfES 2005a:3)	Related 'Key Indicators of Quality' (Ball 1994:54)
(1) Relationships with both children and adults	The development of warm and positive relationships
(2) Understanding of the individual and diverse ways that children develop and learn	A broad, balanced and developmentally appropriate curriculum
(3) Knowledge and understanding in order to actively support and extend children's learning in and across all areas and aspects of learning	A broad, balanced and developmentally appropriate curriculum A well-planned, stimulating, secure and healthy environment
(4) Practice in meeting all children's needs, learning styles and interests	A variety of learning experiences which are active, relevant and enjoyable
(5) Work with parents and the wider community	The development of warm and positive relationships
(6) Work with other professionals within and beyond the setting	The development of warm and positive relationships
	Clear aims and objectives
	A commitment to equal opportunities and social justice for all

'key indicators of quality' in Early Years services that had been identified by the 'Start Right' report in 1994. Table 11.1 attempts to suggest how these earlier 'key indicators' relate to the 'key elements' identified by KEEP.

Both sets of quality indicators emphasize the importance of developing and maintaining working relationships of high quality, both with children and their carers and with other involved professionals. Both sets of quality indicators also suggest that such professional relationships are helped by having (a) clear and explicit aims, objectives and principles, and (b) well-planned practice. In other words, professional communication, co-ordination and integration are all helped by the existence of a common frame of reference, a common professional language, a shared sense of purpose and a high degree of professional respect for individuals.

KEEP consisted of all these things. It set out explicit 'Principles for Early Years Education' (DfES 2005:11) which drew attention to specific quality indicators such as practitioners' understanding of child development, the necessity for a well-structured, relevant Early Years curriculum and staff able to implement such a curriculum's requirements, and the importance of building on children's already-established skills and knowledge. These principles would be familiar to many Early Years practitioners who worked with either Birth to Three Matters or the Curriculum Guidance for the Foundation Stage (both precursors of the current Early Years Foundation Stage), and served to underpin the six 'key elements' listed above.

The intention was that Early Years practitioners' expertise in these six 'key elements' would 'develop, demonstrate and continuously improve … through initial and on-going training and development' (DfES 2005:3) and it can be seen that these categories address a wide range of professional considerations which could have specific training attached to them. For example, training about element 1 in Table 11.1 could include developing understanding of attachment theory, technical advice about operating a key-worker system, training about working within or leading a team and tips about communicating with parents and carers. Similarly, element 3 seems to involve practitioners' knowledge and application of appropriate curriculum frameworks, particularly the Curriculum Guidance for the Foundation Stage's 'Areas of Learning' and Birth to Three Matters' four 'Aspects of the Child'. The sixth element seems explicitly to do with improving multi-professional communication, co-ordination and integration.

KEEP and professional expertise

KEEP was clear and highly accessible to staff at all levels of training and expertise. Every local authority now had a substantial vehicle for shaping professional development and internal quality assurance. KEEP was also to be used to 'develop job descriptions' (DfES 2005:8) and 'inform setting development plans' (DfES 2005:8). In other words, new staff would be selected partly on the basis of their potential and capacity to offer good practice in line with KEEP's six key elements, and services themselves would need to develop in ways that demonstrated a strengthening of these key elements too.

But who would lead such training of personnel and development of services? Early Years services were still staffed by personnel with a vast variety of qualifications, training and levels of expertise, and the existence of KEEP was, in itself, not enough to transform this situation overnight. In 2006, after consultation with local authorities, the government's Children's Workforce Strategy published its intention to develop an integrated qualifications framework for the children's workforce. The intention was to create a coherent unity between all the various professional Early Years qualifications available, and, more centrally, 'to provide the level of quality of service that parents and carers demand … [*by creating*] a stable, committed and highly competent workforce' (DfES 2006b:2). This workforce would be led by dedicated, highly trained personnel, who would provide the managerial, pedagogic and organisational skills and knowledge necessary for the development of quality and vision, and who would be granted proper status and authority in recognition of this.

Put together, all these considerations would lead to the establishment of EYPS (2006) and the creation of the Early Years Professional Standards that a person awarded such status would have needed to achieve.

EYPS and the question of leadership

The government's ten-year strategy, 'Choice for Parents' (H.M. Treasury 2004) had already identified how significant the quality of leadership was in influencing the overall quality of any Early Years setting. This was the starting point of the Children's Workforce Development Council, who, along with the Training and Development Agency in the first instance, set to work to draft a standard for the 'skills, knowledge and practice experience to be required of someone taking a leading role' in Early Years services (DfES 2006c:30).

This emphasis on leadership was to set the tone for the entire nature of the EYPS Standards and the expectations of the role, responsibilities and level of training of an Early Years professional holding EYPS. Establishing high-quality leadership of Early Years services was seen as the most effective way of increasing their quality quickly and reliably. It was intended that the new Early Years professionals would be agents of change, rather than people who would simply replicate services as they already existed.

Key expectations of Early Years professionals

These new Early Years professionals would be expected to lead integrated and co-ordinated Early Years services (most typically through their line management of children's centres), exemplify good practice (as now defined by the new Early Years Professional Standards – see below) and to be responsible for other staff's continuing professional development. The government's aim 'to have EYPs in all children's centres offering Early Years provision by 2010 and in every full daycare setting across England by 2015' ('A Head Start for All': EYPS Candidate Information Pack, CWDC 2006b:6) showed just how central the leading role played by these new Early Years professionals was intended to be.

These very high expectations of the new Early Years professionals meant that not every childcare worker would be eligible to become one. Certain prerequisite requirements were laid down.

Prerequisite requirements for Early Years professionals

First of all, Early Years professionals would also have to offer evidence of a certain minimum level of literacy and numeracy, assessed through the requirement for GCSEs at Grade C or above in Mathematics and English (or recognised equivalents). Second, before being awarded EYPS, prospective Early Years professionals would have to have completed all the EYPS Standards. Finally, and significantly, the necessity for graduate-level training at a minimum was established. This followed the long-established example of QTS being available only to graduates or postgraduates. It was deemed that EYPS would become a graduate-level award too, in order to raise both the quality and status of Early Years provision.

The *quality* of Early Years provision would be enhanced by the requirement for leaders of such provision to have demonstrated degree-level competence – ideally (but not exclusively) in subjects such as 'Childhood Studies', which would involve both honours-level study of relevant considerations such as child development, and placement experience that would be assessed at a higher level than BTec and other level 3 qualifications. Establishing leadership of this quality would go some way towards mitigating against the potentially poor effect of having a largely untrained or minimally trained Early Years workforce, as degree-level leadership would be likely to be quite sophisticated and professional in tone and attention to detail.

Similarly, the *status* of Early Years work and provision would be enhanced by the requirement for degree-level leadership of all the new integrated children's centres being promoted and developed. Not only that, the CWDC and the DfES made statements suggesting that EYPS would have equal status to QTS. However, at the time of writing, the real-life status of the EYPS award and its relationship to QTS are not at all clear (see below).

While the requirements for a degree and a GCSE Grade C level of literacy and numeracy set a certain minimum threshold for those eligible to train for the EYPS award, there was still a proper concern for ensuring that EYPS was within reach for (degree level) staff with differing amounts of childcare experience in their background. For example, existing childcare staff could include recent 'Childhood Studies' graduates with minimal post-degree work experience as well as staff who had worked in professional childcare settings for a number of years.

EYPS training and assessment

The CWDC decided upon the strategy of offering a range of training 'pathways' to achieve EYPS. These were:

- a three-month part-time **validation** pathway for those close to achieving the Standards;
- a six-month part-time extended professional development pathway (**short EPD**);
- a 15-month part-time extended professional development pathway (**long EPD**);
- a 12-month full-time **full training** pathway.

(DfES 2007:18)

It was hoped that this range of pathways would allow appropriate staff from a range of backgrounds and employment histories to meet their potential for achieving EYPS in ways that recognised and built upon their previous training and work experience. Common to all the pathways would be the requirement for candidates for EYPS to provide sufficient evidence of meeting the Early Years Professional Standards (see below). Regardless of which pathway has been undertaken, all candidates would provide such evidence through the following tasks:

- a 'Standards Reflection' (the candidate's written reflection on his/her professional practice and how it relates to the EYPS Standards);
- a 'Gateway Review' (comprising four exercises involving the candidate in role-playing particular aspects of the work of an Early Years professional, complemented by some written reflection on this process. The 'Gateway Review' needs to be completed successfully become the candidate continues on to the rest of the assessment process);
- five 'Written Tasks' (each of which discusses particular aspects of the role of the Early Years professional in practice in certain contexts);
- a 'Setting Visit' (when each candidate is interviewed twice by an assessor, has his/her file scrutinised and when three witnesses of the candidate's practice are interviewed about the candidate's qualities and professional work in the setting).

The important thing to note is that the emphasis of the assessment process is on candidates' ability to reflect on their professional practice, particularly with regard to the forthcoming expectations of *leadership* that will be made upon all those awarded EYPS. In fact, the three key skills looked for during the 'Gateway Review' are the candidates' decision-making abilities, their capacity to lead and support other staff, both in their work and their own professional development, and their ability to work and communicate well with others (Colloby 2008).

It could easily be argued that no good leadership or management could take place without the existence of these skills. In fact, the emphasis on leadership potential is made quite explicit by the CWDC's own 'Guidance to the Standards for the Award of Early Years Professional Status' document (2008), which persistently refers to the necessity for candidates for EYPS to provide evidence of both *reflective personal practice and leadership and support of others*. This document identifies specific examples of what this evidence would consist of:

- working skilfully with others;
- good listening;
- sensitivity to colleagues needs and 'readiness for change';
- ability to explain the rationale for any proposed changes;
- can influence, inspire and negotiate with others;
- can apply these skills for the sake of improving outcomes for children.

Of course, what this statement does not do is identify the various difficulties that Early Years professionals might encounter when trying to accomplish any of the above: for example, they might encounter resistance to proposed changes, or find that what colleagues 'know and can do' requires significant improvement, or find that differences in colleagues' opinions about professional issues are hard to reconcile in a way that improves outcomes for children. As well as sensitivity, good communication skills and good judgement, strong leadership also requires authority. The official hope is that the achievement of graduate-level EYPS underpins any authority denoted by rank or job description by suggesting that an Early Years professional deserves such authority by his/her own achievement of the EYPS Standards through sufficient demonstration of reliable and informed knowledge, skill and understanding. In other words, the leadership of an Early Years professional is something that should be able to be trusted and carry weight. This might make all the difference to the success of any integration or co-ordination of childcare services, such as that ideally offered by children's centres. If a leader can carry his or her staff with him or her, then things are much more likely to run smoothly and in a coherent direction than if he or she cannot (Whalley 2008).

The EYPS Standards

During their assessment process, prospective Early Years professionals have to demonstrate achievement of thirty-nine different but related Standards. These are organised into six groups and prospective Early Years professionals have to demonstrate sufficient evidence of achievement against each *group*, rather than against every single Standard explicitly. It is interesting to note that this is quite unlike the situation for prospective teachers who have to demonstrate explicit evidence of meeting each *individual* Professional Standard for QTS. The QTS Standards were the most direct model for the EYPS Standards, and it might be of some significance with regard to the overall status of EYPS in society that this differing requirement was decided upon (see below).

The six groups of EYPS Standards

The six groups of EYPS Standards are as follows:

1 *Knowledge and understanding* (about key aspects such as common Early Years principles, child development, national frameworks such the Early Years Foundation Stage and Every Child Matters, legal requirements, and the range of personnel working in childcare services);

2 *Effective practice* (the technical skills of providing a safe, purposeful environment, appropriate child-centred routines, selecting and using resources, and so on);

3 *Relationships with children* (the skills of establishing safe, fair, trustworthy relationships with children, listening to and communicating with them well and modelling the positive values, attitudes and behaviour expected from children);

4 *Communicating and working in partnership with families and carers* (the understanding of parents' and carers' expertise about their children, and the skills of working with parents and carers in proper partnership and communicating with them professionally and thoroughly, both formally and informally);

5   *Teamwork and collaboration* (the most explicit 'leadership' group of Standards, requiring the ability to shape the culture and policies of a setting, to work with and lead multi-professional groups of staff, and to take responsibility for the organisation and development of other staff's roles and responsibilities);

6   *Professional development* (the most explicit 'reflective practitioner' group of Standards, requiring the ability to reflect on and evaluate practice, develop personal skills in literacy, numeracy, and information and communication technology, and respond constructively to innovation and be prepared to adapt practice when outcomes for children could be improved).

The first thing to note is how these groups of Standards and the attributes that they concern themselves with relate closely to the six 'Key Elements of Effective Practice' identified by KEEP (DfES 2005); in fact, they seem to be more detailed variations of KEEP together with an added emphasis on leadership – which in itself, as has been demonstrated, has a history going back to the 'Start Right' report (1994). The EYPS Standards are clearly based upon research findings over time (such as those of the EPPE Project) and seem to be well-judged in terms of range and content. None of the expectations made by the EYPS Standards would have come as a surprise to anyone who had followed the development of Early Years service and research over the previous 15 years. This suggests that they have an extremely large potential to act as a common frame of reference, a common professional language, and a common set of Early Years quality indicators and professional expectations. Such potential would seem to be very helpful towards supporting the development of smooth professional communication and the successful leadership and integration of Early Years services typically found in children's centres.

The EYPS Standards and the QTS Standards compared

The second thing to note is how closely some of the EYPS Standards relate to the current QTS Standards that need to be achieved by all those recommended for the award of QTS, especially in light of the official suggestion that these QTS Standards and the EYPS Standards have equal status (see above). In fact, some of the EYPS Standards seem virtually identical to their QTS counterparts.

Table 11.2 Similarities between EYPS Standards and QTS Standards

EYPS Standards	QTS Standards
S7: Have high expectations of all children and commitment to ensuring that they can achieve their full potential S25: Establish fair, respectful, trusting, supportive and constructive relationships with children	Q1: Have high expectations of children and young people, including a commitment to ensuring that they can achieve their full educational potential and to establishing fair, respectful, trusting, supportive and constructive relationships with them
S29: Recognise and respect the influential and enduring contribution that families and parents/carers can make to children's development, well-being and learning	Q5: Recognise and respect the contribution that colleagues, parents and carers can make to the development and well-being of children and young people and to raising their levels of attainment
S39: Take a creative and constructively critical approach towards innovation, and adapt practice if benefits and improvements are identified	Q8: Have a creative and constructively critical approach towards innovation, being prepared to adapt their practice where benefits and improvements are identified

Consider the examples in Table 11.2. There seems almost nothing to choose between them (though the phrase 'raising their levels of attainment' gives a clue to the concern with educational standards found within the QTS Standards). This, in itself, suggests that the two sets of Standards do have parity with each other. However, each set of Standards has a quite different emphasis. The QTS Standards, as expected, focus on the educational role of the teacher rather than on good practice in the Foundation Stage. The EYPS Standards are much more explicit about what constitutes such good practice (consider the examples in Table 11.3).

Key similarities and differences

It can be seen that the EYPS Standards in Table 11.3 are much more precise about features of good practice that apply particularly to the Foundation Stage, while the QTS Standards above are very generic and imprecise in comparison. For example, EYPS Standard S11 emphasises the desirability of child-led learning and play, and the importance of good use of the environment (three consistently important features of good Early Years practice), while QTS Standard Q10 asks for a range of teaching strategies to be used, but does not in any way indicate what these might be. This is not a complete surprise, given that the QTS Standards are meant to be broad

Table 11.3 Differences between EYPS Standards and QTS Standards: good practice

EYPS Standards	QTS Standards
S11: Plan and provide appropriate childled and adult-initiated experiences, activities and play opportunities in indoor, outdoor and in out-of-setting contexts, which enable children to develop and learn	Q10: Have a knowledge and understanding of a range of teaching, learning and behaviour management strategies and know how to use and adapt them, including how to personalise learning and provide opportunities for all learners to achieve their potential
S2: [Secure knowledge and understanding of] The individual and diverse ways in which children develop and learn from *birth to the end of the foundation stage* [my italics] and thereafter	Q18: Understand how children and young people develop and that the progress and well-being of learners are affected by a range of developmental, social, religious, ethnic, cultural and linguistic influences

enough to apply to all teachers, whether Early Years, Primary or even Secondary, but it does suggest that the EYPS Standards are, in fact, superior when it comes to discussing, assessing and sharing expectations for professional practice centred in the Early Years. (Certainly, trainee Early Years teachers for whom I have been responsible have all found the EYPS Standards much more useful in shaping the actual nature of their work than the generic QTS Standards which have officially applied to them.) The substantial 'Guidance to the Standards for the Award of Early Years Professional Status' document (CWDC 2008) serves to underline this further by offering very accessible, useful and precise exemplars of good Early Years practice and giving clear advice about expectations of high quality.

In addition, the EYPS places much more emphasis on leadership than this set of QTS Standards (Table 11.4), which emphasize good teamwork rather than any leadership qualities (other than directing teaching assistants).

This increased emphasis on leadership qualities also suggests that the EYPS Standards are meant for Early Years practitioners at a high level in their career, as compared to the QTS Standards for newly qualified teachers, which are meant for teaching staff at the beginning of theirs.

The potential problem

What has also often been missed by teachers and headteachers in Foundation Stage training sessions that I have led is that the EYPS Standards (2006)

Table 11.4 Differences between EYPS Standards and QTS Standards: leadership and teamwork

EYPS Standards	QTS Standards
S34: Ensure that colleagues working with them understand their role and are involved appropriately in helping children to meet planned objectives	Q33: Ensure that colleagues working with them are appropriately involved in supporting learning and understand the roles they are expected to fulfil
S35: Influence and shape the policies and practices of the setting and share in collective responsibility for their implementation	Q32: Work as a team member and identify opportunities for working with colleagues, sharing the development of effective practice with them

actually preceded the current version of the QTS Standards (2007). Many of the teaching staff I have talked to had made the assumption that the EYPS Standards were an adapted version of the QTS Standards, and were quite astonished when it was pointed out to them that it was the other way around, and that the current QTS Standards are actually an adaptation of the EYPS Standards. This seems to serve as further evidence that the EYPS Standards are now the definitive frame of reference for professional work in the Foundation Stage.

But are they? Early Years professional work falls into two camps: work that takes place in maintained schools (which the majority of four-year-olds now attend, at least part-time), and work that takes place in services based outside these schools (such as most children's centres). As just demonstrated, the professional standards that need to be achieved by Early Years professionals differ from those that need to be achieved by Early Years teachers. Questions remain about the relationship between the two sets of standards and the two sets of practitioners, and it seems likely that the future success of the intention to establish integrated childcare services will depend upon how these questions are resolved.

One Early Years Foundation Stage or two?

The first thing of significance to note is that the CWDC regards Early Years professionals and all Early Years practitioners based in mainstream schools (whether they are Early Years teachers or teaching assistants) as quite different personnel. In fact, the training and assessment routes towards achieving EYPS are only 'open to people with degrees in or joining the Early Years workforce in all settings *other than maintained schools*' (DfES 2007:18, my italics).

Early in 2007 this prohibition on maintained-school staff training for EYPS was queried by James Rogers, the Executive Director of the Universities Council for the Education of Teachers (UCET). Beverley Hughes, the then Minister for Children, Young People and Families responded to his query stating that the government's first priority was to have an increased number of graduate Early Years professionals in private, voluntary and independent full daycare settings, on the grounds that these settings were generally of the poorest quality (Hughes 2007). In other words, the new Early Years professionals were to be used and required in a targeted fashion.

The suggestion was, it seemed, that maintained schools already had graduate staff who had met a set of professional standards, so the priority was to develop the quality of services outside such school settings. This was all well and good, but it did mark a division of the Early Years workforce that KEEP, for example, had been so good at avoiding. This division was potentially exacerbated by the CWDC's statement that 'CWDC believe that over time, *only those with EYPS* should lead the delivery of the new Early Years Foundation Stage' (CWDC 2006b:6, my italics).

So what does all this mean for Early Years teachers working within mainstream schools? Does it mean that their own high-level training and expertise would be seen as second-best, rather than equivalent, to those holding EYPS? Or does it mean that they would be responsible for leading the delivery of the Early Years Foundation Stage, but only as it manifests itself in mainstream schools? Either option seems problematic: the first would suggest that EYPS has a higher status than QTS (even though the assessment requirements to achieve QTS are much, much more difficult, rigorous and extensive than those required to achieve EYPS), while the second would suggest the existence of two *different* Early Years Foundation Stages in practice – one school-based Foundation Stage and one all-other-settings Foundation Stage, each potentially operating in different directions and with different priorities. Neither of these options seems particularly helpful towards the cause of integrated childcare services.

To give the CWDC some credit, it did state:

> The CWDC also believes that the relationship between QTS and EYPS should be clarified in time for the introduction of the new EYFS in 2008. The Government agrees that further clarity is needed. The Government and CWDC wish to ensure that people with QTS are attracted to and are retained in the Early Years workforce.
>
> (CWDC 2006a:5)

Unfortunately, such further clarity has been rather sparse. In 2007, James Rogers reported that a UCET member had received a statement from the DfES about the relationship between qualified teachers and Early Years professionals, which seemed to suggest the following:

- Early Years professionals would not replace qualified teachers in schools.
- The professional standards for EYPS and QTS are based on different sets of skills for what are anticipated to be different workforces.
- Early Years professionals would need more practice experience of working with children aged 0-3 than teachers.
- Early Years professionals would need more understanding of child development than teachers.
- Early Years professionals would need to have more expertise in working with parents and carers, and currently required to obtain QTS.
- The Early Years professional's role is different to that of a qualified teacher.

Unfortunately, such apparent messages from the DfES raise more questions than they answer. It is not at all clear that Early Years teachers require less knowledge of early child development than other Early Years practitioners, for example, nor is the assumption that Early Years teachers need less knowledge and experience of working with parents and carers a well-grounded one. (Of course, if one went by the letter of the QTS Standards, then perhaps these conclusions could be reached, but this only serves to demonstrate the inability of the generic QTS Standards to properly reflect what is known about good Early Years practice.) So the questions about the relationships between QTS and EYPS and between EYPs and Early Years teachers remain. Early Years professionals cannot be employed as teachers, even teachers working in the Foundation Stage, while Early Years teachers are not deemed to have EYPS.

Conclusion: suggestions for a possible way forward

The Early Years Foundation Stage became statutory in September 2008, and, for the first time, the Foundation Stage was formally constituted as being from birth to five years of age. All funded Early Years services (including both maintained schools and children's centres) now have to follow the EYFS. With this in mind, the following suggestions for progress are put

forward (though the likelihood of their being followed seems rather minimal at present):

- *Suggestion 1.* The Training and Development Agency (TDA) should
  reconstitute what they consider to be Early Years teacher training. At
  present the TDA's official definition of 'Early Years' is three to seven
  years of age (i.e. the old Foundation Stage and the existing Key Stage
  One). 'Early Years' should now correspond to the new EYFS requirements and be reconstituted as birth to five years of age.

- *Suggestion 2.* Given this, Early Years teachers should now be given a
  distinct set of QTS Standards that relate explicitly to the education and
  care of children aged birth to five, rather than the current generic set
  of standards. These new Early Years QTS Standards should define clear
  and explicit expectations of good Early Years teaching practice. This
  new set of Early Years QTS Standards would have a much closer match
  to the EYPS Standards in their detail, and teachers who achieve the
  new Early Years QTS Standards should be deemed as also having
  achieved the EYPS Standards. These measures would prevent the frag-
  mentation of Early Years services into two separate Foundation Stages
  (as discussed above), and would help promote shared professional
  understanding, expectation and communication between schools and
  other childcare services. They would go quite a long way towards ful-
  filling the CWDC's wish to 'ensure that people with QTS are attracted
  to and are retained in the Early Years workforce' (Early Years Professional
  National Standards, CWDC 2006a:5). Finally, they would also open
  up the possibility of Early Years teachers leading integrated children's
  centres alongside their Early Years professional colleagues.

- *Suggestion 3.* The status of the EYPS Standards should be enhanced by
  (a) making it quite clear that they are the leading and exemplar standards for good Early Years practice, and (b) making achievement of
  them more challenging than at present.

The second point needs to be explained. As an Early Years teacher educator,
I am very aware of the rigour and extent of the achievements that need to
be demonstrated for student teachers to gain the award of QTS, and, to me,
the requirements for achieving the award of EYPS are much lower. This can
be easily demonstrated by comparing the assessment requirements of QTS
to the assessment requirements of EYPS (Table 11.5).

Table 11.5 Comparison of assessment requirements in QTS and EYPS

QTS requirements	EYPS requirements
Constant lesson evaluation and formal reflection of progress against the QTS Standards in each block of school experience (at least 90 days in total for PGCE programmes and 120 days for three-year undergraduate programmes)	A 'Standards Reflection and a 'Gateway Review' Variable requirements for the number of days of work experience necessary
Typically, at least three assignments totalling 12,000 words, plus a series of written school-based tasks, totalling approximately 2,000–3,000 words. Many PGCE courses are also now at Masters degree level	Five 'Written Tasks', approximately 6,000–7,500 words in total
Constant and regular (often weekly) lesson observations by assessors. Each block of school experience is formally assessed and graded	One 'Setting Visit' by an assessor
Successful completion of the TDA 'Professional Skills Tests' in Literacy, Mathematics and ICT	

If the wish is for EYPS to truly have a high status in society (and be of at least equal status to QTS), then perhaps EYPS should be made as challenging and creditable to achieve in the first place. If not, then there might always be a feeling that EYPS is a lesser animal. This would have the potential to be very damaging towards professional relationships across the Foundation Stage, and might serve to fragment schools from other Early Years services in an unhelpful manner.

These suggestions are offered to help iron out some existing issues relating to the EYPS award, but it still remains the case that the EYPS Standards themselves are extremely well thought out and exemplified by the 'Guidance to the Standards for the Award of Early Years Professional Status' (CWDC 2008). It also remains the case that the emphasis given to Early Years professionals' leadership of childcare services is very well founded and likely to pay dividends.

There is certainly a pressing need for Early Years professionals. In 2008 Ofsted reported that: 'The quality of childcare varies widely across different areas of the country … overall, quality is generally poorer where there is most poverty and social deprivation' (Ofsted 2008:11).

Good Early Years professionals who have achieved the EYPS Standards will be the catalysts to change this situation. Ofsted point out that in the best childcare settings:

Leaders have a clear sense of purpose, an ambition for excellence, and a clear vision for the future of the setting ... [*they*] are self-motivated, good communicators and able to get the best from those they work with. They regularly review what they do and plan for improvement .... In the best run settings there is an atmosphere of infectious enthusiasm where adults are highly motivated and c ommitted to providing the very best support for children. Adults have extensive knowledge and skills in promoting children's welfare and supporting their learning and development.

(Ofsted 2008:20)

It is notable that all the above qualities identified by Ofsted are precisely those that would serve to promote the successful integration of childcare personnel and services: good communication, a strong sense of vision and purpose and high levels of knowledge and commitment. These qualities are exactly what the introduction of the EYPS and its Standards is intended to achieve. If the issues noted in this chapter can be dealt with successfully, then the emergence of this professional award and its Standards (alongside the common framework of the EYFS) seems very likely to enhance the quality of integrated childcare services and children's centres considerably.

References

Ball, C. (1994) *Start Right: the Importance of Early Learning*. London: Royal Society of Arts.

Colloby, J. (2008) *The Validation Process for EYPS*. Exeter: Learning Matters.

CWDC (2006a) *Early Years Professional National Standards*. Leeds: CWDC.

CWDC (2006b) *A Head Start for All: EYPS Candidate Information Pack*. Leeds: CWDC.

CWDC (2008) *Guidance to the Standards for the Award of Early Years Professional Status*. Leeds: CWDC.

DfES (2005) *Key Elements of Effective Practice*. Norwich: HMSO.

DfES (2006a) *Improving Outcomes for Children in the Foundation Stage in Maintained Schools: Process-based Targets in the Foundation Stage*. Nottingham: DfES.

DfES (2006b) *Children's Workforce Strategy: Building an Integrated Qualifications Framework*. Nottingham: DfES.

DfES (2006c) *Children's Workforce Strategy: the Government's Response to the Consultation*. Nottingham: DfES.

DfES (2007) *Local Authority Briefing Pack for the Early Years Foundation Stage*. Nottingham: DfES.

H.M. Treasury (2004) *Choice for Parents, the Best Start for Children: a Ten Year Strategy for Childcare*. Norwich: HMSO.

Hughes, B. (2007) Letter from Beverley Hughes (Minister of State for Children, Young People and Families) to James Rogers (Executive Director of the Universities Council for the Education of Teachers), 26 February. Ref: 2007/0009397POBH.

Ofsted (2008) *Early Years: Leading to Excellence*. London: Ofsted.

Sylva, K., Melhuish, E., Sammons, P., Siraj-Blatchford, I. and Taggart, B. (2004) *The Effective Provision of Pre-school Education (EPPE) Project: Final Report*. Nottingham: DfES.

Whalley, M.E. (2008) *Leading Practice in Early Years Settings*. Exeter: Learning Matters.

Woods, M. (2005) In Taylor, J. and Woods, M. (eds) *Early Childhood Studies: an Holistic Introduction* (2nd Edition). London: Hodder Arnold.

Further reading

Ball, C. (1994) *The Start Right Report: the Importance of Early Learning*. London: Royal Society of Arts.

DfES (2005) *Children's Workforce Strategy Consultation Document*. Nottingham: DfES.

Dryden, L., Forbes, R., Mukherji, P. and Pound, L. (2005) *Essential Early Years*. London: Hodder Arnold.

Joslyn, E., Such, C. and Bond, E. (2005) 'Social policy, the state, the family and young children', in Taylor, J. and Woods, M. (eds) *Early Childhood Studies: an Holistic Introduction* (2nd Edition). London: Hodder Arnold.

Osgood, J. and Sharp, C. (2000) *Developing Early Education and Childcare Services for the 21st Century (LGA Research Report 12)*. Berkshire: NFER.

Wyness, M. (2006) *Childhood and Society*. Hampshire: Palgrave.

CHAPTER 12

Accountability and inspection

Carole Beaty

This chapter will look at the highly complex issue of evaluating the work of Sure Start children's centres and the difficult task of establishing whether or not they really do make a difference in terms of improving outcomes for children and for families. It will consider the often rather cumbersome way in which a base line for accountability has been established and the highly delicate and thought-provoking manner in which anecdotal and case-study evidence might be used to establish good practice. It will consider the nature of ongoing reflective practice which is so essential if true integrated work is to form the backbone of children's services. It looks at the role of the Self-Evaluation Form (SEF) in establishing an ongoing dialogue with partner agencies and with accountable bodies.

When the original Sure Start centres were set up, there was an emphasis on innovative and original practice, with each centre setting its own agenda and its own way of working. The notion was to begin to gain an understanding of the unique needs within the local community and develop innovative and often radical ways of creating services which might in some way address those specific needs. A key element of this practice was to ensure that local parents had a say in what they wanted and the way in which this might be delivered. Sure Start centres tried out new ideas and new ways of meeting local community needs. They were not hidebound by bureaucracy and by endless conformity to targets. The notion was that money spent early on specific informal interventions would have benefits for individual children and communities. This drew upon the work of Head Start and the Nurse-Family Partnership, which found that appropriate early intervention really can make a difference. This ultimately would be a cost-saving exercise, and would support the development of increasingly sustainable communities.

Sure Start was by any measure ambitious and radical. There was originally the scope and the funding to try out new ideas and to be adventurous.
In fact, for many of us working in the original Sure Start programmes, it
caused almost some level of embarrassment to have such a high level of
funding attached to our work that could seem indulgent to other hard-
pressed partner agencies. However, what lay at the heart of many of these
initial programmes was the importance of the child and the community
from which they came. Of course there were targets to do with reach,
mostly concerning the number of families that signed up to the programme,
breast-feeding, and smoking-cessation. However, services generally were
not driven by these targets. There was room to breathe and to reflect upon
practice. There was scope to work around difficulties and create new ways
of working.

However, the original Sure Start programmes worked along quite a rigid
demarcation in terms of geographical area, so that reach was decided
by post code and numbers of families who signed up and who attended
services. This could lead to very needy families missing out on excellent
services, and there needed to be an imaginative approach to the implementation of such rules and regulations. The Sure Start programmes initially
were not tied to the local authority in every instance; although it might
have some say, Sure Start's generally remained outside the general heavy
hand of the local authority. Most important for all who have worked in the
Sure Start programmes has been the role of parents and families in shaping
services and ways of working that are appropriate for them and their
children.

The whole area of integrated practice by its very nature is complex,
perhaps almost impossible to analyse; the nuances of a programme create a
subtle interplay that can make a tremendous difference, yet are difficult to
establish in terms of specific measureable outcomes. Another important
issue is the fact that like many early intervention programmes like Head
Start and High/Scope positive outcomes are not always apparent in the
short term. It takes many years to see a real difference. Together with the
fact that an early intervention programme is just that, a proactive approach,
how can you measure your success if you are hoping to stop something
happening? However, Sure Start children's centres are committed to a
reflective approach to professional practice in which cross-disciplinary
forums begin to question each other when establishing what works for
children and their families, and learn from each other as they develop in

sophistication and expertise. Sure Start was built upon a sound research-based approach that valued evidence-based practice.

Inspection and accountability: the background

Many of the early Sure Start programmes used specific research practice to investigate particular projects and to provide feedback for both parents and practitioners. For example, West Sussex made use of the research expertise offered by the National Children's Bureau to examine key initiatives and to draw out what worked in terms of innovative practice and what all professionals might learn in moving partnership work forward. This was an exciting way of working that gave useful and pertinent comment upon often quite radical approaches to delivering services. What was particularly valuable about these studies was the way in which they reflected the parent's views and looked at how the quality and impact of the service affected the service-user. It was also valuable that the researchers always involved the practitioners in centres in the research design. Parents were also a key part of the process.

Children's centres are primarily about building more sustainable communities and strengthening a sense of place and purpose. Leaders of children's centres and their partnership groups need a sound grasp of what is going on within a local area, what needs and opinions are out there. This type of research can help in developing that understanding:

> Children's Centres have the potential to transform the way in which families gain access to and can benefit from local services. The head of a Children's Centre must have a comprehensive understanding of their local community and its strengths. Developing the capacity of community organisations and individuals will support sustainable community development.
>
> (DfES 2007:9)

Having a researcher to investigate the views of parents and of partner agencies can provide valuable, informative insights that can enhance and develop practice. In the spring of 2007, Jinny Briant from the National Children's Bureau carried out an evaluation of a parent training project for the Littlehampton Programme Board that looked at parent participation and development and included a weekend way as a family, getting to know each other and reviewing practice, and looking at what went well and what could be improved. The training also included a more formal governor training that helped to tease out issues raised and explored on the original weekend away. Parents were able to be frank and open in their responses to an outside evaluator:

> This evaluation has shown that the parent training was very successful in terms of its aims and objectives. It gave them an opportunity to bond as a team and helped their confidence. It also enabled the parents to gain a better understanding of the services provided, about the management of the centre, and of roles and responsibilities of those providing services within the centre. In addition, it provided the parents with an opportunity to forge friendships with other parents on the Board and to observe other parental styles and gave them quality time with their children.
>
> (Briant 2007:13)

However, this study also showed that partner agencies on the Board had provided little feedback from this project and that parents sometimes felt that they were reluctant to engage in a professional dialogue with parent members. This caused frustration and at times alienation, an important issue in terms of community development, and in the development of the Partnership Board and the efficacy of its work. Studies such as these have been invaluable in forging and refining practice and have proved a purposeful tool for ongoing evaluation and accountability.

More informal means of gathering feedback can also prove helpful; providing a message board or 'post-it' wall can help to give useful insights into the way in which services are perceived and what else local people might want. It is important to ensure that such means of gathering opinions and ideas are accessible to all, providing relevant translation services, for example. What is also essential is that such comments are not just gathered and then ignored, but shared across teams and then fed back to the community, through parent forums or newsletters, and that while comments and ideas are acknowledged they are also taken forward. This is what you asked for, this is what we are doing in response, so that ideas do not just languish unremarked but are used in a dynamic manner to really shape practice.

The 2004 Children Act provided the legal underpinning for the transformation of children's services as set out in the 'Every Child Matters: Change for Children' programme. Section 10 of this Act provides the statutory basis for the Children's Trusts (the duty to cooperate). A revised version of this guidance was published in November 2008. The 'relevant partners' under the 'duty to cooperate' are: district councils, the police, the probation board, the youth offending team, the Strategic Health Authority and Primary Care Trusts, Connexions partnerships, and the Learning and

Skills Council. Partners are placed under an obligation to cooperate in making arrangements to improve well-being and have the power to where necessary pool budgets as well as other resources.

The Children Act 2004 was a catalyst for change in the way in which children's services were inspected:

> Integrated inspection of children's services, replacing inspections of individual services, is a driver of improvement and a key part of the effort to rationalise planning, accountability and performance management.

> Services are monitored through two inspection processes. The first is an annual performance assessment (APU) of each council's children's services. The second is a programme of joint area reviews (JARs), which involve greater depth than the APU and also range beyond council services to include for example, health and police services. Both processes look at how services are working together locally to improve outcomes for children and young people. They are intended to:

> *Target inspection activity on clear outcomes for children, and to be focused on the user, unconstrained by service boundaries*

> *Make arrangements for the effective coordination of inspection activity to prevent duplication and to reduce burdens and pressures of those inspected.*
> (www.everychildmatters.gov.uk/strategy/inspection
> 12/4/2009, my italics)

This joint inspection provided an impetus for more considered joint working and gave thought-provoking feedback in terms of clarifying different roles and responsibilities when working with families. It provided status and credibility for more effective integrative services.

Both joint area reviews and annual performance assessments came to an end in December 2008 and were replaced by the comprehensive area assessment (CAA), which came into action on 1 April 2009. The CAA focuses most particularly on people and places with different inspectorates jointly evaluating how well local services work together to support the needs of local children and their families. The CAA will identify specific strengths and weaknesses and assessments will be based upon a national range of indicators (the National Indicator Set). The CAA will provide a further impetus to more effective partnership working and will focus on local community need:

Vision of Comprehensive Area Assessment

- A catalyst for more effective improvement of local services for citizens, especially those in need

- Area based and outcome focussed
- Relevant to local people
- Supporting improved accountability
- Constructive and forward looking.

(Nottingham City Council 2009:2)

Should you be preparing for CAA?

- Ask yourself, and your partners . . .
- How well do we understand our local communities?
- Is this understanding shared among our partnership?
- Is it reflected in our shared priorities?
- How well do we understand our performance and is this clearly focused upon on outcomes?
- How well do we understand the challenges ahead and are we working effectively together to meet these and improve priority outcomes?

(Ibid.:12)

The CAA provides a real opportunity for inspection to provide an increasingly dynamic role in helping to create more sustainable communities, helping to create a creative inspection framework which reflects local needs.

The Self-Evaluation Form

While children's centres will form part of a more general inspection of children's services in their area, centre Managers and their team will be expected to record their progress and to log outcomes using the Self-Evaluation Form (SEF). This document should provide a framework for an ongoing dialogue with the centre's accountable body and should provide a tool to support ongoing reflective practice and uses:

- Data about children's centre performance, to benchmark progress and to review impact.
- Analysis, giving a rounded picture of practice and the local context against which progress should be judged.

(DCSF 2008a:2)

Centres are asked to populate the form with factual information about the centre. They are then asked to look at their reach in relation to national standards. So they are asked to provide information on the percentage of the following groups with whom the centre has established contact:

- teenage mothers and pregnant teenagers;
- lone parents;
- children in workless households;
- children in black and ethnic minority groups;
- disabled children;
- fathers;
- children of disabled parents.

A key element of the children's centre movement is to help address the whole issue of social exclusion and of social isolation. Although this might be seen as a crude device for gathering data, it at least highlights the issue and requires that the centre explores the way in which services are offered to ensure that all groups feel included:

> The central role that children's centres have to play in improving outcomes for children as part of Every Child Matters is well established. The role of children's centres in 'reducing the inequalities in outcomes between the most disadvantaged children and the rest' which forms part of the over-arching vision for children's centres has been further reinforced in the Sure Start children's centres Planning and Performance Management Guidance (DfES 2006). This builds on the Guidance issued in 2005 and includes a specific focus on supporting children from those families most in need within the community and highlights the importance of centres delivering responsive services which are more tailored to their needs.
>
> (Together for Children 2007:3)

Such an emphasis is valuable across the whole area of integrated practice as it keeps the focus most clearly on families who feel marginalised. Having it as a central plank of the evaluation document enables more focused part-nership working around this area of need. However, gathering relevant and useful data can be a sensitive task.

The SEF goes on to ask centres to record information about the services that they provide under the headings of 'Every Child Matters':

- be healthy;
- stay safe;
- enjoy and achieve;
- make a positive contribution;
- achieve economic well-being.

Centres are asked to look at their overall effectiveness in meeting individual outcomes and to rate themselves on a three-point scale:

Grade 1: Outstanding – for exceptional settings that have excellent outcomes for children

Grade 2: Good – for strong settings that are effective in promoting outcomes for children

Grade 3: Satisfactory – for settings that have acceptable outcomes for children but which have scope for improvement

Grade 4: Inadequate – for weak settings that have unacceptable outcomes for children

(DfCSF 2008a:5)

Clearly making such a judgement is highly subjective, and while such considerations are a valuable point of reflection and discussion they cannot be an exact science. The nature of integrated children's centres, when effective, requires a shift in emphasis on practice, and the way in which service-users receive that practice. Outcomes are very hard to quantify and the discrete nature of the children's centre contribution needs to be considered, most particularly when they are working in clear partnership.

Making use of the SEF to improve access

As discussed before, the role of the children's centre should be to help to break down barriers and to help the most excluded groups to gain good access to services and to become a part of moulding those services. The Together for Children 'Toolkit' would urge practitioners and parents to consider the way in which services are offered and to evaluate whether or not it is in fact the services which are inaccessible. Many service providers are concerned when services are poorly attended or are only utilised by certain sections of the population; maybe this is telling us something about the service and when, where or how it is offered.

Rather than trying to identify specific groups as 'priority and excluded families' it is important that we first consider if your service is 'hard to reach' for some individuals such as those who:

- Have competing things to do with their time, like working
- Dislike 'groups' or don't like or approve of the group care offered to their young children
- For whom English is an additional language

- Cannot use some buildings or transport or find it hard to leave the home
- May feel culturally isolated, alienated, suspicious or fearful of unwanted 'interference'
- Worry that they may be criticised or judged
- Are geographically isolated or living in temporary accommodation or refuges
- Are living with a long-term illness or disability, their own, a child's or a family member's
- May prefer, trust and rely on the network of support they receive from family and friends
- May have negative experiences in their own childhood such as physical, sexual or emotional abuse within the family or poor experiences of services

(Together for Children 2007:3)

A key element of the evaluation process most particularly through the SEF is to be able to revisit the fundamental vision and values that underpin a centre's practice and do this with all the practitioners involved and with parents and families. The example above provides the starting point for helping evaluation explore the issue of exclusion, helping all of us to focus on that notion of 'hard to reach'. What do we mean by 'hard to reach' and are we actually offering inaccessible services or inaccessible practitioners to our clients? Anyone who has had to access public services at some time in their lives knows what it means to have experienced almost impenetrable services.

Case study: children's centre manager

When I first saw the SEF, I was truly daunted by it and it seemed to me to be just another piece of bureaucracy that had to be got through. However, now I see that it is something that we have to do, yes, but that it is a method of focusing all of our minds upon change. It is something that can be used with real creativity to look at the way that we provide services and for all agencies to take responsibility, to be involved. This focusing down on what seems like small details has been of immense value and has brought different agencies closer together. It has been a really valuable and enlightening process. However, while it is a valuable tool for bringing services together it is very difficult to isolate pieces of evidence and say yes it was us who made a difference here, for that is the very nature of integrated work.

(Children's centre manager)

However, the complex and difficult thing about Sure Start children's centres is that a great deal of the work that they undertake is not quantifiable. It is about subtle shifts in emphasis for individuals and for communities. It is about the establishing and the nurturing of relationships over time, which may lead to different behaviours and so to very different outcomes. For children it must be about living within sustainable communities in which services are built around their needs, not the needs of the service provider. It is about going back to Bronfenbrenner's circles of influence, looking at the contexts in which children grow and learn and helping these to become increasingly nurturing.

Measuring this gentle, but powerful way of working is very challenging. The danger is that we concentrate too much on what is measurable rather than allowing real situations to unfold. The sensitive attuned manager is able to judge these shifts and developments; however, it is difficult to capture and to record. Those responsible at a strategic level for the running of children's centres need to be aware of this powerful, yet subtle work and need to know how it works in each and every centre, for it will be different. The annual conversations that they have with centre managers need to clearly reflect the wide-ranging work that may or may not have been achieved.

The National Evaluation of Sure Start

> I would like to see the research world opening its doors much more fully to practice and practitioners, embracing the messy chaotic world of the young child and trying to work with it in order to understand it more fully.
>
> (Pascal 1996:5)

From the outset the Sure Start programme was committed to working with an evidence-based approach, encouraging practitioners to learn from the results of new and innovative practice and to learn from each other. External evaluation and evidence has proved a valuable tool in developing practice. The National Evaluation of Sure Start (NESS) was commissioned early in 2001, to provide robust, independent research which could be used to modify and to challenge developing practice (DCSF 2008b). Until now, 26 studies have been undertaken and published, all of which can be accessed through the National Evaluation website.

The study 'The Impact of Sure Start Local Programmes on Three Year Olds and Their Families' (NESS Team 2008) provides some pertinent information on the way in which programmes are making a difference to children's lives. This study was significant in that it demonstrated a marked difference in terms of positive outcomes for children and families from the cross-sectional study published in 2005. Parental attitudes were a particular focus of the 2008 study and here in the areas studied there was a marked improvement:

> Parents of three-year old children now show less negative parenting and provide their children with a better home learning environment. Three year old children in SSLP areas display better social development with higher levels of positive social behaviour and independence/self-regulation. These SSLP effects appear to be a consequence of the SSLP benefits on parenting. Three-year old children in SSLP areas have higher immunisation rates and fewer accidental injuries than children in similar areas without a SSLP (though it is possible these last two effects could reflect a difference in time measurement). Families living in SSLP areas use more child- and family-related services than those living elsewhere.
>
> (DCSF 2008b:7)

While celebrating the achievement of the Sure Start programmes and the developing children's centres this report also emphasises the need to move the agenda forward and most particularly highlights the need for centres to provide a strong lead on speech and language development. This is an area that has been an essential theme elsewhere in this book, and one that is paramount if we are to make a difference to young children's life chances.

Current study

Currently the NESS team led by Professor Edward Melhuish at the Institute for the Study of Children and Families and Social Issues, is working upon a National Evaluation of Sure Start. This evaluation will study the effectiveness of all Sure Start programmes in England (524 programmes) and will last for six years.

Sure Start children's centres are starting to demonstrate their worth, but we all need to have confidence in this imaginative, fantastic, subtle, empowering way of working:

> Patience from policy makers is required, as Sure Start's strongest effects may emerge over decades. Results from a similar American programme, part of President Johnson's Head Start called Perry High/Scope, were phenomenal, but took a long time to show up.
>
> (Toynbee and Walker 2008:139)

Ofsted inspection of children's centres

Inspection of all children's centres by Ofsted began in January 2010, following a pilot programme of 60 centres, which was completed in the autumn of 2009. It will always be challenging to provide a consistent approach to the inspection of children's centres, which are diverse nature, most specifically as they offer a subtle approach to supporting families. However, it is important that there is a sense of capturing the way in which centres are performing and how they are adding value to their communities. Each centre will be inspected for a day, together with time for preparation and for reporting.

The Ofsted consultation document identifies the focus of the inspection process, which will focus on:

- An evaluation of the services provided by a centre
- Whether these are matched to local need
- How well they are integrated and managed
- The success of any outreach services and training for adults

(Ofsted 2009:5)

The consultation document suggests that the inspection will make use of specific questions to shape the evaluation process:

- How good are outcomes for those served by the centre?
- How good is the provision?
- How effective are the leadership and management of the centre?
- What is the centre's capacity for sustained improvement?
- How effective overall is the children's centre in meeting the needs of and improving outcomes for those served by the centre?
- What does the centre need to do to improve?

(Ofsted 2009:6)

The inspection process will need to draw heavily upon the SEF and supporting evidence. It will be important for centre managers and staff to demonstrate a good knowledge of their local area and the particular issues that arise for families and how they might help to address these. Some of that knowledge will be drawn from statistical data related to targets, such as breast-feeding, but other important information will be about local knowledge and understanding. This local knowledge must be about getting to know the community, the voluntary services, libraries, schools, nurseries, childminders, health services, police services, etc., that serve that community. However, above all it is getting to know local families and what they need from these services.

Evidence

As discussed elsewhere in this book, we need to provide evidence for the work that we do in children's centres and we need to show that children's centres can and do make a difference. However, as discussed elsewhere in this book, much of the work that we do is not short-term work, but is likely to show an impact in years to come. We will need to show quantitative evidence of impact through changes in outcomes for children and families and more qualitative data through case-study material and direct statements from families and from partner agencies.

Good practice in providing case-study material

Effective case-study material will need to describe how pieces of work or ongoing relationships offered a tangible improvement. This might be a change in an individual's life and circumstance or it might relate to how joined-up working is being facilitated and managed.

Most particularly case-study material will need to provide:

- links to the centre's business plan and vision statement;
- reference to the five outcomes for Every Child Matters;
- the context to the piece of work;
- who was involved and why;
- a clear time-line;
- a narrative;
- an evaluation related to outcomes;
- detailed reference to what has changed with particular examples;
- a suggestion for a way forward;
- the voice of the parent and/or the practitioner;
- how a centre is helping to empower parents to change their own and their children's lives and change the way in which services are provided;
- has the intervention/support made a difference.

The role of centre managers

Centre managers know where and how their centres are making a difference; they also know where they need to improve. What managers need to do is to be diligent about capturing the evidence. Sometimes the vibrant work that goes on in centres is fleeting and fragmentary, like cupping sea water in your hand it is gone in a moment. We all need to be diligent about capturing that evidence, through discussion and interview, through asking parents for their thoughts, their experiences, maybe photographs of events or video evidence; we need it to illustrate just how children's centres are working. Managers at every level also need to be realistic and patient; we are in this work for the long haul not the quick fix.

In her seminal work *Involving Parents in Their Children's Learning*, Margy Whalley (2001) outlines some important principles when we are fully working side by side with parents in the process of evaluation and development that all agencies would do well to keep at the front of their thinking:

> As we work hard to develop even more effective ways of working with children and parents we need to recognize:
>
> - the great untapped energy and ability of parents and their deep commitment to supporting their children's development;
> - the importance of developing a mutual understanding based upon shared experiences;
> - the need to have a clearly articulated pedagogical approach – when we are clear about our own beliefs then we can share them with parents;
> - the need to employ staff who are confident, articulate, well trained and excited about working with adults as well as working with children;
> - that it takes time to establish an equal partnership where parents decide what interests them; parents may write beautiful 'baby biographies' for a year at a time or just attend one session on understanding their children's educational needs. Parents need to get involved in their own time and in their own way;
> - that working with adults in this way is always political. In Chris Pascal's (1996, p. 2) words, 'we want to encourage parents to stop accepting their lot and start creating the world they'd like to be part of'. In the words of Paulo Freire, it is about opening up for parents a 'language of possibilities' (Freire, 1970, p. 68).
>
> (Whalley 2001:34–5)

Perhaps what is most important when we consider the nature and the basic contribution that evaluation can make to the overall effectiveness of a children's centre is quite simply is it working for local children and families, does it make a difference to their lives? We can endlessly fill in tick-boxes and provide endless quantities of statistical data, but ultimately it is the evaluation that we do with our partner agencies and with local families that must shape our practice. When we are working with families out in the community we know what is working and what is not and we can keep asking the question. It has not always been comfortable to so fully involve service-users in the process of shaping the agenda, and for some agencies it is clear that it is an alien concept. However, now is the time to build upon the excellent work that Sure Start programmes have begun and really have parents at the very centre of our work.

References

Briant, J. (2007) *An Evaluation of an Early Excellence Project: Parent Training*. London: National Children's Bureau.

DCSF (2008a) *Self-evaluation Form for Sure Start Children's Centres*. Department for Children, Schools and Families.

DCSF (2008b) *The Sure Start Journey: a Summary of Evidence*. Department for Children, Schools and Families.

DfES (2006) *Sure Start Children's Centres Planning and Performance Management Guidance*. HMSO.

DfES (2007) *National Standards for Leaders of Sure Start Children's Centres*. HMSO.

Freire, P. (1970) *Pedagogy of the Oppressed*. Harmondsworth: Penguin.

NESS Team (2008) *The Impact of Sure Start Local Programmes on Three Year Olds and Their Families*. Department for Children, Schools and Families.

Nottingham City Council (2009) *Comprehensive Area Assessment*. Young Nottingham Select Committee.

Ofsted (2009) 'Inspection of Children's Centres', consultation document.

Pascal, C. (1996) Lecture at Pen Green Centre (unpublished).

Together for Children (2007) *Toolkit for Reaching Priority and Excluded Families*.

Toynbee, P. and Walker, D. (2008) *Unjust Rewards*. London: Granta.

Whalley, M. (2001) *Involving Parents in Their Children's Learning*. London: Paul Chapman, Sage.

Further reading

NCSL (2004) *NPQICL Community Development: a Framework for Thinking*. Corby: Pen Green Training and Research.

Websites

Every Child Matters:
www.everychildmatters.gov.uk/strategy/inspection

National Evaluation of Sure Start:
www.ness.bbk.ac.uk

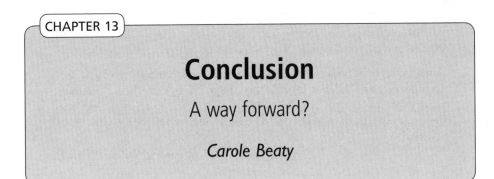

CHAPTER 13

Conclusion

A way forward?

Carole Beaty

In 2009, during those bright beautiful early summer days that so perfectly capture the idyllic nature of the English countryside, the metaphorical storm clouds were gathering. During the middle of an economic recession there was a huge political scandal unfolding every day in our papers. The scandal of politicians and their expenses reverberated around the country and led to a feeling of scepticism and mistrust. For some politicians the plight of the poor and the need to address child poverty, and the entitlement of every child, has clearly not been at the front of their minds. Public confidence waned rather faster than usual, and it occurred to many of us that politicians who spend so much of their energy pursuing personal gratification at the taxpayers' expense do not have much understanding of a world in which many of our children are growing up.

With the Labour party no longer in power after the 2010 election, what will become of the once-proud flagship of the Labour government? We need to keep saying it, this is an excellent way of working, let people know, let us be proud of the achievement of integrated centres, let us all ensure that every child has the right to expect the services of truly child-centred, joined-up services.

We have the duty to protect the more vulnerable members of our society. While child poverty may not be so apparent today in the twenty-first century as it has been in previous generations, it is still with us and it is still making a difference to children's lives, denying them the opportunities of their more fortunate counterparts. Polly Toynbee and David Walker describe how the Fabian Society gathered together a group of voters from middle England (these were people who were neither to the extreme left or right politically) to discuss child poverty:

> At first they expressed the typically British view that poverty is due to laziness and personal failings. They thought no children were poor . . ..
>
> After a couple of hours attitudes were shifting. Participants heard a factual account of how children brought up under the poverty line were three times more likely than average to die as babies, five times more likely to die in accidents, at higher risk of mental illness and destined to have shorter lives.
>
> (Toynbee and Walker 2008:69)

The growth of inequality causes unhappiness and unrest, yet Sure Start and, later, children's centres were put in place to address issues of child poverty and of the iniquity of denying children a proper chance in life. Now the government has required a children's centre in every area, to provide a gateway for all to more comprehensive, child-centred services that are truly integrated. While some children's centres continue to serve their local community with strength and conviction, offering parents a real chance to take charge of expanding services for young children, some provide a very reductionist view of that original brave vision of reconfiguring services on a child-centred model. Moving across to many local authorities taking the lead has ensured a reduction in some areas in funding to individual centres, and in many cases a one-size-fits-all model of staffing, funding and often, delivery. We are starting to see the benefits of this integrated approach to early support and intervention; we know from other models of early support programmes around the world that it takes a long time to change practice and to see the effects on individuals and on communities. Some centres have moved away from the notion of offering universal services and early intervention to a more targeted model. We hope to see children's centres become part of the landscape as they become a statutory service, in the near future and become embedded in all our ways of working. What we need are truly universal services in every community that can offer child and family friendly services in health, education and care, and provide a gateway for more specialised, targeted services.

Key messages

- Children's centres need to become a statutory service with status within every community and with a set of services and a vision that everyone will recognise and be proud of. They need to be offering universal services to all, and reflect the makeup of the local community and its needs.

- Integrated children's centres need to make much more use of the expertise on community participation and development offered by the voluntary sector.

- We must keep faith with the Sure Start vision for supporting the child within the context of family and community. In the long run this will show an economic and social benefit.

- We need to provide excellent childcare and education for all two- to five-year-olds and to ensure that places are heavily subsidised, and in the future free to all. Those running Early Years centres and nurseries need to be highly trained to degree level and have Qualified Teacher Status equivalence. Those working in nurseries need to be highly trained and be rewarded accordingly. All those working with young children need to have a sound education in early development and in pedagogical practice. As in Scandinavian countries and in Reggio Emilia they need a good background in social and emotional learning and the way in which the arts challenge children's thinking.

- If we are going to make a difference to children's life chances then we must provide a creative, child-centred curriculum for the under-fives based upon play and experiential learning. We need to build upon the way in which children learn naturally, helping children to extend those dispositions for learning which will be with them for life.

- Children's centres need to be places of inspiration and innovation with families having a key role in setting the agenda for change in children's services. All services need to be offered in a dynamic, child-centred manner.

- Staff at children's centres, whether they are part of the immediate Sure Start children's centre team or are part of the wider partnership team need to have appropriate training for the work that they are required to do. This is highly skilled and diverse work and needs staff with a good understanding of young children's development and they need to be assured and competent when working with adults. Staff will also need an understanding of the Common Assessment Framework and of safeguarding children procedures. Currently in some centres, because of the diminished level of funding, staff are being asked to take on complex roles as front-line staff for which they are neither trained nor paid for.

- Children's centre managers need to have the status of head teachers and be paid accordingly; they need to come from a clear background of working with young children and families. Research has demonstrated

that centre mangers with a health background are particularly successful in meeting the needs of communities and individual children
within them. Centre managers need to be prepared and equipped to
cause that "disequilibrium" that Margy Whalley speaks of, to unsettle
the status quo, the need to be political creatures, and they need to have
a clear voice within the community. Most importantly, centre managers
themselves need to be empowered through excellent supervision, support and training to be advocates for local children. The NPQICL is a
great start, but training needs to be ongoing and to be specific as centre managers have a huge remit and need particular training on such
issues as financial management, supervision across different agencies.

- All families need access to excellent integrated provision; however, this
  is most particularly the case for families with specific needs.

- Excellent integrated practice that promotes a shared vision and reflective practice really can make a difference to every child and to every
  community, but there needs to be a clear commitment to this way of
  working from every agency, at every level; education, health, social
  services and from the voluntary sector. We must be prepared to learn
  from each of these agencies, most particularly from the voluntary
  sector, in ensuring that true collaboration happens.

- Services from children's centres cannot just be centre based, but need
  to reach out to the local area through outreach services and through
  home-visiting services.

- The role of staff already working with families in the earliest years of
  life, in peoples' homes, most specifically the health visiting service,
  needs to be strengthened and expanded to ensure a more responsive
  service for families in need.

- Children's centre managers must not be left alone to change the way
  in which services are designed and delivered. They cannot do this without a clear lead from above. All agencies in health education, social
  services and the voluntary sector need to be committed to integrated
  practice and provide front-line workers with a clear powerful and
  informed lead.

If you visit a children's centre or you work in one, you will know what we
are talking about; they are and must continue to be beacons of excellence for
improving the life chances of every child in every community. Society will
reap the rewards if we can keep developing innovative, exciting, irreverent,

challenging, inclusive, dynamic, serious, fun, happy, extraordinary, collaborative centres for all our children. We will also reap the consequences if we let this extraordinary way of working slip through our fingers.

Reference

Toynbee, P. and Walker, D. (2008) *Unjust Rewards*. London: Granta.

Index